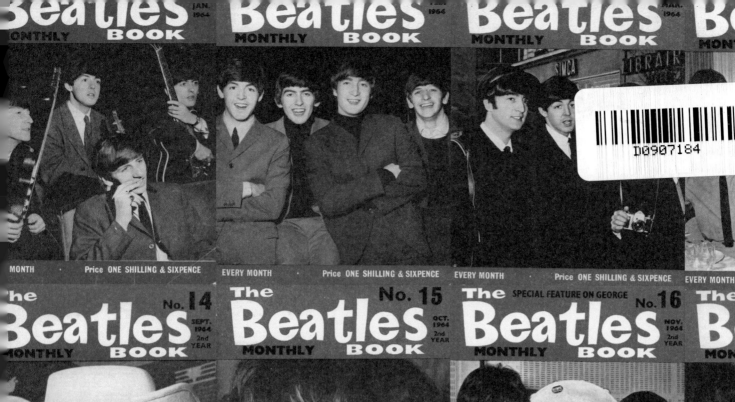
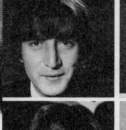
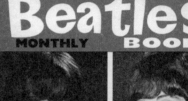
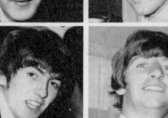
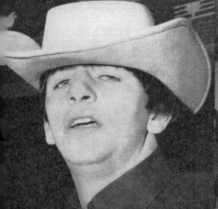
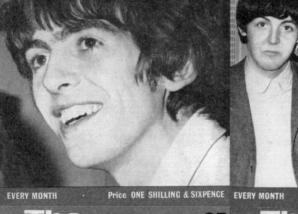
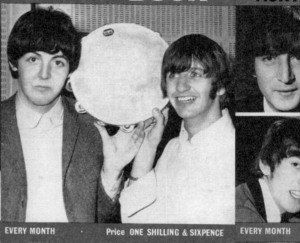
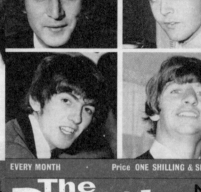
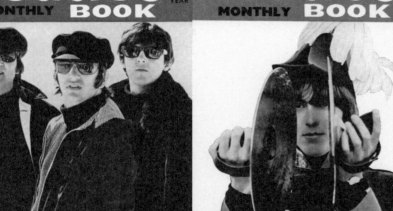
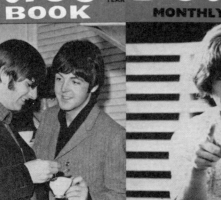
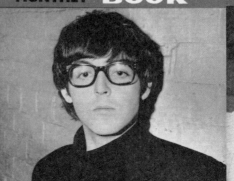
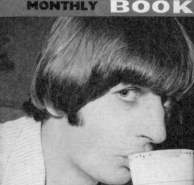

LOOKING THROUGH YOU

RARE & UNSEEN PHOTOGRAPHS FROM THE BEATLES BOOK ARCHIVE

LOOKING THROUGH YOU

RARE & UNSEEN PHOTOGRAPHS FROM THE BEATLES BOOK ARCHIVE

FOREWORD

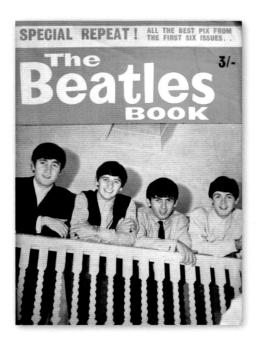

I REMEMBER THE day my father, Sean O'Mahony, showed me his Beatles archive for the first time. It was in 2004, shortly after he retired. Just a year before, he had published the final issue of *The Beatles Book*, the group's official magazine he had edited for almost forty years. The Beatles came up in conversation over a family lunch. My father said he had a few photos of them in his office, so my husband Tom and I went up to have a look. Only then did we begin to fully realise the part he and the magazine played in the whole Beatles story.

On a shelf were dozens of boxes of Ilford 'Ilfobrom' photographic paper, glossy, brilliant, double weight, each one labelled. He took one down, '*L477 Help Austria*' in black permanent marker down the side, opened it up and started pulling out a selection of ten-by-eight inch black and white prints.

They were extraordinary; dozens of photos from behind the scenes during the shooting of *Help!* Top hats, capes and skis. Leading ladies and stunt doubles. Another box. '*L368, Sheffield*': Paul mucking about for the camera backstage, gurning, sweeping up, as well as onstage. My father was on a roll. '*Recording Sgt Pepper*'. '*Live in the US*'. '*At Home with Ringo*'. The photos led us to the magazine, *The Beatles Book* that originally ran for 77 issues from August 1963 to December 1969.

The first edition was snapped up by fans. In an era before pop idols could be seen through the click of a mouse, *The Beatles Book* was a lifeline for Beatle People desperate to see fresh pictures and read news of their heroes. At its height it was selling 330,000 copies a month.

While my father worked under the pseudonym Johnny Dean, *The Beatles Book* official photographer was Leslie Bryce who completed over 40 photo sessions with the group. Some were 'open' – press conferences and the like – while others were private, including invitations into The Beatles' own homes, recording at Abbey Road and unguarded backstage moments.

Each session Leslie shot, using both medium format and 35mm, was given an 'L' number, running from *L25*, the first, in Margate in July '63, to '*L1174 Yellow Submarine Premiere*' in July '68. The term 'session' is slightly misleading though. Some shoots appear to be just a couple of hours spent with the group (for example, *L1151* on June 4, 1968, where only 12 photos were taken of the band working on 'Revolution 1' at Abbey Road), whereas others, such as '*L131 First American Tour*', saw the magazine spend an extraordinary week with the group as Beatlemania hit the US. That box consists of over 600 photos. Looking closely, what struck me was how few photographic 'misses' there were in the collection. From the set up portraits to the off-guard captured moments, so many of the photographs were fantastic, a testament to Leslie's skill behind the lens.

The photographs record how the group developed from "the toppermost of the poppermost", to serious, experimental, gifted musicians. Towards the end of the sixties, my father found the band difficult to contact, more and more reluctant to be photographed and rarely together as a foursome in one place. The last official exclusive photo session was in June 1968, although the magazine carried on for just over a year more, combining photographs from others – road manager Mal Evans especially – along with images already in the archive.

A few years ago my father passed the photo collection on. Tom and I felt it important to digitise the collection as a back-up for the negatives that may slowly deteriorate over time. The more we saw though, the more we realised its importance. Hundreds of images from the archive were published in *The Beatles Book* in its various guises – the magazine was relaunched in the seventies and eighties – and some have been seen in other publications, including, of course, *The Beatles Anthology*. But there are others from these same shoots that have never been seen before.

However, we think there's more to this collection than just unseen images. These photographs are of great historical importance and this book provides not just an opportunity to showcase these marvellous images of The Beatles but to demonstrate that my father and *The Beatles Book* were a vital part of their story too.

Jo Adams, London, March 2015

INTRODUCTION BY ANDY NEILL

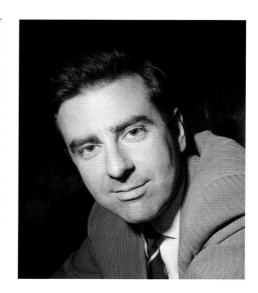

THE BEATLES BOOK was the only periodical authorised by the group. While millions of words about their lives filled countless newspapers and magazines, the glossy compact monthly publication proved to be the bible for all Beatles fans throughout the sixties – and beyond. At its height *The Beatles Book* was distributed worldwide with a readership running into millions and it still ranks as the most respected fan magazine ever published. Being official, it had license to take Beatles fans behind the scenes while documenting the Fab Four's extraordinary career as it occurred, featuring invaluable contributions from many of their closest friends and associates who provided unique facts, stories and insights. Additionally, while the average reporter could get only so far, *The Beatles Book* was granted privileged access – visiting the group backstage, in the recording studio, on film sets and even in their homes.

This was all thanks to the entrepreneurial foresight of one man who founded and edited the magazine throughout its original tenure, successfully reviving it several years later to take it into the eighties and beyond. Born in London in 1932, Sean O'Mahony originally started out in the mid-fifties' music biz, demoing his own compositions and taking them around London publishing houses. "I was writing pop songs of the time," he recalls. Throughout this period, old-school managers and music publishers ruled the roost. The record producer – or A&R man – would 'discover' the up and coming star and the music publisher would supply the song. There's some delicious irony in that Sean would later devote an enterprise to the artists who turned this practice on its head.

As well as writing his own songs, Sean was employed in the advertising department at ABC Television. "I wasn't directly involved in the programming but I used to go along and see *Oh Boy!* at the Hackney Empire. It was new, fresh, original and very exciting."

Through a contact in the business, Sean started working for Australian expat Robert Stigwood, the future manager of Cream and The Bee Gees and successful theatrical producer. At this time, on top of being a record producer, manager and agent, Stigwood co-owned a magazine called *Pop Weekly*, with Albert Hand, the publisher of *Elvis Monthly*. The eccentric Hand was unapologetically fanatical about Presley and had started his magazine – the first of its type – in 1960. Sean was installed as the advertising manager at *Pop Weekly*, working with music journalists David Cardwell and Peter Jones who provided most of the copy. Jones would be a valued participant in Sean's next venture.

"*Pop Weekly* didn't have a lot of credibility. I never knew the whole picture but it didn't sell that many copies. It was read by girls, like all pop magazines were. We always offered new acts a write-up in *Pop Weekly* provided they took a little ad at a cost of about £25. I rang EMI and they gave me Brian Epstein's number so I contacted him to see if he would be interested in taking out an ad for The Beatles' first single. I was used to getting rough managers who didn't want to spend money but Brian was very different. It was an extraordinary phone call – he was so charming, and he said yes, he'd be happy to take an advertisement for 'Love Me Do'."

While at his desk job Sean saw the possibilities that lay round the corner. "Everyone in the business was always looking for the next big thing and I was convinced the group thing was going to be it," he recalls. In late 1962 he approached Albert Hand and IPC to interest them in the idea of a new magazine. Both turned him down. Undaunted, Sean left *Pop Weekly* that December to set it up. "I rented an office at 244 Edgware Road, two doors down from Stigwood, which he was unhappy about. It was only me and my secretary Sheila Klein who was [future Rolling Stones manager] Andrew Oldham's girlfriend [later wife] at the time."

With a fresh start came a fresh pseudonym. "Johnny Dean came from my name on a record mailing label, sent from either Pye or Philips, but instead of Sean they'd made it Dean," he explains. "I liked it, then added Johnny, which is Sean anyway."

Its editor having adopted this new name, the first issue of *Beat Monthly* came out in May 1963. Inside was a competition, organised with Brian Epstein, offering the winner 'A Day With The Fabulous Beatles'. The print-run of 40,000 sold out very quickly. The Shadows were on the cover but, tellingly, the second issue featured their usurpers The Beatles. "When 'Please Please Me' was launched [in January 1963] I realised there was something totally new there – an incredible different sound to 'Love Me Do'. Follow-ups were usually sound-alikes."

Sean was well-aware of how successful *Elvis Monthly* had been for Hand and was confident a publication devoted to this new pop sensation from Liverpool could do equally as well. However he'd only just chanced his arm by launching one music-related magazine, so the prospect of backing another so soon seemed financially foolhardy. But with The Beatles' third single 'From Me To You' and first album *Please Please Me* resting at number one in the respective British singles and albums charts, and with potential competitors set to beat a path to Epstein's door, Sean knew he had to take decisive action.

"I went back to Brian and suggested the idea. He said 'You'll have to meet the boys.' It took a while to happen but then I met them at the Playhouse Theatre [on May 21]. The whole point of that first meeting was for them to give me the once over. They didn't want just anyone editing their magazine, wandering around close to them in the studio…

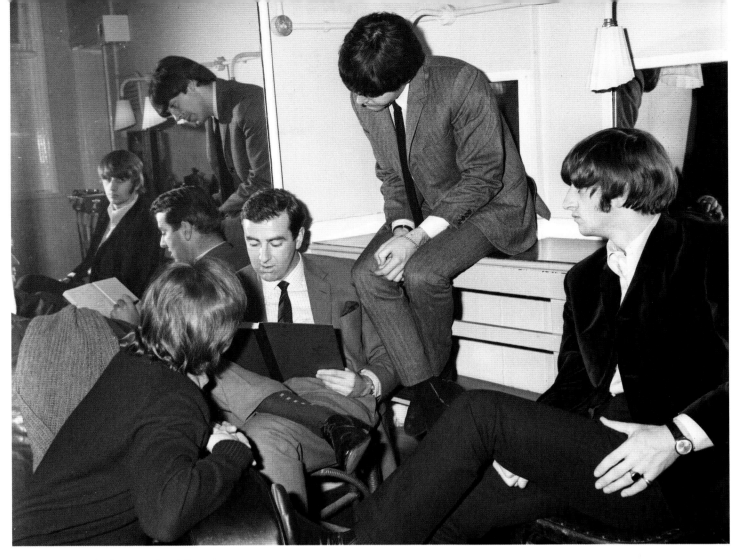

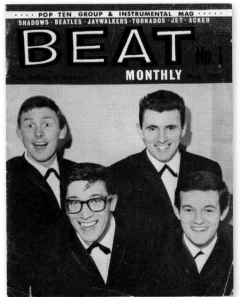

Top: Sean O'Mahony with The Beatles in their dressing room at the Hippodrome, Brighton, October 25, 1964.

Above: The debut issue of Beat Monthly, Sean's first venture into publishing just prior to The Beatles Book.

It was a very easy conversation. George asked how much the magazine would cost to buy. Paul wondered 'How are you going to fill it every month?' and I just said 'Leave that to me.' I told them, 'The great advantage of the magazine is that it will always promote The Beatles positively.' And I kept to that."

With the verbal approval of The Beatles and their manager, the formalities were confirmed in a letter from Epstein's company NEMS Enterprises Ltd dated June 14, 1963. The Beatles' only concerns were about presentation and accuracy. One condition stated that exclusive publishing rights would be granted for three years provided that either party may terminate the agreement on each anniversary of the date and that notice was given three months in advance. In view of the magazine's sales over its first three years it was considered unnecessary to revisit this clause.

Sean was present on July 1 at EMI Studios when the next Beatles single 'She Loves You' was being recorded. He brought with him Philip Gotlop, an experienced showbiz photographer. Gotlop was just one of several taking pictures that day as Sean recalled two years later in *The Beatles Book*: "John wasn't keen on them being there. Trouble was that he had to wear his glasses simply to be able to see what was going on, and it just wasn't easy to keep whipping them off every time a camera clicked. Also the boys sensed that this was a particularly important session as far as their future was concerned." Sean had brought along four copies of a questionnaire to be completed for use in the first issue which each Beatle obligingly sat and completed in the studio's foyer.

Not long afterwards Brian advised Sean that Gotlop had met with The Beatles' disapproval. "I think they thought he was too old for them." It was through an introduction via his wife Jackie that Sean met Leslie Bryce. Born in 1933, Bryce , an Associate member of the Royal Photographic Society, was once personal assistant to Baron (Sterling Henry Nahum), a Court Photographer to the Royal Family. From there Leslie branched out with another of Baron's assistants, Tony Armstrong-Jones (Lord Snowdon) and worked for Shell-Mex and BP, taking photos for annual reports and staff magazines, and as a freelance photographer for promoter Harold Pendleton's *Jazz News*. Basing himself from a studio at 36a Blandford Square, Bryce's first Beatles assignment was photographing them at the Margate Winter Gardens and at their seaside hotel, The Beresford in nearby Birchington-on-Sea, with support act (and fellow NEMS artistes) Billy J Kramer with The Dakotas.

Bryce next attended an EMI session on July 30 but it would appear no photos were taken that day. In view of Lennon's irritation at the number of photographers present during the 'She Loves You' recording, it was probably for the best.

On August 1, the first issue of *The Beatles Book* was published. "The title was my idea," Sean confirms, "and calling it that appealed to them. It was a magazine but it was called a Book. I think John liked this – it was a bit quirky." The distinctive white-lettered logo, designed by Bob Gibson who would also contribute the novel cartoon drawings featured in the magazine, sat above a Dezo Hoffmann photo of the boys in their collarless suits. Sean's opening address, written by 'Johnny Dean,' as they all would be, set the magazine's positive tone from the outset. "I must begin my first editorial for *The Beatles Book* by thanking all of you who wrote to me, or to The Beatles themselves, because it was your letters more than anything else

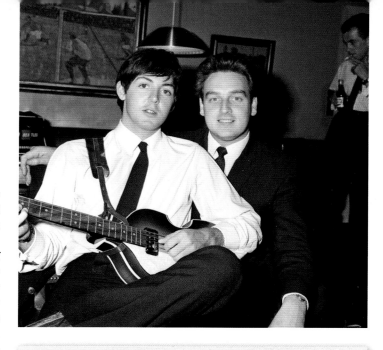

which helped to give George, John, Paul and Ringo their own monthly magazine. I, personally, am very honoured to be their editor, because I think they're just about the greatest thing that ever happened to British pop music."

Right from this first issue the magazine incorporated the majority of features that would be included throughout its six-and-a-half year run – a letters page including the occasional personal Beatle reply (ghosted by the editor), a Beatle News page and the month's Beatle song. Pages four and five were devoted to the Fan Club's national newsletter, beginning the symbiotic arrangement between *The Beatles Book* and The Official Beatles Fan Club. Back in June, Beatles press officer Tony Barrow decided that the Fan Club should have a London-based National Secretary operating from Barrow's press office address at 13 Monmouth Street. Until then Southern area fans had kept in touch through Bettina Rose in Surrey while Freda Kelly had looked after the North from Liverpool. The new National Fan Club secretary was Anne Collingham, a fictitious name Barrow made up as a cover-all for the ever-rotating staff who helped to answer the mountains of mail as membership continued to increase. (Collingham was based on Barrow's secretary's address in Earls Court; Anne was his wife's middle name.)

Issue one also featured potted biographies of each Beatle as well as Brian Epstein and George Martin. Eagle-eyed fans were swift to point out the embarrassing blunder committed by printing George's birthdate as February 25, 1942, and stating Paul was the youngest Beatle. Nor was there any mention of John's wife and son, hardly surprising in those 'available pop star' days. "One day after the first issue was out, I got calls telling me about Cynthia," Sean recalled. "I immediately rang Tony [Barrow] and he groaned. It was silly – The Beatles couldn't possibly keep it quiet."

The initial print run of 40,000 copies, with a cover price of one shilling and sixpence, swiftly sold out, thus creating a demand from fans who had missed it. In his second editorial, Sean promised to include as many readers' comments and suggestions in future editions and a rotational system of individual Beatle photographs would appear in the pull-out centre pages, prompting irate fans of their non-represented favourite to write in and complain when this was not adhered to.

The second issue also featured the first part of a serialisation entitled 'A Tale Of Four Beatles', written by Billy Shepherd, alias journalist Peter Jones, Sean's contact from *Pop Weekly* who also wrote for *Beat Monthly* and the weekly paper *New Record Mirror*. Much of the group's off-duty time during a season at Bournemouth's Gaumont Cinema in August was spent recounting their lives thus far to Jones at the Palace Court Hotel. As well as being serialised in *The Beatles Book*, Shepherd's early account of The Beatles' rise to prominence was published in expanded form as *The True Story Of The Beatles*. Issued in March 1964, it remained the only reference work on the group until Hunter Davies' more substantial biography appeared in 1968.

Tony Barrow employed his *Beatles Book* pen name Frederick James for an illuminating article regarding Lennon and McCartney's songwriting. Echoing similar sentiments he expressed in his sleeve notes for *The Beatles Hits* EP, Barrow wrote: "If at some future date – possibly around the year 2014 or 2016 – The Beatles ceased to be popular with the disc-purchasing public they'd be quite content to fall back upon a variety of other occupations." He jokingly suggested Ringo would turn to motor racing while George would become a traffic warden but John and Paul "would stick together and write songs from now until Doomsday".

AS THE REMARKABLE year of 1963 ended the list of Beatle statistics was staggering – 'She Loves You' spent four weeks perched atop the British singles charts, falling back at one point but then regaining the pole position for another two weeks at the end of November before being displaced by 'I Want To Hold Your Hand', both singles selling well over a million; *Please Please Me* had been knocked off the top of the album charts by its successor *With The Beatles*; and *Twist And Shout*, an EP with four tracks from their debut LP, made EP sales records with over 250,000 sold. Launched with modest intentions, *The Beatles Book* was swept along in Beatlemania's incredible slipstream. In January 1964 the magazine's sales peaked at an astounding 330,000, three times the amount *Elvis Monthly* had ever attained.

Top: Paul with Beatles Book *photographer, Leslie Bryce, in Holland June 1964*

Above: copy of the original agreement between Brian Epstein's company NEMS Enterprises Ltd and Sean O'Mahony

In the wake of the magazine's success Brian Epstein asked Sean to launch a similar publication to promote another of his NEMS artists, speculating that Billy J Kramer's good looks would shift copies, although as Sean recalled, "Brian saw me as the publisher and I had to take the risk." Sean reluctantly acquiesced, but instead chose Gerry & The Pacemakers as the magazine's subject. The first issue hit newsstands in March but good fortune, like lightning, rarely strikes in the same place and *Gerry And The Pacemakers Monthly* folded after only four issues. "I found it very difficult to do," Sean admits. "I tried hard but it didn't work."

Meanwhile, *The Beatles Book* was going from strength-to-strength without recourse to outside advertising, although attempts to launch overseas versions of the magazine invariably foundered. America and Canada expressed interest without committing while a French version, *Les Beatles*, lasted just three issues. This had little effect on the bigger picture. A year on from the first issue, Sean's editorial stated *The Beatles Book* was being distributed to over a million people worldwide. Subscribers and Fan Club members received an extra treat when 50,000 copies were printed of the Club's special summer 1964 *National Newsletter Magazine*. The Official Beatles Fan Club membership had reached its peak – 80,000 were officially enrolled Beatle People in the

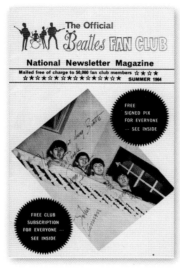

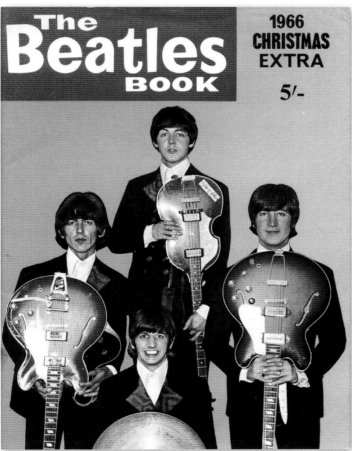

UK, and besides the two first floor offices of 13 Monmouth Street, the club now occupied the entire second floor.

Such was the weight and importance already being attached to The Beatles' career that in September 1964 a Behind The Spotlight column commenced in *The Beatles Book* looking back at events occurring exactly two years before. The most interesting for historians was the four-part series starting in the August 1965 issue examining The Beatles' childhoods which was researched with the aid of their parents and John's Aunt Mimi, as well as early friends and former schoolmasters. Alongside a wealth of hitherto unknown information were invaluable pictures including John aged eight on his first two-wheeled bike, Paul on holiday with brother Mike, George posing with his first guitar, and young Ringo and pal garbed in fancy dress. The following year, Iain Hines, formerly of The Jets, Tony Sheridan's backing band, contributed an interesting article examining The Beatles' early experiences in Hamburg.

Competitions became a regular *Beatles Book* attraction with not only cash prizes being awarded for the best entries but also the chance to win personal Beatles items such as drumsticks used by Ringo and a string from John, Paul or George's guitars. Readers' polls similarly proved popular. As an example, in the September 1965 issue *Beatles Book* readers were asked to vote for the most popular *Help!* album track and the best Beatles song ever. The results ranked Paul's 'Yesterday' as best from the LP and, somewhat inevitably considering it was their newest single, 'Help!' as best-ever song (although curiously it rated only ninth in the *Help!* album poll).

A Christmas bonus came with a special 64-page *Beatles Book Extra*, featuring copious colour and unpublished pictures – only a small percentage of the photos Leslie took made it into the monthly magazine. The limited print run sold out so the experiment was repeated the following year. The "personal articles by the Beatles themselves", which appeared in both specials and the magazine's Beatle Talk column, were the work of either 'Billy Shepherd' or 'Frederick James' asking questions designed to get specific answers. "The Beatles were very easy to work with but their angle was 'you're doing this, do it, and bother us as little as possible'," Sean recalls. "Paul actually said that to me after about a year. Pretty quickly they didn't welcome formal interviews, which we did at the very start. So we'd spend time with them and make notes, and get answers to questions by making them informal, just in conversation. The Beatles never saw the issues until they were out. What they mainly did was look at the pictures. No one ever discussed format, style, or choice of writers."

Tony Barrow's job was made slightly easier as he was able to transcribe recordings made at The Beatles' press conferences he was chairing. Tony was then asked to ghostwrite a regular column for Beatle aides Neil Aspinall and Mal Evans, the first of which appeared in the April 1966 issue. Again this provided a wealth of detail regarding the group's professional and off-duty activities.

The year 1966 was all change for The Beatles who were fast outgrowing their image as cheeky, cheery moptops. In August of that year, they made the private decision to cease live concerts – permanently as it turned out. This presented Sean with a problem. *The Beatles Book* relied heavily on a ready supply of photographs showing the boys' up-to-date activities but what had once been a torrent had now slowed to a trickle. At some point – in late 1966/early 1967 or possibly even earlier, in June 1966, when the original three-year agreement with NEMS expired – Sean met with Brian Epstein to review the situation.

Brian was now in the unenviable position of keeping the outside world at bay. Breaking the previous three-year cycle, there was no new Beatles' single and album in time for Christmas. Fans had even picketed his Belgravia home demanding to know why a British concert tour had not been planned for the end of 1966. The pressure on him to satisfy the demands of fans, press, recording company and Beatles was immense. During the course of their conversation, Epstein informed Sean that the boys now thought the magazine didn't portray them as they really were. To this, Sean could only point out that if he did portray them as they really were, he would have to print various indiscretions they wouldn't want revealed.

A compromise of sorts was reached and the magazine continued. However, for a brief period during the lack of access, and in a desperate move, Sean was forced to retouch old photos by getting an artist to pencil in moustaches to keep up with The Beatles' changing image. "When I next went along to Abbey Road there were quite a few funny comments from The Beatles about the drawn-on moustaches."

In his editorial for the April 1967 issue, the first with fresh Bryce pictures of The Beatles recording *Sgt. Pepper*, Sean promised: "The boys and Brian Epstein feel that almost all of the photographs in every issue from now on should be bang up-to-date and taken within a couple of weeks of publication." Not all readers were happy with The Beatles' progression. Letters flooded in complaining about the Fab Four's new-look and in a *Sgt. Pepper* opinion poll, the all-female responses printed were from the type of fan now gravitating toward the uncomplicated pop and clean image of The Monkees.

In the May *Beatles Book*, a letter from Mary Watson of Macclesfield, Cheshire won her a free subscription: "Dear Johnny, I love The Beatles very much, and of course, think they're marvellous; but I'm also very proud of them... we've NEVER heard of any of The Beatles being mixed up in all this drugs business... I know if Paul took drugs, I'd be worried sick for him, but I know he is too sensible."

Just weeks later, the BBC banned 'A Day In The Life' because of drug connotations and hysterical press headlines met McCartney's admission in *Life* magazine that he'd taken LSD. As a gesture of support, the magazine reprinted the explanation Paul gave to ITN on June 19. The majority of readers polled came out in his favour. "I didn't like the drug taking at all," Sean says now. "It was very difficult for us to deal with. I wasn't pretending it didn't happen, I just ignored it. *Beatles Book* readers didn't want that. I'd promised Brian I'd keep the magazine positive."

The magazine's cover went colour for the first time in June to mark the release of *Sgt Pepper* – a special wraparound cover featuring one of Michael Cooper's photos supplied by EMI from the album cover session.

Just over four years had passed since Brian Epstein gave Sean the authority to publish the magazine – a fact brought home with a resounding jolt when the news came through in August that The Beatles' manager, mentor and friend had died. "Although he had his faults, Brian was still a person they could rely upon to say things intended to be for their good," Sean asserts. "After he died it became more and more difficult to get to the boys. You got the strong impression that things were falling apart. It wasn't run anymore, it was whim and fantasy... Looking back I wish we'd fought harder. They were happy with Mal Evans and John Kelly there taking photos, so we used theirs more."

Mal (and occasionally Neil) was still filing Tony Barrow-ghosted reports from various Beatle adventures including the *Magical Mystery Tour*, the trip to Rishikesh, and George's excursions to America to see Ravi Shankar. However, as Sean observed, the cracks were appearing. Ironically, shortly after the May 1968 issue appeared, carrying a glossy colour shot of Paul with Jane Asher taken in India, the first time a Beatle partner appeared on a *Beatles Book* cover, the couple split up. That month, John's marriage to Cynthia ended when he took up with Yoko Ono.

When the news became public Sean's position (in the August editorial) remained as resolute as ever: "We received a tremendous flood of letters this month about John and Yoko. But, as always *The Beatles Book* regards this as part of John's private life.... I don't think it's fair to either John or Cynthia to say anything about what is a very private affair between them. That's been our policy up to now and we are going to stick to it."

In October 1968, Sean's operation moved offices from 36-38 Westbourne Grove to 58 Parker Street, in Covent Garden. Alongside *Beatles Monthly* and *Monkees Monthly*, which Sean had launched in early 1967, he was still publishing the successful *Beat Instrumental*, the popular monthly magazine that had evolved from *Beat Monthly*.

The biggest news for Beatles fans at the end of the year was the possibility of the band returning to the stage for a one-hour television show to be staged in front of an invited audience. A banner on the cover of the December issue promised: 100 Beatles' Show Tickets To Be Won. With a venue still to be decided, in January The Beatles started rehearsals at Twickenham Film Studios for *Get Back*, an ill-fated project that started with good intentions. The Beatles would be filmed for the TV special, rehearsing new and old songs with the planned concert (wherever it might be) providing the grand finale. Personal tensions, musical disagreements and the cold atmosphere at Twickenham conspired to make proceedings difficult. Consequently, the show never happened.

At the end of 1969, Sean realised *The Beatles Book* had reached a natural conclusion. "When I ended the magazine, there was no one to relay my decision to. It just finished and I quietly told the NEMS office." Curiously enough, the December 6 issue of music paper *Disc & Music Echo* carried a small news piece revealing that Paul McCartney planned to launch a new Beatles publication in the New Year. An existing undated document drawn up by Paul at an Apple business meeting reveals he definitely had ideas of launching some kind of Beatles magazine. The document details projected sales, cost breakdowns, and

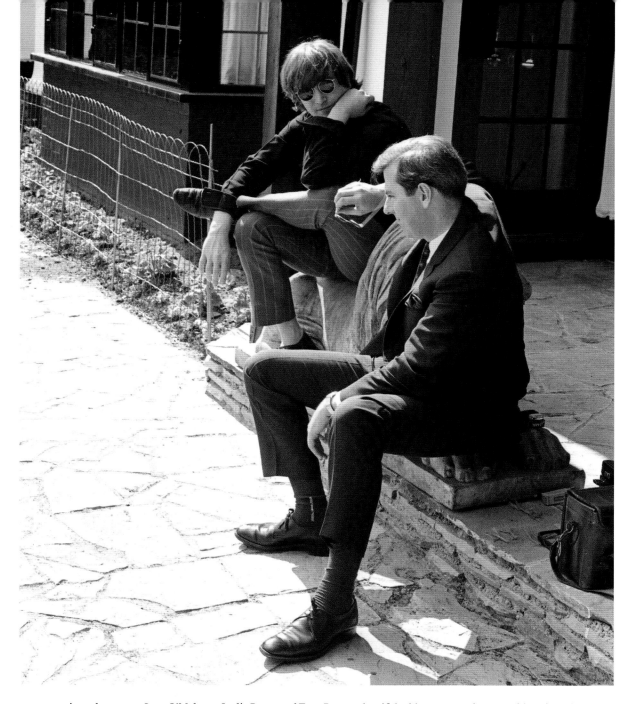

Above: John and Sean during a photo shoot at Ringo's home Sunny Heights, Weybridge, May 31, 1966

even mentions the names Sean O'Mahony, Leslie Bryce and Tony Barrow, but if the idea was a serious consideration, the whole suggestion was irrelevant when The Beatles were breaking apart.

In a press statement issued in *Record Mirror* (dated December 13), Sean declared: "*The Beatles Book* belonged to the sixties when the boys were in their twenties. Now, as they approach their thirties, I feel, and I believe they do too, that we can't produce the same sort of magazine in the seventies. Sadly this is the end of The Beatles era. I think I must be one of the few publishers to close a magazine while it is still showing a profit!"

"The whole thing had literally collapsed," Sean says now. "I think the circulation of the last ever issue in December 1969, number 77, was about 50,000. It had been dropping steadily since it peaked at over 300,000."

It was a sad end to a quality product that had become an important monthly fixture on the calendar for a great number of Beatles fans. As the first of each month drew nearer, an element of excitement grew – what would this month's issue contain? The loyal readership was rarely disappointed. The best tribute the magazine can be paid is perhaps what Sean wrote back in 1967 when it hit 50 issues: "I can very well remember that when I got down to putting together the very first *Beatles Book* in May 1963, I felt that it would run for many years because I was absolutely certain that The Beatles had such tremendous talents that they would still be world beaters for a long time to come."

S EAN'S ADVENTURES IN publishing continued throughout the seventies and beyond with new titles including *Hit Songwriting & Recording*, and other fan magazines devoted to subjects as diverse as The Police and *Starsky And Hutch*. In 1979, he successfully founded the vinyl bible *Record Collector*. With a wave of Beatle nostalgia after the re-release of their singles catalogue by EMI in 1976, Sean resurrected *The Beatles Book* in May of that year, reprinting the original magazines in sequential order with four surrounding pages updating the ex-Beatles' current activities. Owing to continuing demand from Beatles fans, a 'new' magazine was launched in October 1982 (coincidentally the 20th anniversary of the release of 'Love Me Do') when the original series of 77 issues came to its conclusion, and continued on for a further 242 issues before Sean ended the magazine permanently on his retirement in January 2003.

"Looking back I still believe The Beatles were the greatest phenomenon to ever hit the music world," Sean declares. "Anyone connected with them, be it in the studio, on stage or in the audience, felt privileged to be involved, to be part of it. I'll never forget it."

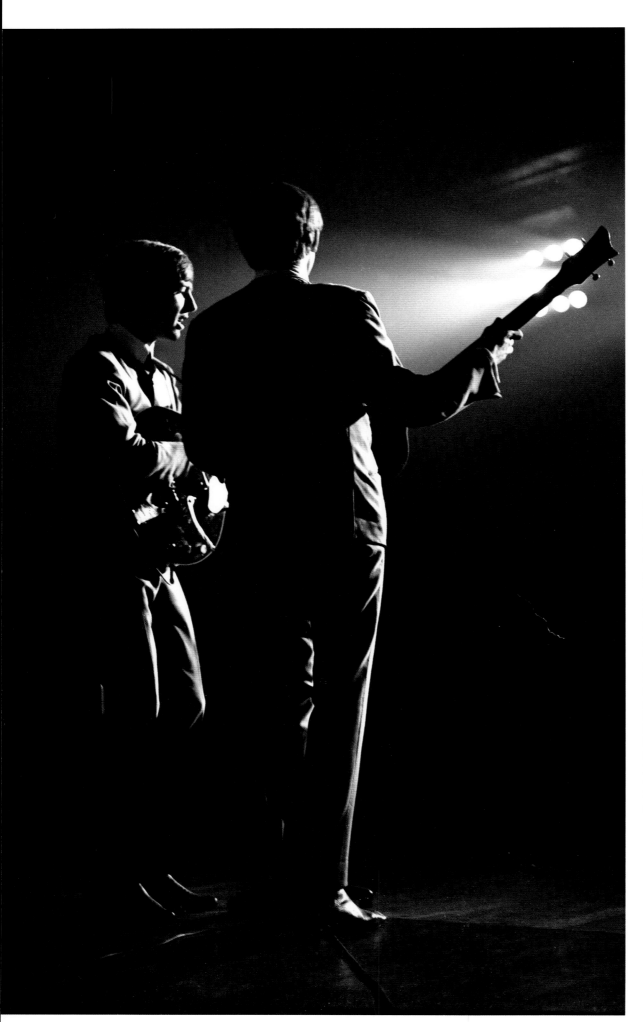

WINTER GARDENS, MARGATE
JULY 8–13, 1963

Leslie Bryce's first *Beatles Book* assignment took him to the Kentish coastal town of Margate where The Beatles were playing a week's residency at the Winter Gardens. "It was all very odd at first," Bryce recalled. "I really only knew The Beatles existed... certainly I didn't know them by name... The general public barely knew them – only the fans." That was all soon to change and Leslie's photos mirror how the Fab Four's following saw the group on stage throughout the spring and summer of 1963; Ringo behind his Ludwig kit, Paul in distinct left-handed stance with Hofner violin bass, George proudly cradling his Gretsch Country Gentleman and John alternating between his Gibson electric-acoustic J-160E and black Rickenbacker, each dressed in light grey Pierre Cardin collarless suits.

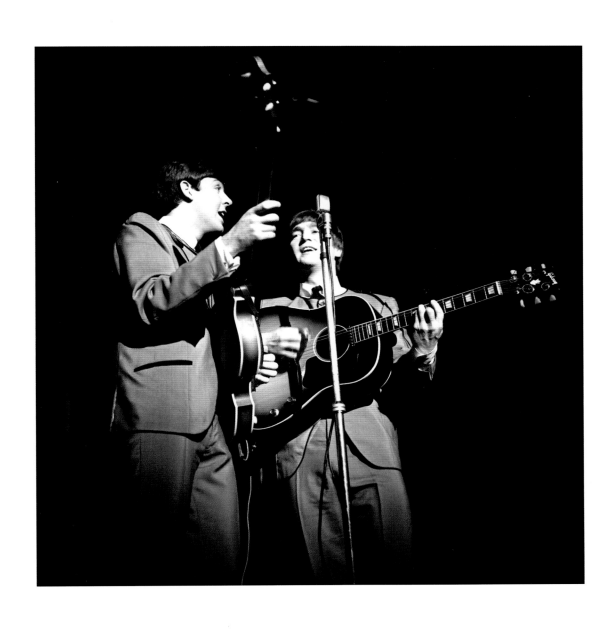

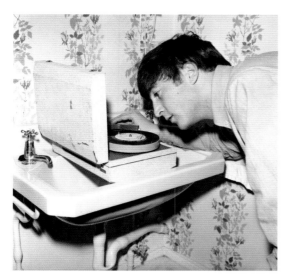

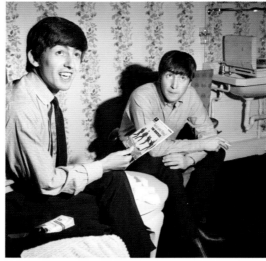

MARGATE
JULY 8–13, 1963

The Beatles killing time between performances – a short-sighted John getting up close to drop the stylus on a pre-release test pressing of their first EP *Twist And Shout* on the portable record player that travelled with the group on tour; gazing at their reflections for a Bryce-arranged pose; PR savvy Paul meeting admirers outside The Beresford Hotel and grooming himself for a show while George reads a fan letter.

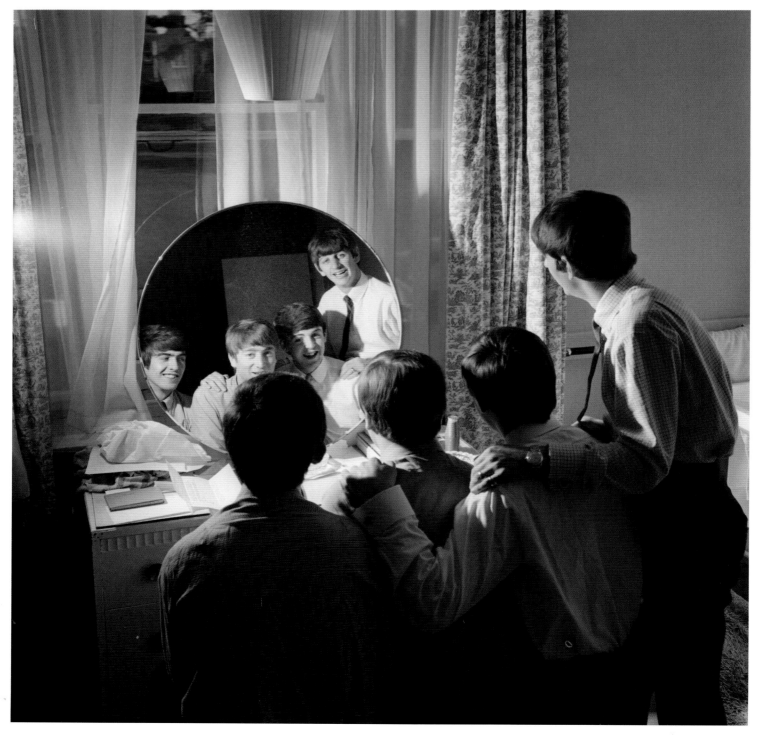

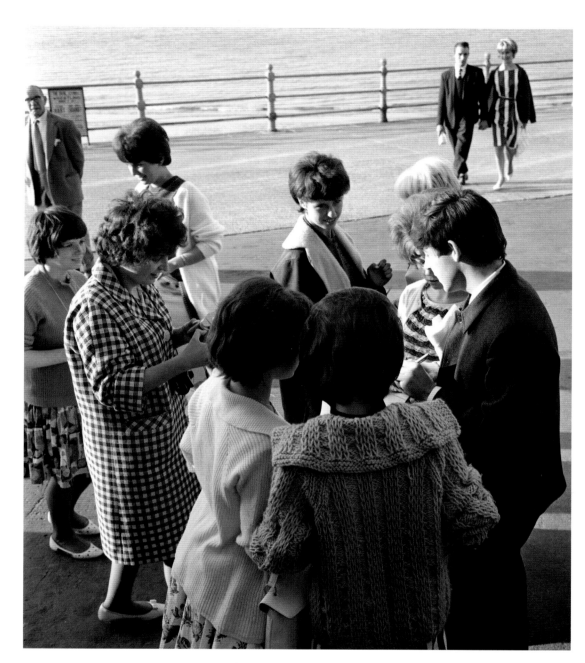

MARGATE
JULY 8–13, 1963

Sean O'Mahony, who accompanied Leslie Bryce to Margate, remembers how The Beatles appreciated the novelty of sleeping in the same bed at the same hotel for a whole week and the facilities on offer such as a swimming pool and table-tennis. Leslie Bryce: "I remember getting them to fix a huge striped umbrella outside [the hotel] by a table – it would have made a good picture but the manager roared out and told us to stop."

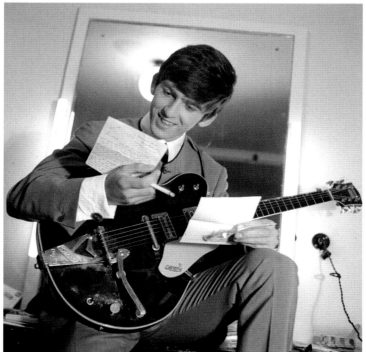

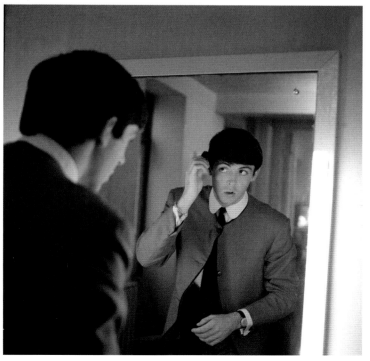

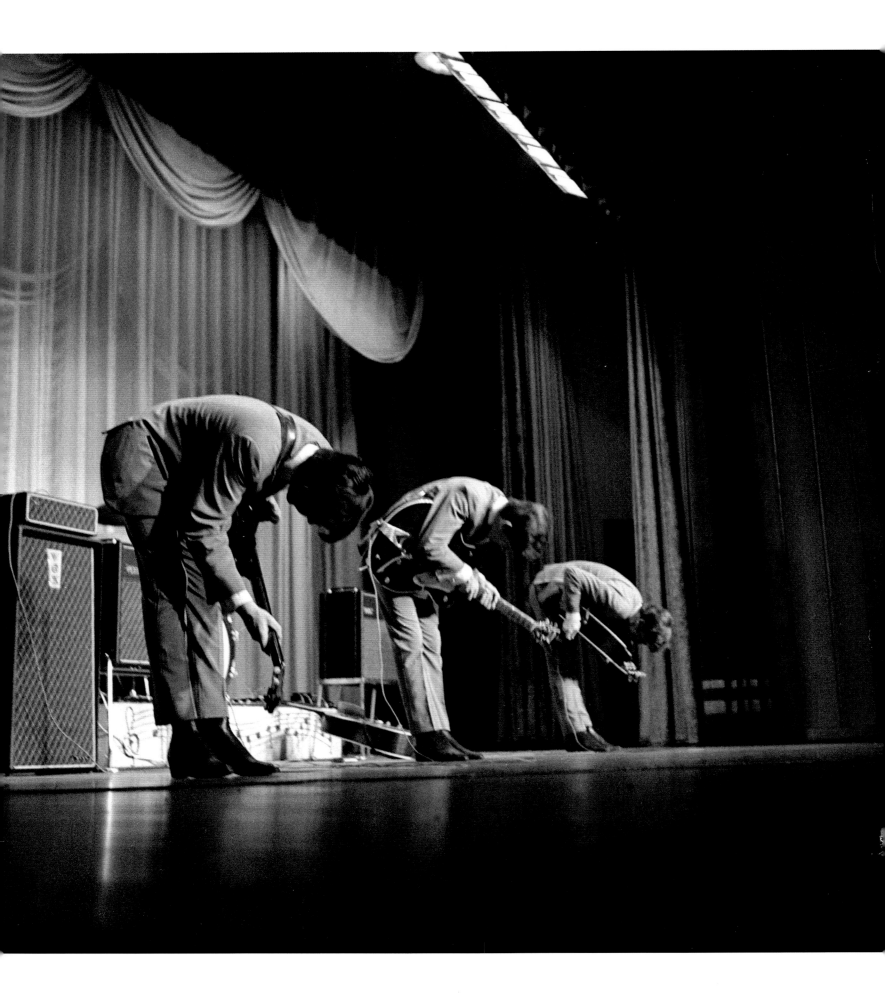

WINTER GARDENS, MARGATE
JULY 8–13, 1963

Tuning up and taking a bow. In an age when foreign travel was still considered a luxury, Britain's seaside resorts were the favoured destinations for most British holidaymakers. Consequently, with a readymade audience, entertainers – whether comedians, jugglers or pop stars – frequently performed summer seasons at coastal theatres, playing two "houses" daily on multi-artist bills. Sean remembers the shows he and Leslie attended not being sold out; The Beatles weren't yet household names. As well as Margate, in the summer of 1963 the group played week-long stints in Weston-super-Mare, the Channel Islands, Llandudno, Bournemouth and Southport.

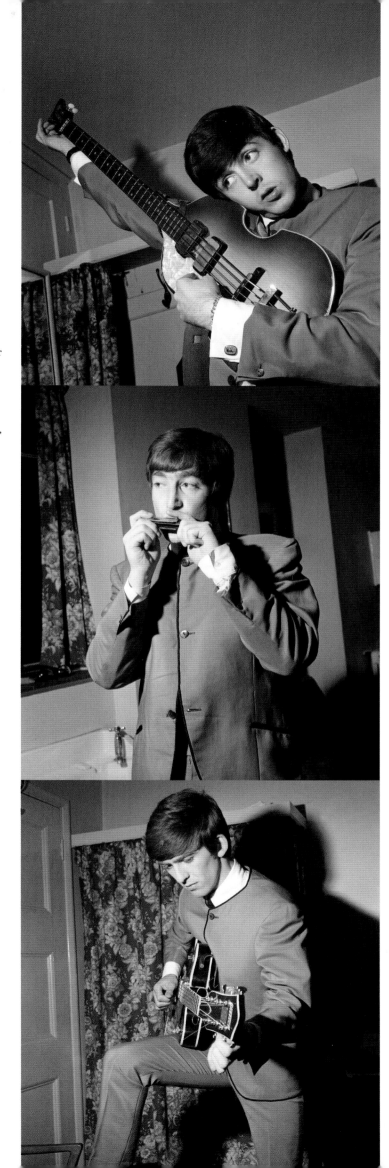

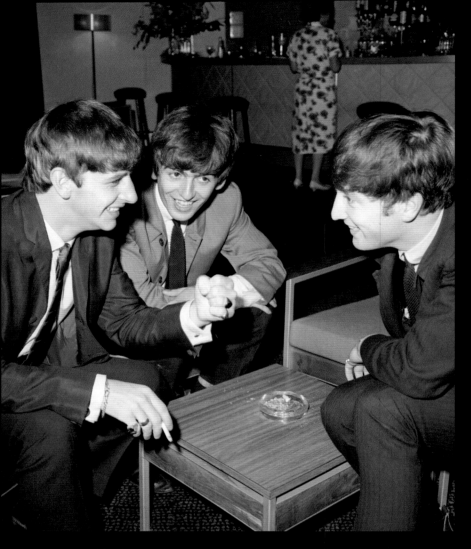

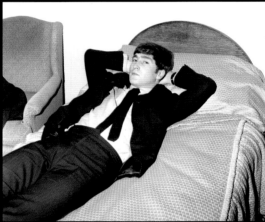

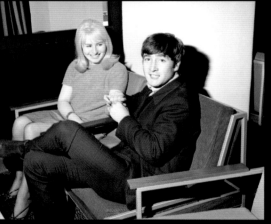

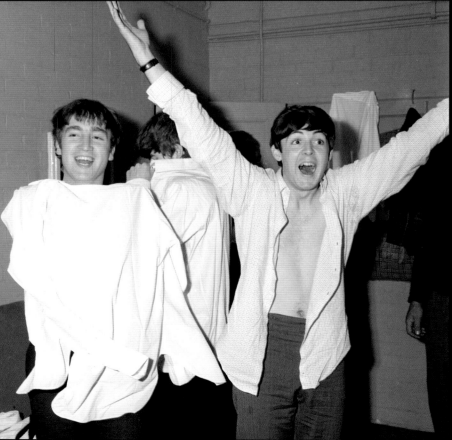

The Beatles off-duty at the Palace
Court Hotel during a six-day season
in Bournemouth. Cynthia Lennon
left baby Julian in the care of an
aunt of John's and travelled down
from Liverpool to the South Coast to
spend a first wedding anniversary
with her busy pop star husband.
George Harrison, laid up in bed with
a cold, composed his first song 'Don't
Bother Me' which was recorded for
the group's second album *With The
Beatles*, released in November.

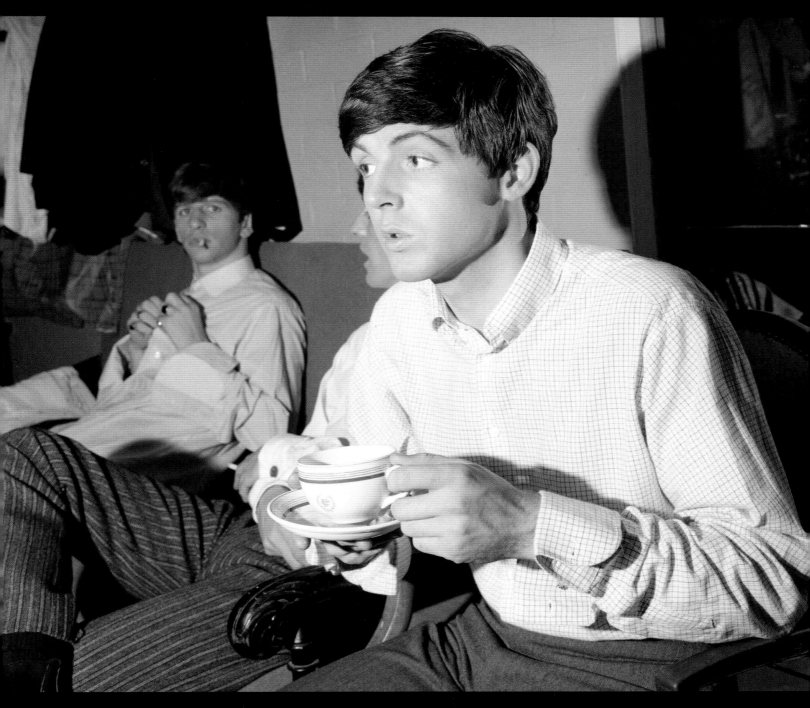

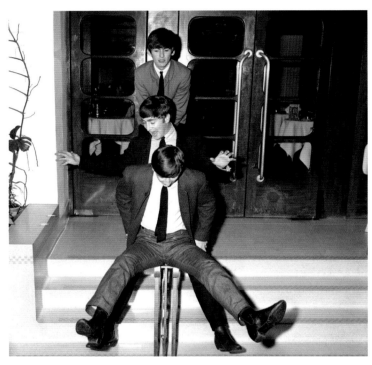

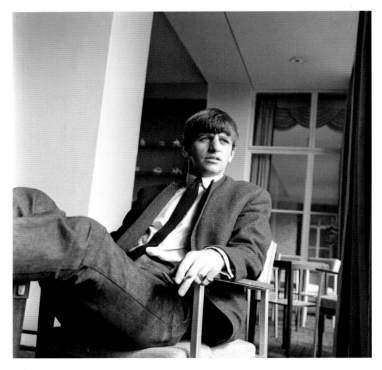

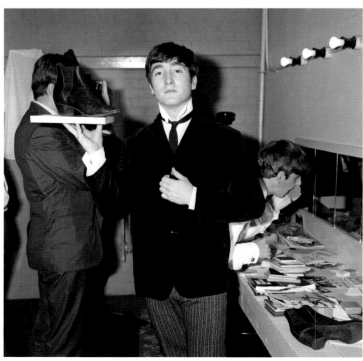

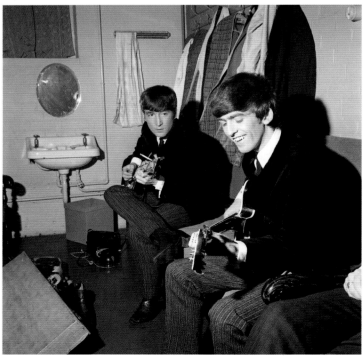

BOURNEMOUTH
AUGUST 22, 1963

For the *With The Beatles* sleeve shot, photographer Robert Freeman took the distinctive black and white half-shadow portrait in the hotel dining room (seen in the background of the photo top left, *opposite*) using the natural light coming through the heavy drape curtains. The image was directed by The Beatles themselves, inspired by the innovative images their friend Astrid Kirchherr had taken of them in Hamburg that incorporated a similar effect. The backstage pictures at the Gaumont Cinema reveal the cramped conditions in The Beatles' dressing room. They also show the group changing into their short-lived stage outfits of velvet jackets and pin-striped trousers. Ever willing to oblige Bryce's requests for spontaneous zany shots, waiter Lennon serves up an impromptu delicacy of *une Beatle botte*. It wasn't all larks in Bournemouth; at one performance, a large metal pin was thrown, narrowly missing Paul's eye, prompting an impassioned plea via the pages of *The Beatles Book*: "Please don't let people throw things at us on stage."

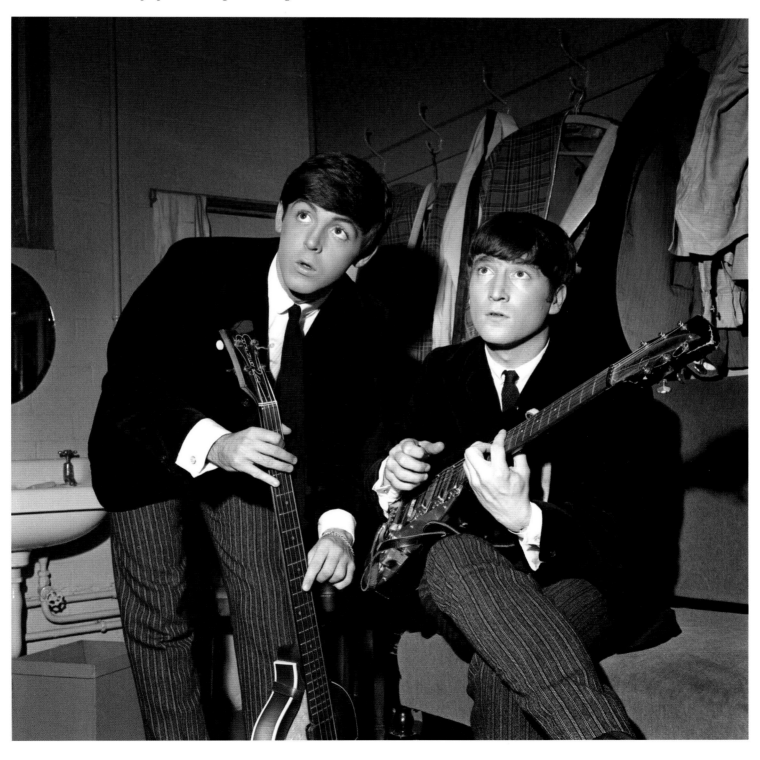

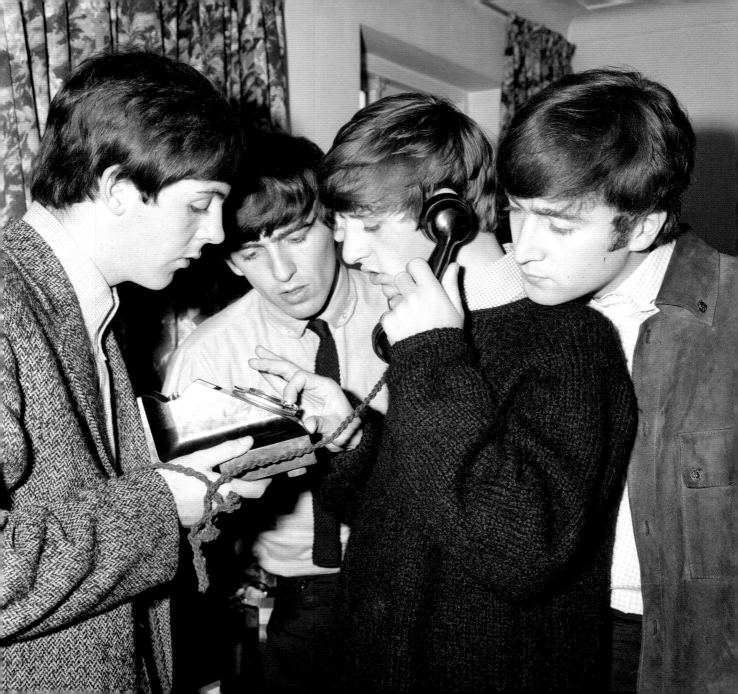

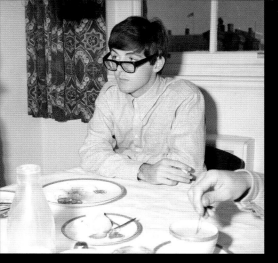

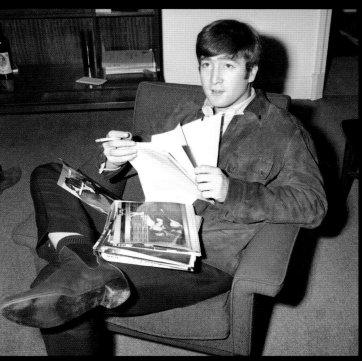

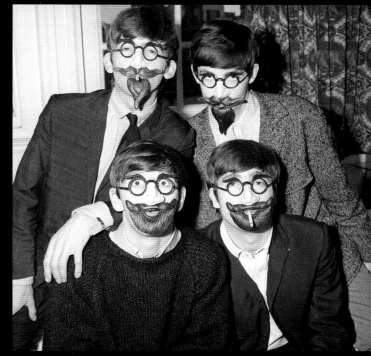

GREEN STREET, LONDON OCTOBER 16, 1963

For a very brief period in the autumn of 1963, all four Beatles shared a fourth floor flat at 57 Green Street, in the refined area of Mayfair. Sean and Leslie arrived in the afternoon as the boys were just getting up for breakfast. For the shoot, the four lounged around the flat, at the kitchen table sifting through some of John's birthday cards (he'd turned 23 on October 9), donning silly plastic masks and at one point Paul popped on John's horn-rimmed specs – a shot which later graced the cover of *Beatles Book #13* – while playing platters on the old-style radiogram. The iconic image of The Beatles on the landing (seen on page 208) remained one of Bryce's favourites. "The staircase photo was Sean's idea. [Sean] held the flashlight for me – and it wouldn't work at first. The boys offered to light matches for me. Then we got a real beauty. In fact, Brian Epstein had 50,000 copies printed for the fan club."

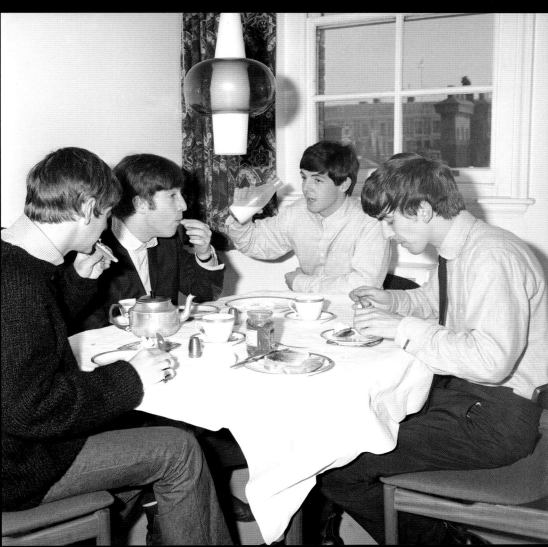

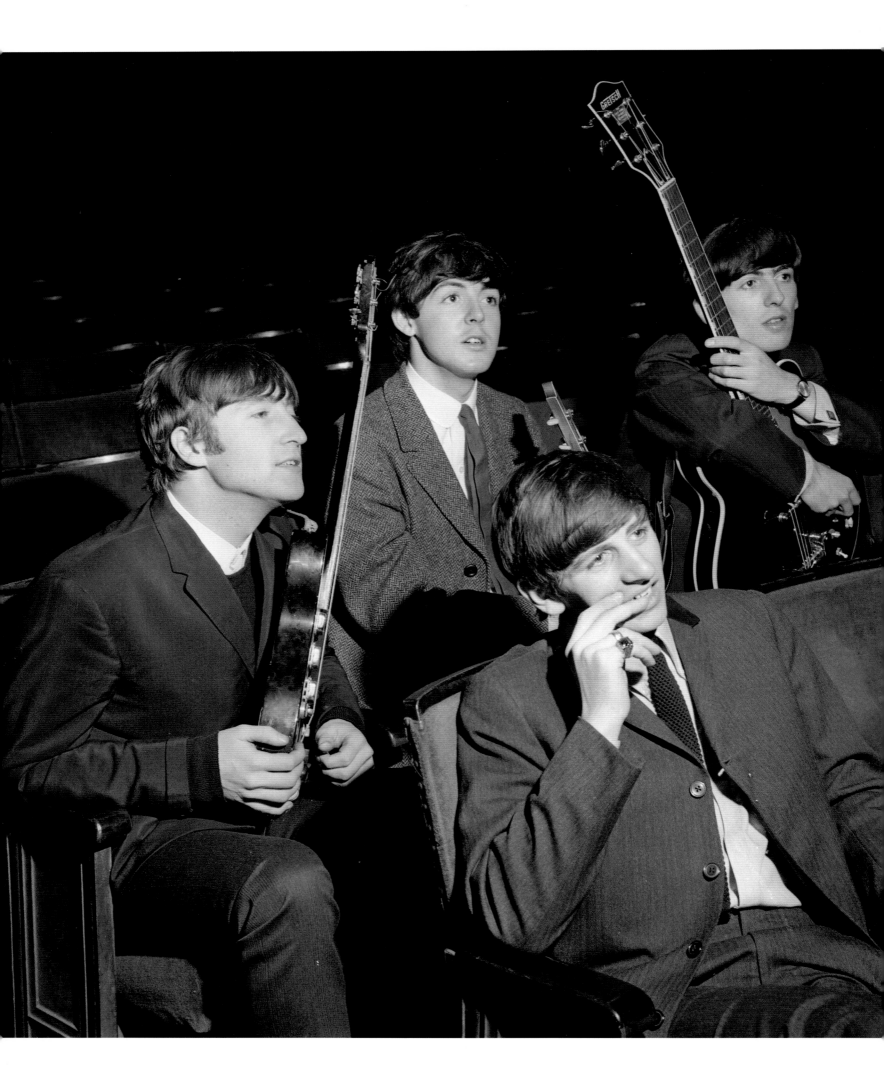

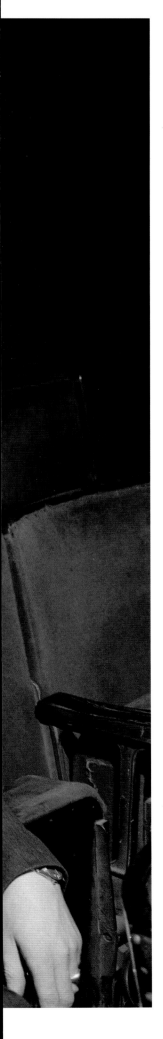

GAUMONT CINEMA, WOLVERHAMPTON
NOVEMBER 19, 1963

Nearly three months had passed since *The Beatles Book* visited a Beatles concert and within those intervening months, Beatlemania, a phrase coined by Fleet Street, had well and truly arrived. The Beatles were midway through their first headlining, hysterical tour of Britain where elaborate, military-style operations to transport the group in and out of each venue were becoming the norm. Locked inside the theatre hours before showtime, The Beatles engaged in an impromptu jam session with some of the support acts on the tour; Ringo stands next to his kit chatting to bandleader Peter Jay (holding cymbal) while John jams with the lead guitarist of the Rhythm & Blues Quartet and "Lolly" Lloyd of The Jaywalkers as NEMS employee Tony Bramwell looks on. While the Gaumont was still empty, Leslie had The Beatles pose on the stage as they would at a normal concert in order to get some close-up "live" action shots.

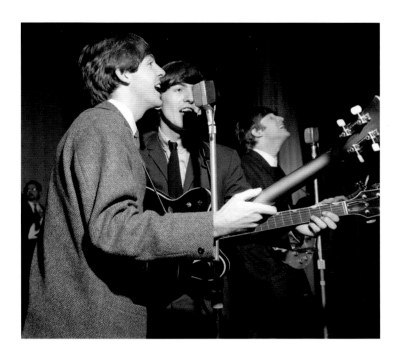

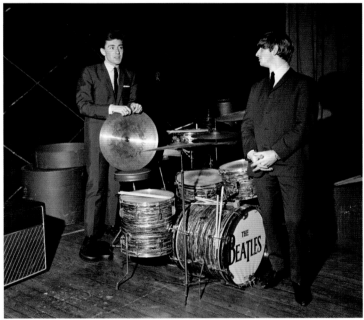

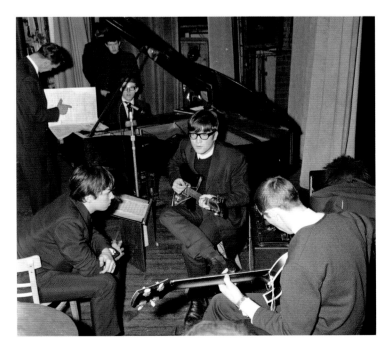

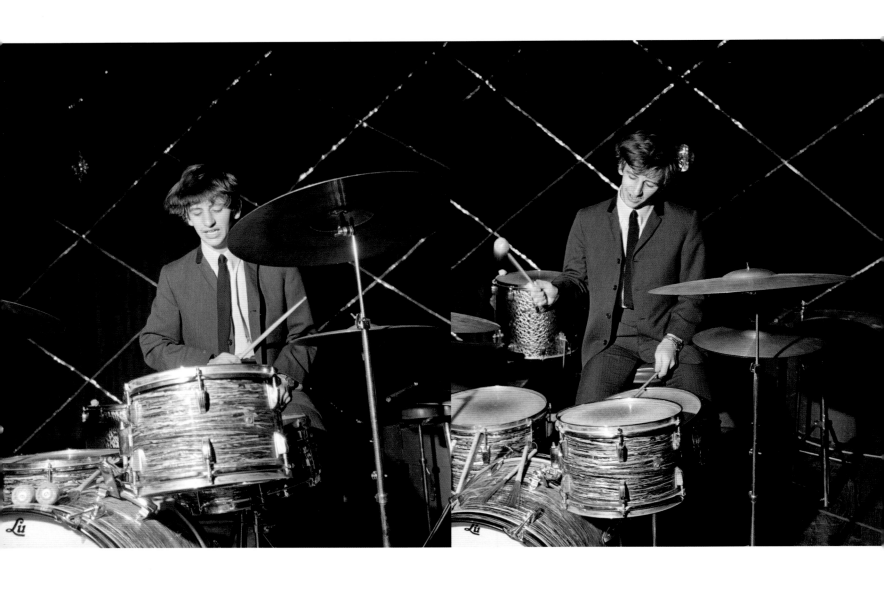

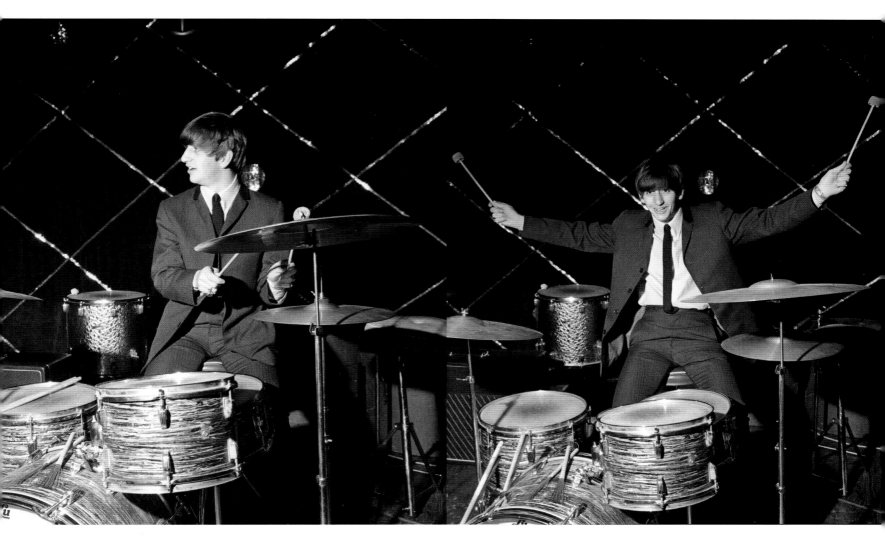

GAUMONT CINEMA,
WOLVERHAMPTON
NOVEMBER 19, 1963

Ringo in action for Bryce's camera.
Being the last to join The Beatles,
he was still unsure of his role in the
group and, because John, Paul and
George had known each other for
the best part of five years, was more
reticent to join in with the others
when answering reporters' questions.
This insecurity didn't last long and
Ringo's fun-loving personality and
percussive talents often singled him
out as many fan's favourite Beatle.

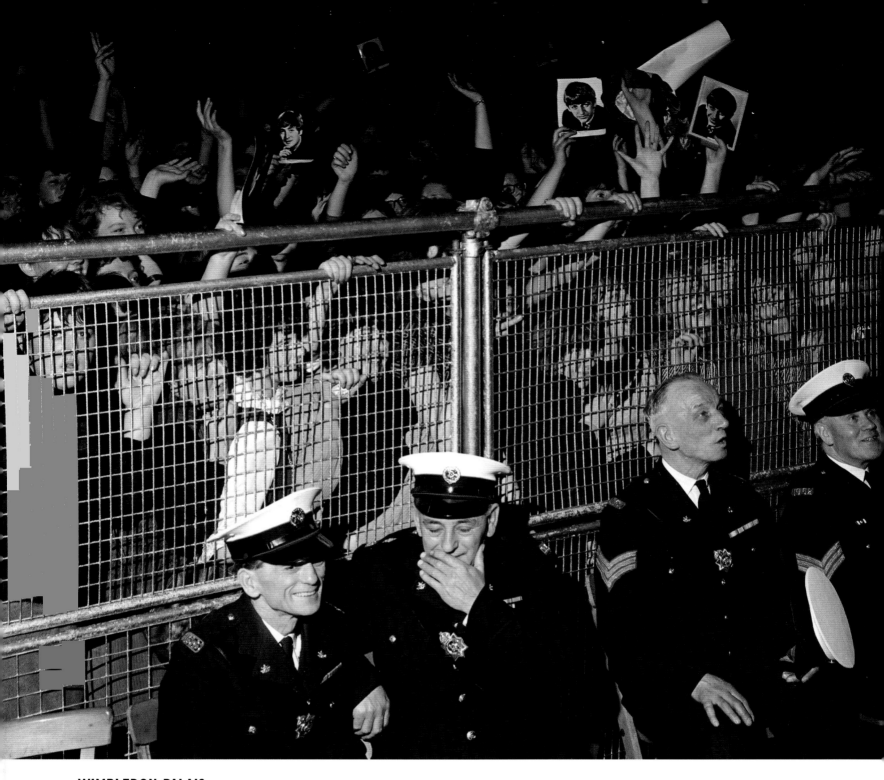

WIMBLEDON PALAIS,
LONDON
DECEMBER 14, 1963

With membership of the official Beatles Fan Club
continuing to spiral, towards the end of 1963 special
plans were made to hold conventions in both the north
and south of England. Liverpool Stadium was tentatively
pencilled in as a venue for October but when this was not
possible, fan club members were invited to the Liverpool
Empire on December 7 to watch The Beatles tape their
appearance on BBC TV's *Juke Box Jury* and the boys' own
live special *It's The Beatles*. The Southern Area Fan Club
Get Together, announced in the October issue of *Beatles
Book* and held during the afternoon at this south London
ballroom, was even more unique and intimate. Fan club
members were asked to complete a special form which
was entered into a ballot draw of 2,000 winners. A limited
number went to the senders of the first applications
pulled out of the postbag while the remaining tickets had
an asking price of 3/6d. Some 3,000 fans queued along a
wooden bar to meet and greet, feel a Beatle fringe and get
autographs. If The Beatles were happy to go along with
this, they were less enthusiastic about the steel cage-like
structure erected around the front of the stage.

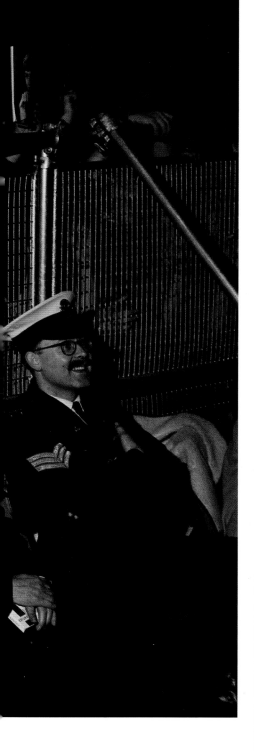
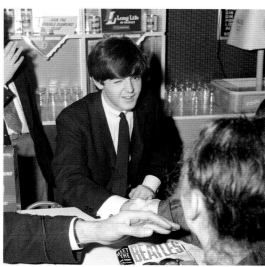
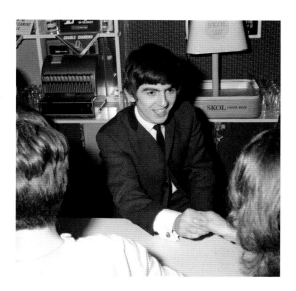
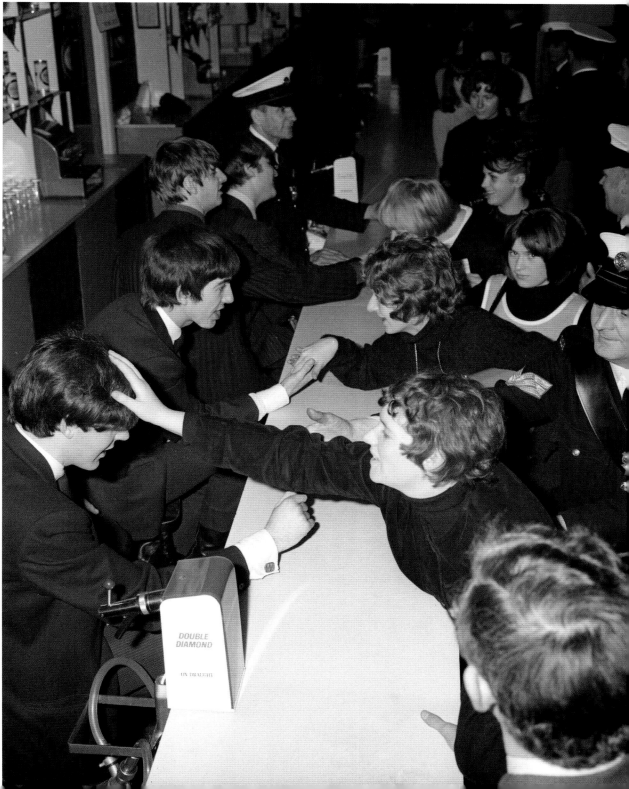

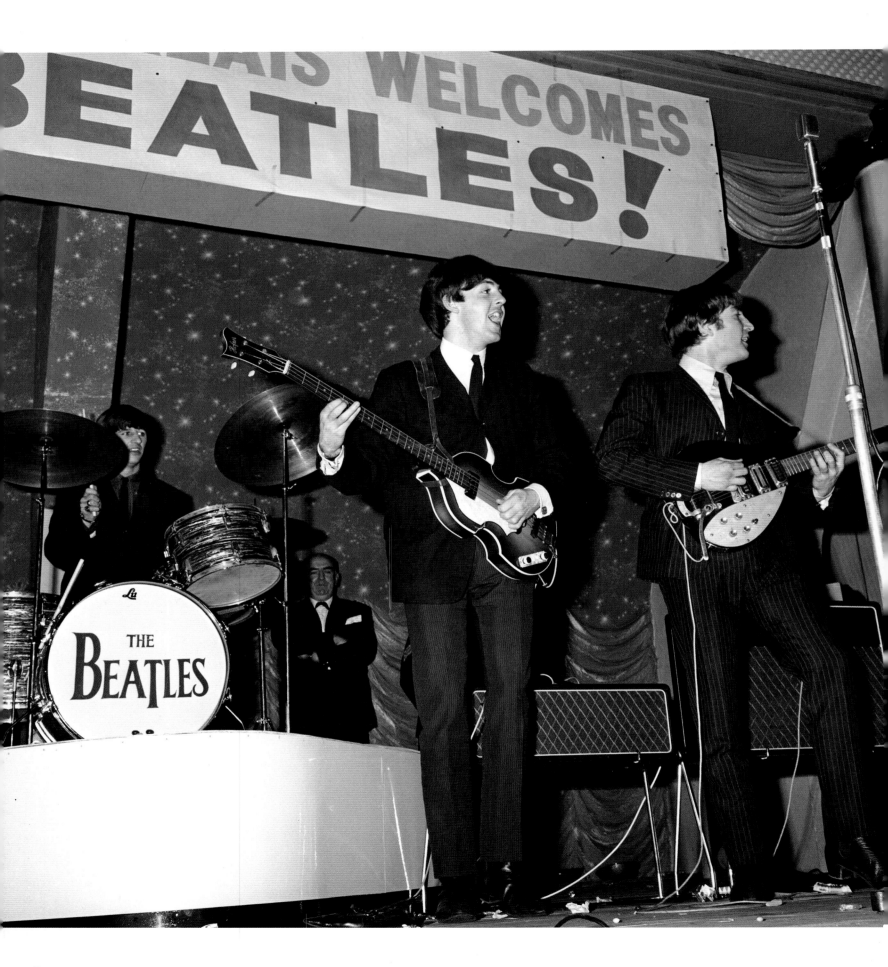

WIMBLEDON PALAIS, LONDON
DECEMBER 14, 1963

Not only were The Beatles unhappy at seeing fans pressed up against a wire barrier, but a wooden extension, hastily built by the venue's management to protect their precious stage, further irritated them. It proved less than sturdy as Mal Evans discovered when loading the gear into place for the afternoon concert. The Beatles performed tracks off their new album as well as, by special request, Ringo's showcase 'Boys'. While The Beatles and aides were aghast at the organisation, the event crowned a memorable year – both for them and the Fan Club, which now boasted a membership of 30,000 Beatle People; 28,000 of whom received a special Beatles Xmas flexi disc – a Yuletide tradition that would last through until 1969.

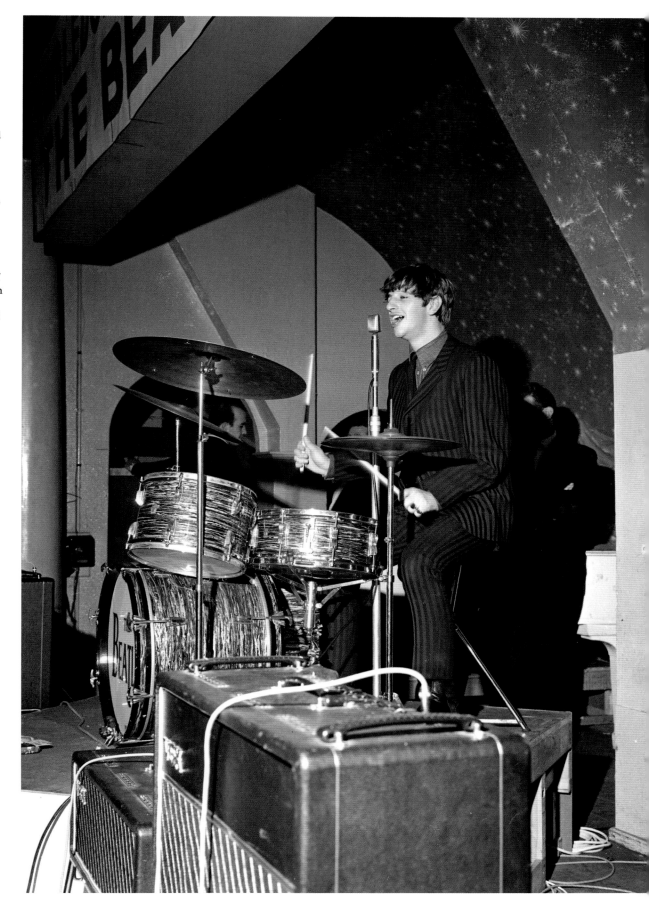

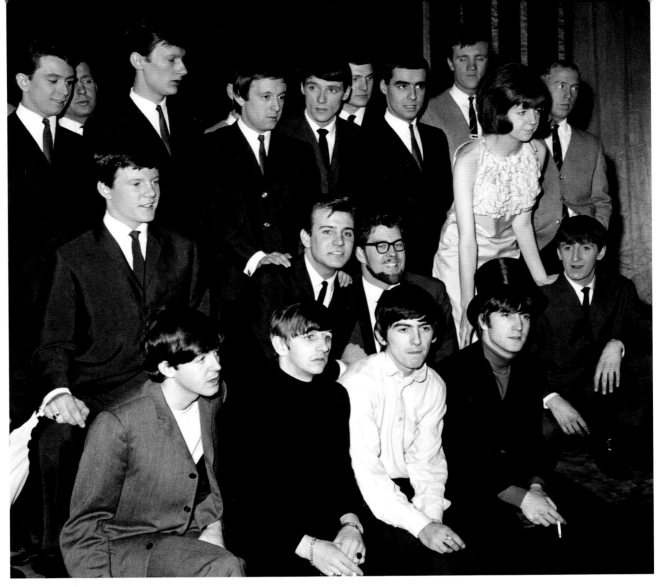
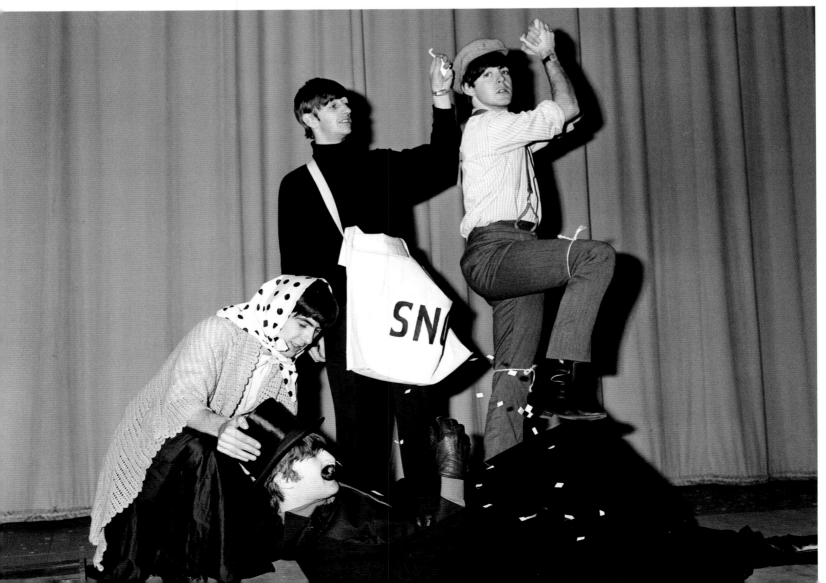

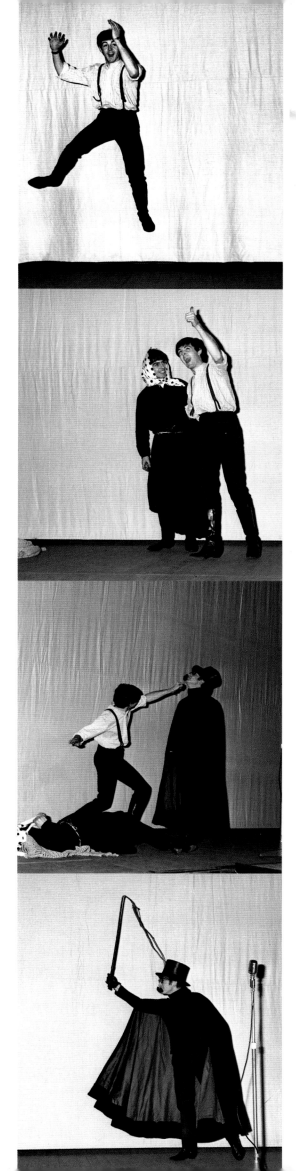

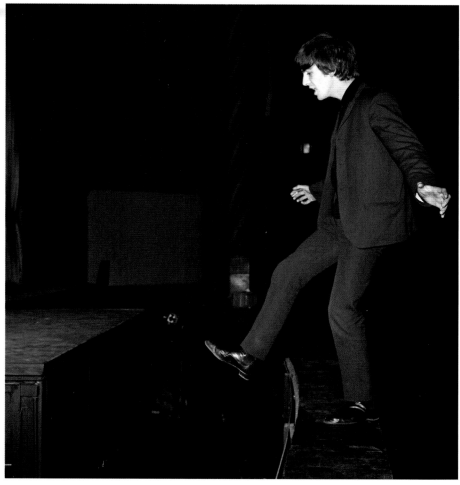

FINSBURY PARK ASTORIA, LONDON
DECEMBER 24, 1963

Lining-up with the cast of 'The Beatles' Christmas Show' which featured The Barron Knights, Tommy Quickly, The Fourmost, Billy J Kramer with The Dakotas, Cilla Black and compere Rolf Harris. The Beatles were in costume to rehearse their roles in 'What A Night', a traditional Victorian pantomime in which John played the villainous Sir John Jasper and George the heroine Ermyntrude, who is saved by 'Fearless Paul the Signalman'. Ringo's role was to run around the stage sprinkling paper snow. Produced by Peter Yolland, 'The Beatles' Christmas Show' commenced with the four Beatles bursting out of a mock Christmas cracker. They were seen again descending from a huge cardboard helicopter 'The SS Beatle' (after the supporting cast had disembarked), complete with BEA travel bags and dark glasses, and appeared in quick-fire skits between acts. The dialogue in the sketches was pre-recorded and played back through the primitive PA for The Beatles to lip-sync to; a futile exercise considering that their voices were drowned in female shrieks as soon as a Beatle opened his mouth. To appease fans up North, two unofficial 'final dress rehearsals', minus the theatrical sketches, took place in Bradford and Liverpool.

Tony Barrow, under his nom de plume of Frederick James, wrote this report (*Beatles Book #7*) that included a barb aimed at the unauthorised mercenary merchandisers now prevalent around Fabdom: "Between Christmas Eve and Saturday 11 January almost 100,000 people trooped out to North London's three-thousand-seater Finsbury Park Astoria to see Brian Epstein's presentation of 'The Beatles' Christmas Show'. Outside the theatre a gigantic photograph of the fabulous foursome grinned down upon 'All Tickets Sold' notices. To cross the pavement and reach the entrance one had to scramble through a small siege of salesmen – the new street-corner spivs of the Beatle era who must be making a small fortune from the shoddy pictures and out-of-date booklets they try to flog in any town where The Beatles are scheduled to appear."

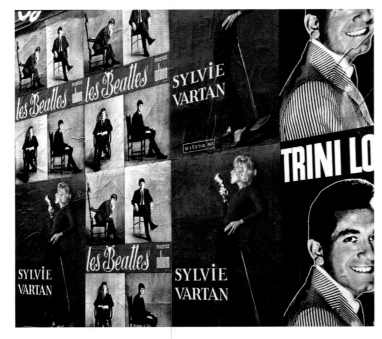
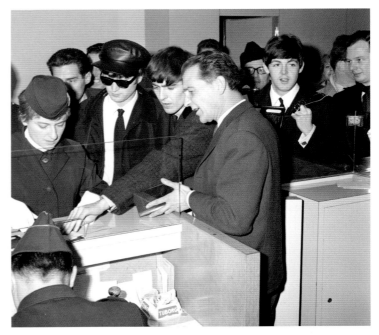
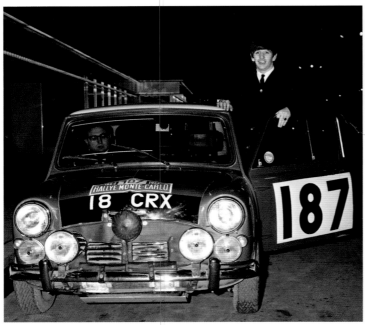
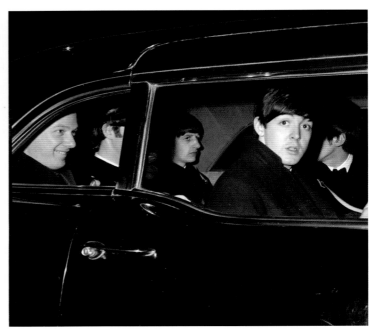
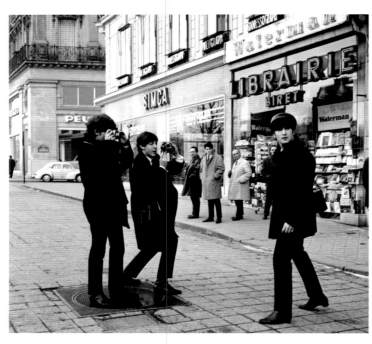
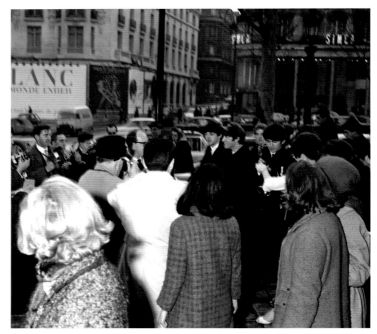

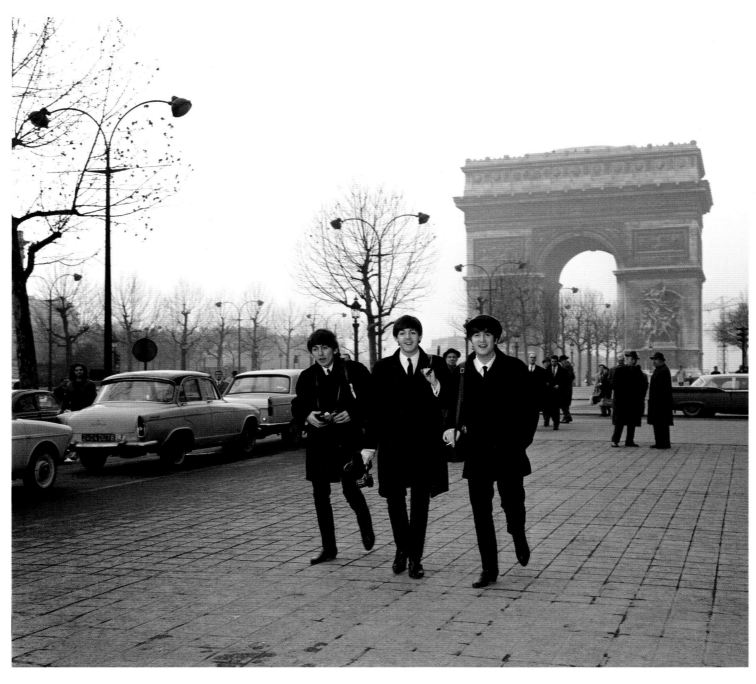

PARIS,
FRANCE
JANUARY 1964

Les Beatles! On January 14, John, Paul and George, along with Brian Epstein, press agent Brian Sommerville and Mal Evans, flew into Le Bourget airport, Paris. Ringo was fogbound in Liverpool and arrived with Neil Aspinall the following day, collected by a souped-up British mini entered in the Monte Carlo Rally, to join the others at the swank George V Hotel close to the Champs-Elysees. In the weeks leading up to the three-week marathon at the Olympia Theatre, the French media had been trying to uncover the 'secret' of the new phenomenon. A typical French response to The Beatles was "the English group with the French hairstyles". The week The Beatles arrived chic Parisian department stores were stocking Beatle wigs. The media frenzy sparked by an afternoon saunter along the Champs-Elysees must have struck John and Paul as ironic; in October 1961 they had spent John's 21st wandering the City of Light as complete unknowns. Much of the pair's leisure time was spent in their hotel suite composing songs required for their forthcoming film, *A Hard Day's Night*.

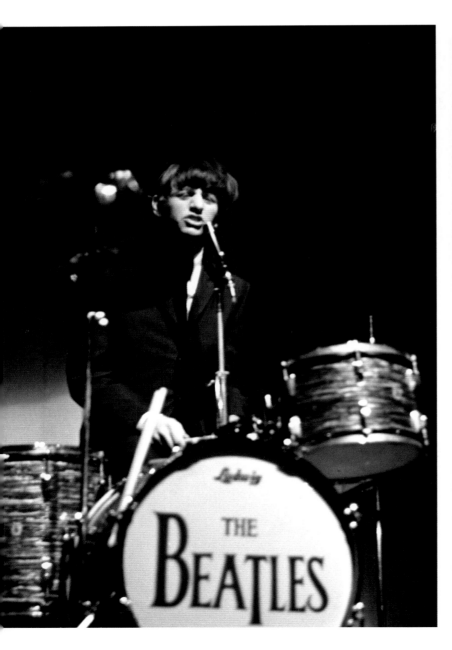
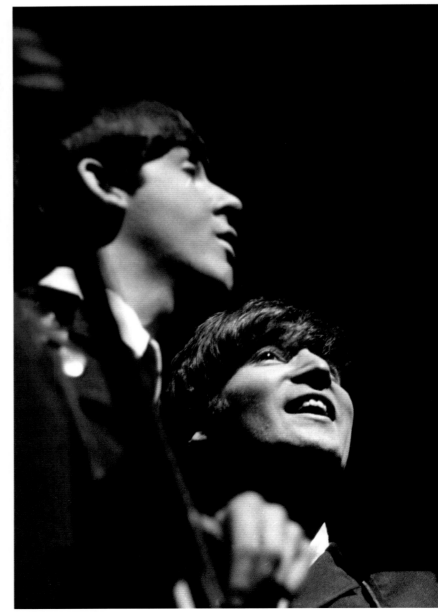

L'OLYMPIA THEATRE, PARIS, FRANCE JANUARY 1964

The Beatles in action at the Olympia, the top music-hall in France. The more vociferous fans packed the matinee shows, while the evening attracted Parisian sophisticates. Initially French audiences appeared indifferent but they soon fell into line. The support acts included Trini Lopez and blonde bombshell chanteuse Sylvie Vartan. If The Beatles expected more examples of va va voom femininity, they were dismayed to find their audiences were mainly comprised of young males. Also high ticket prices, mixed press reviews, overzealous officials, aggressive photographers and the unpredictability of the French electricity supply (which resulted in three power outages on opening night) conspired to make the experience less than satisfying. However any disappointments were overcompensated for by the news that reached them on January 15 – 'I Want To Hold Your Hand' had jumped from number 43 straight to the top of the American *Cashbox* hit parade, the fastest-rising recording ever by a British act in the United States.

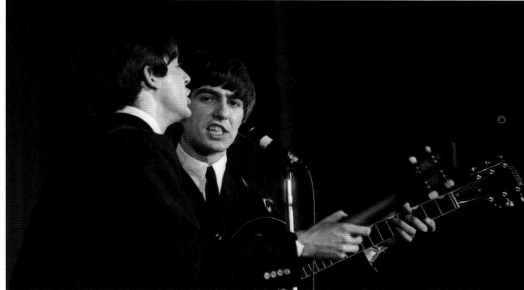

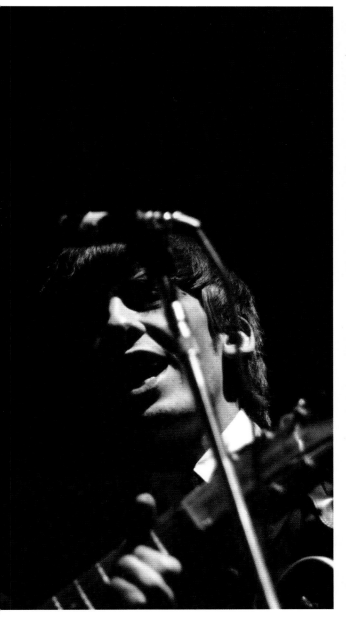

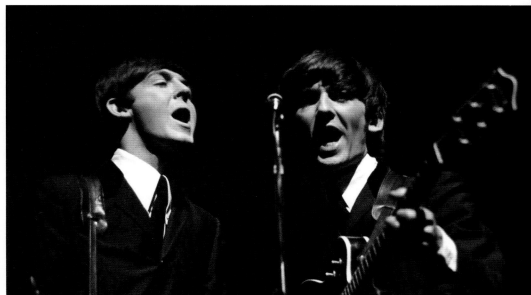

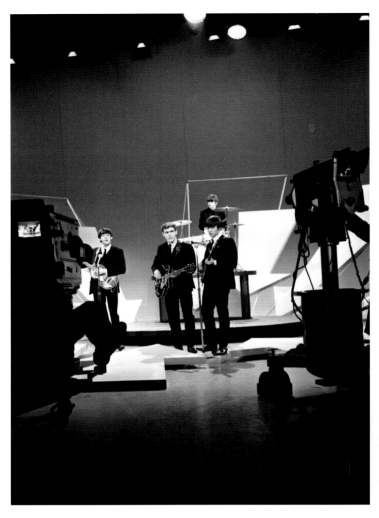

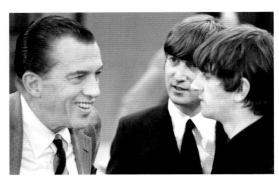

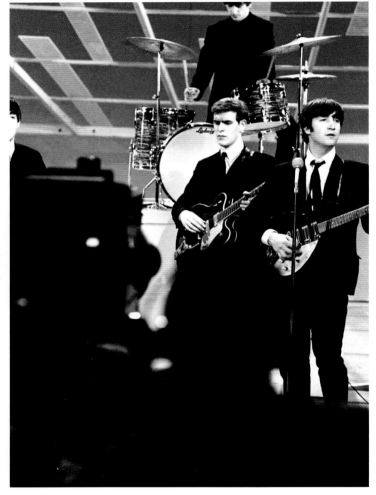

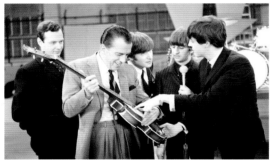

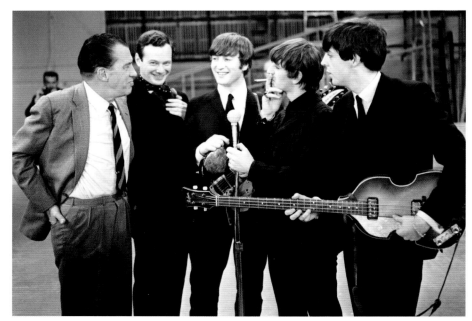

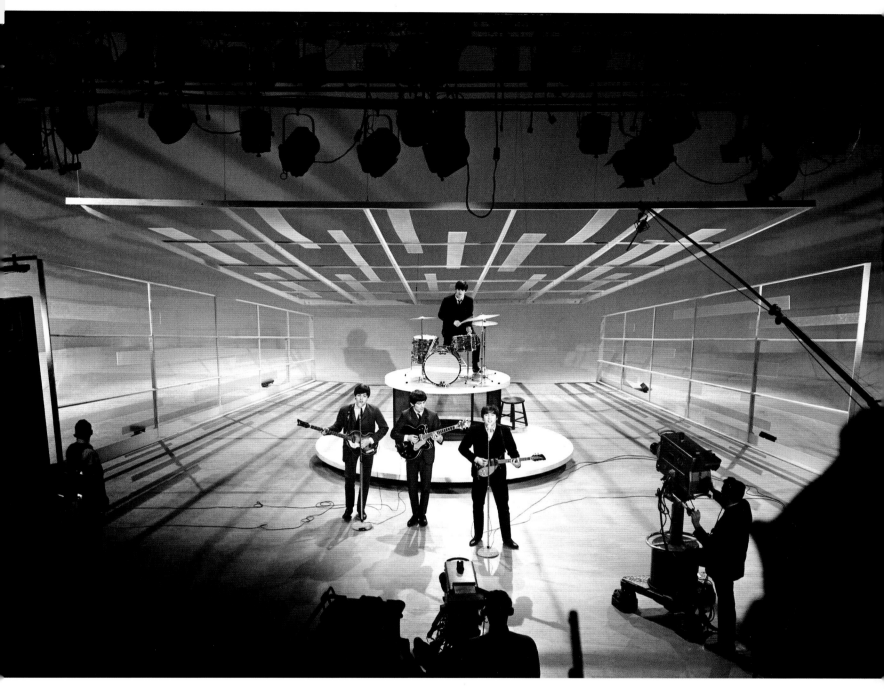

STUDIO 50,
NEW YORK CITY, USA
FEBRUARY 8–9, 1964

The Beatles' first US tour was the stuff of legend from the moment Pan-Am Boeing 707 flight PA 101 left London Airport at 11am on Friday, February 7 with Brian Epstein, Brian Sommerville, Neil Aspinall and Mal Evans on board as well as record producer Phil Spector and a planeload of photographers and reporters. The group arrived at John F Kennedy International Airport to a welcoming committee of over 3,000 fans. The following afternoon, with George back at the Plaza Hotel nursing a sore throat, The Threetles (with Neil standing in) rehearsed at CBS Television's Studio 50 on Broadway between West 53rd and 54th Streets for their prestigious appearance on *The Ed Sullivan Show*. The group had to become members of trade union AFRA first. On the 9th, before a studio audience, The Beatles first pre-taped what would be their third consecutive appearance on Sullivan's networked show (to be aired on February 23 after their departure back to England), followed by their actual live debut, witnessed by an estimated 73 million viewers across America – at the time a record for US television.

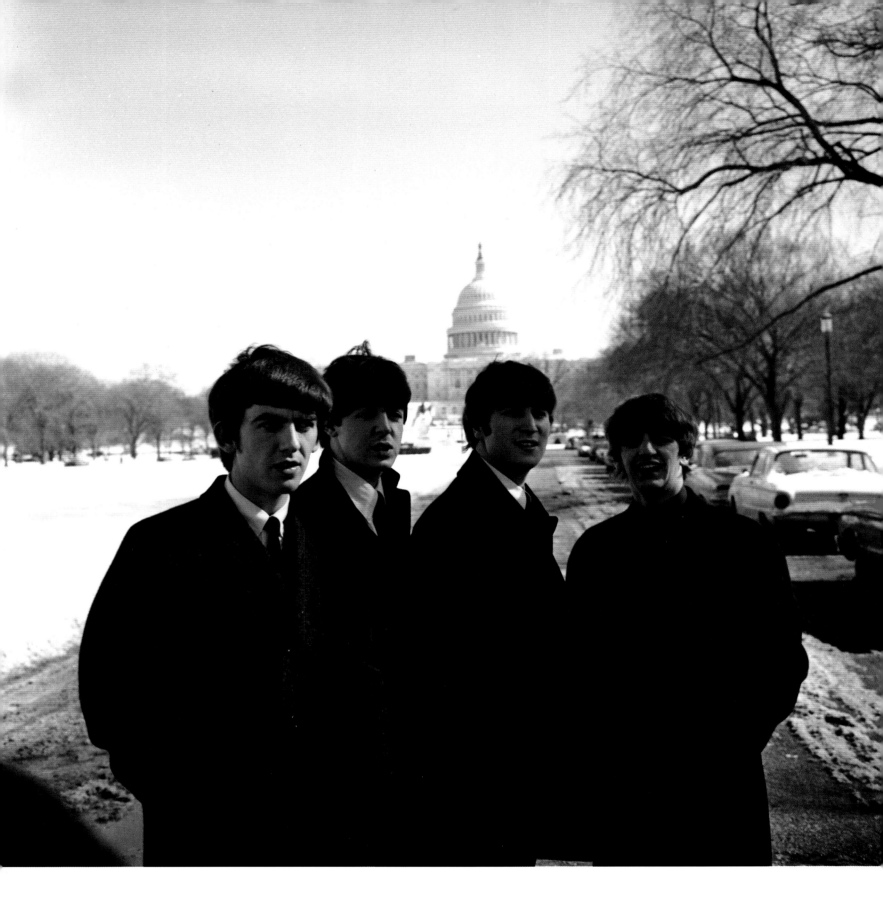

WASHINGTON DC
FEBRUARY 11, 1964

The Beatles' first American
concert was in Washington DC
at the Washington Coliseum.
From a chaotic welcome at Union
Station, The Beatles were whisked
to the venue for a pre-show press
conference – as usual, the four
supplying quick fire quips to some of
the inane questions put to them – as
well as a publicity photo session in
the snow with the iconic Capitol Hill
building as a backdrop.

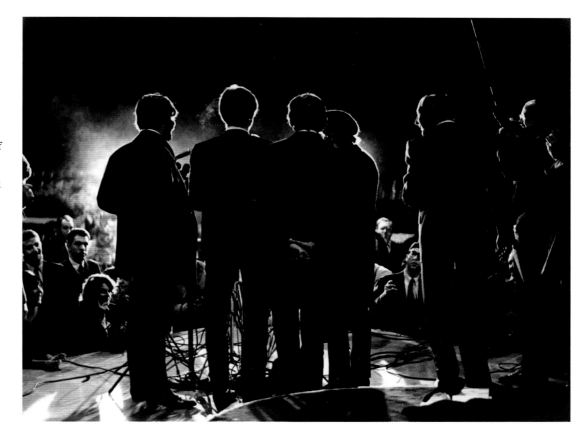

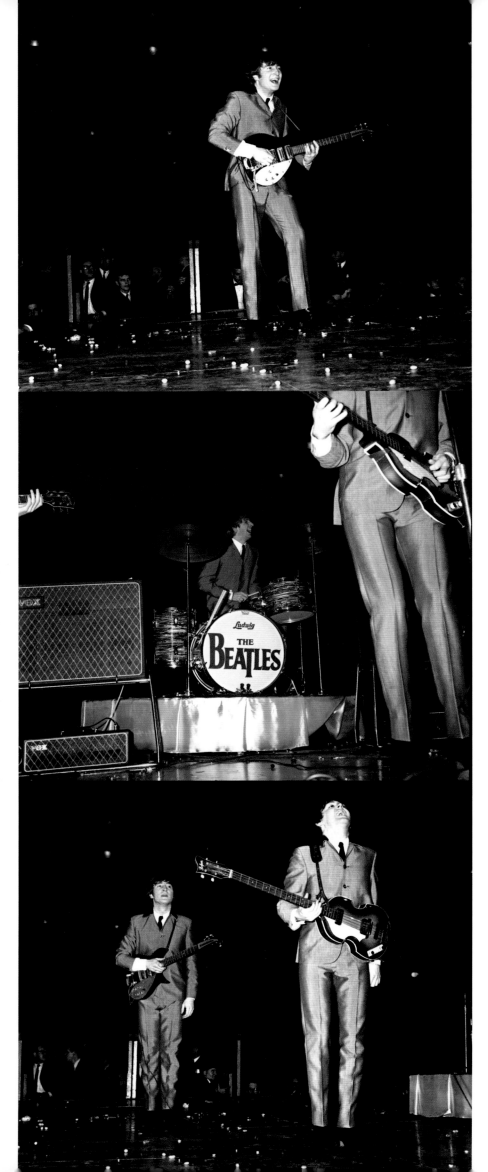

WASHINGTON COLISEUM, WASHINGTON DC
FEBRUARY 11, 1964

The Coliseum concert was notable for
its stage – a boxing ring situated in
the round, with The Beatles having to
run the audience gauntlet through
a gangway to reach it. Also, absurdly,
with the aid of Mal Evans, they were
obliged to turn their equipment
around every few songs to face
different sections of the 8,600 crowd.
As evidenced, jelly beans were among
the missiles showered onto the stage
but, as The Beatles later complained,
American jelly beans were hard-cased
and felt like bullets, unlike the softer
British-style jelly babies.

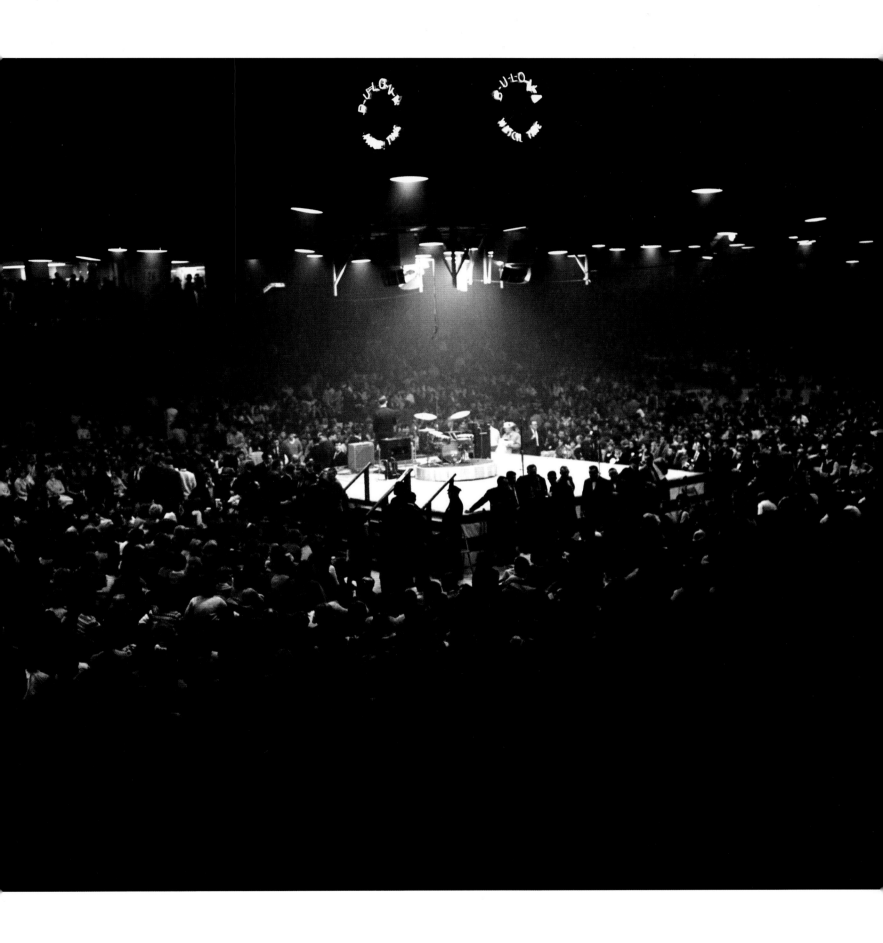

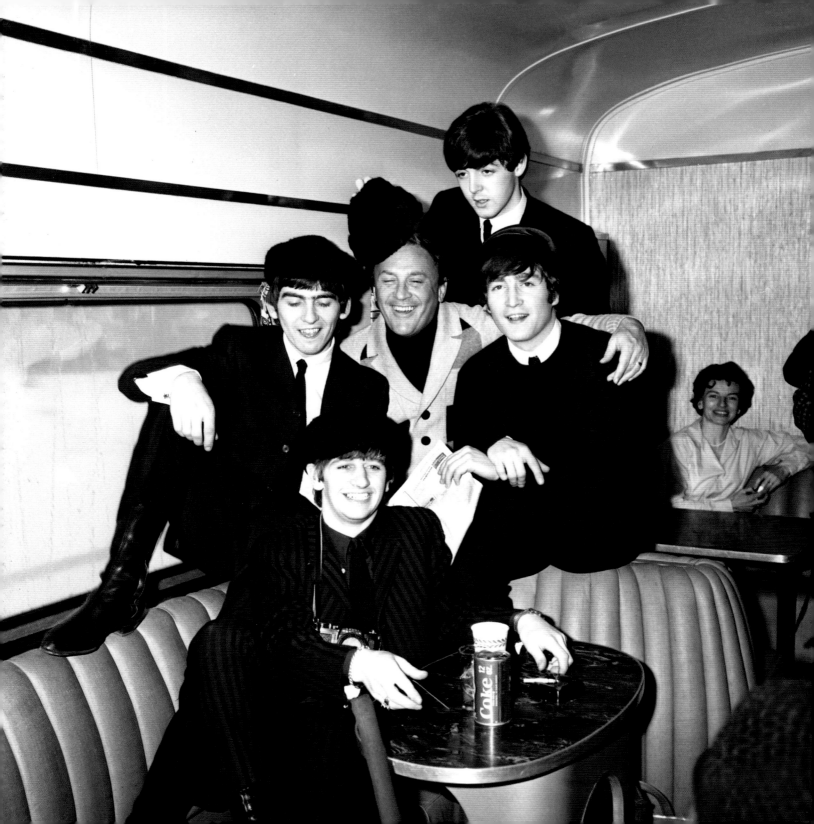

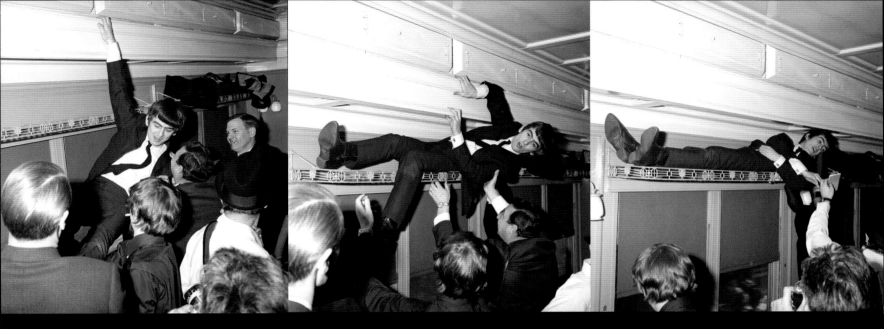

TRAIN FROM WASHINGTON TO NEW YORK
FEBRUARY 12, 1964

Because of snow storms, The Beatles
took a train from Penn Station
rather than fly to Washington
DC. The Pennsylvania Railroad
Company attached a special coach
to the express Congressman,
which was full of journalists and
photographers capturing the Fab
Four's tomfoolery on both legs of
the return journey from New York.
While George is hoisted up into
the luggage rack, his progress is
watched by George Martin, who had
flown over with the intention of
overseeing Capitol Records recording
The Beatles at their Carnegie Hall
concerts on February 12 – a plan
that was scuppered by the American
Federation of Musicians. Also along
for the ride was Murray the 'K'
(*opposite*), a hip-talking New York DJ
on station WINS, who had attached
himself like a limpet to The Beatles'
entourage from the moment they
arrived in America and remained

TRAIN FROM WASHINGTON TO NEW YORK FEBRUARY 12, 1964

More shots from the Washington train journey; George talks transistors with Neil and Mal, Paul makes a new friend while Ringo shares a drink with the train guard and meets a young fan. As well as Leslie Bryce, Beatle-related photographers like Robert Freeman and Dezo Hoffman (both seen opposite in the background), as well as reporters and 'smudgers' from the British dailies, made the journey over the Atlantic to document The Beatles conquering America. Ringo borrowed their cameras for another zany scene captured in Albert and David Maysles documentary production *What's Happening! The Beatles In The USA*, as press officer Brian Sommerville (glasses and cigarette) looks on.

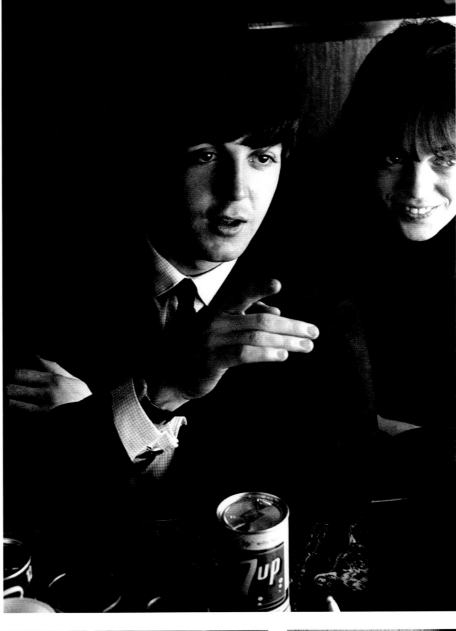

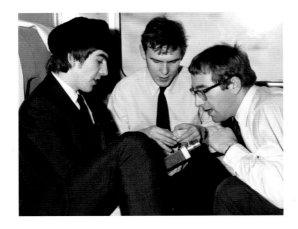

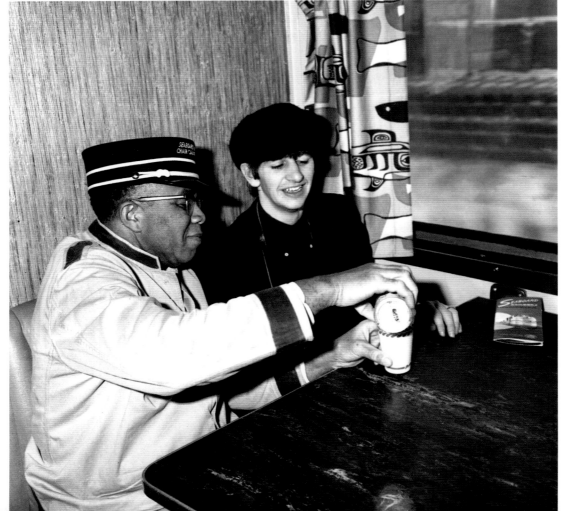

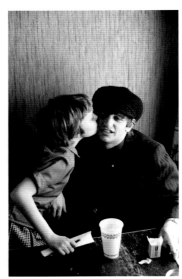

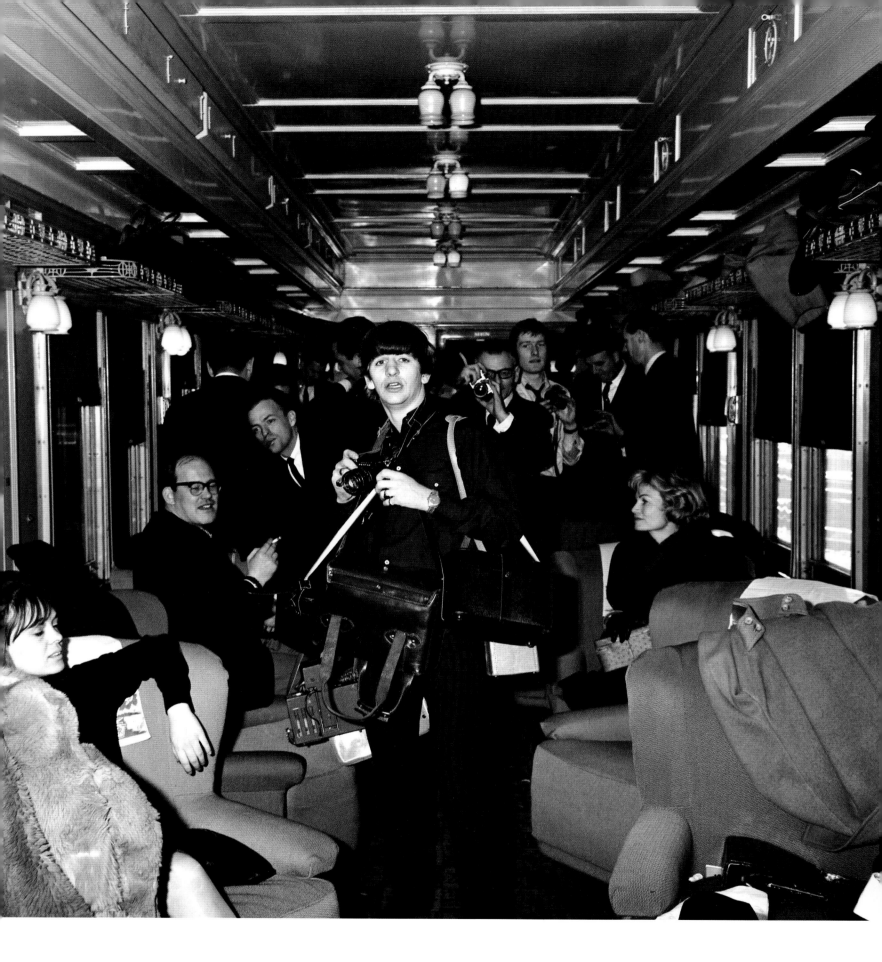

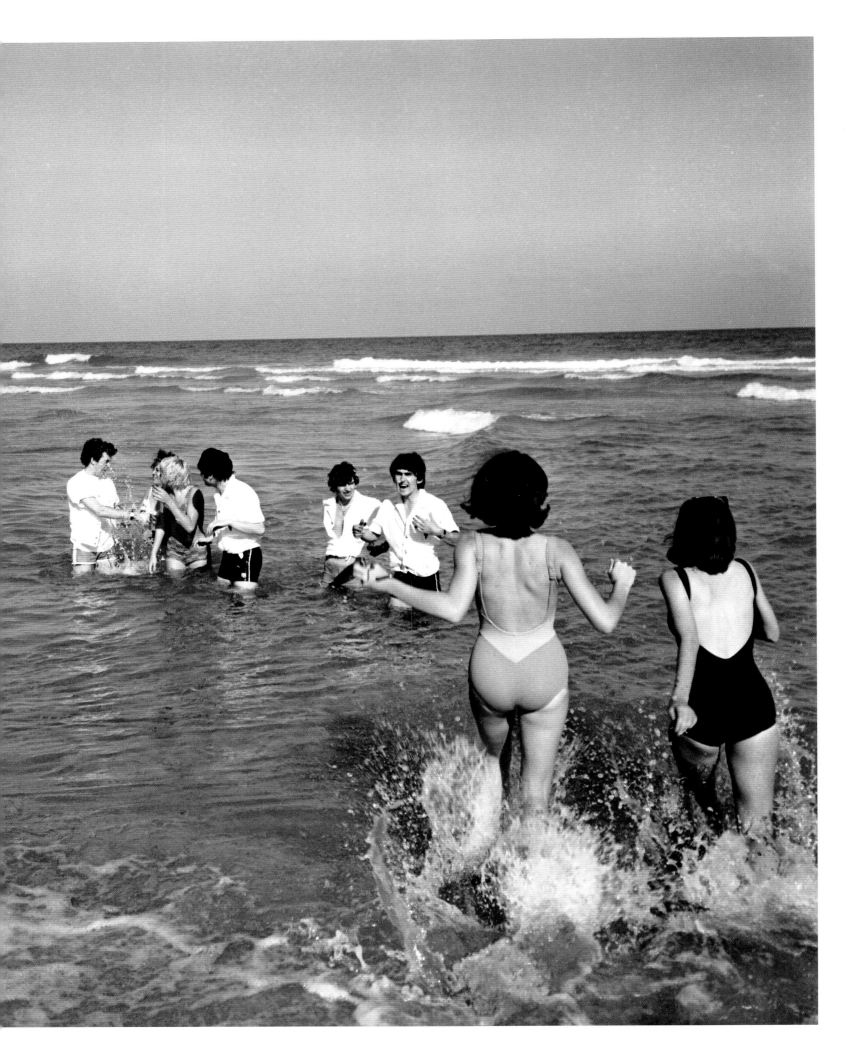

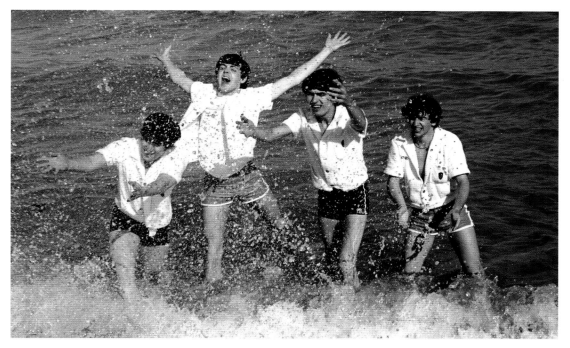

MIAMI BEACH, FLORIDA
FEBRUARY 13–16, 1964

On February 13, The Beatles left New York for the sunshine of Miami, staying at the Deauville Hotel where they were to make their return appearance on *The Ed Sullivan Show*. On the 14th, the group visited a private swimming pool for a group shot later used on the cover of *Life* magazine. The rest of the day was spent aboard a luxury houseboat loaned by Mr Bernard Castro that was surrounded by cruising boats manned by fans or press hoping to catch a closer glimpse. The following day, a publicity paddling session was held in the Miami surf where the splashing Beatles were soon joined by a bevy of bathing beauties.

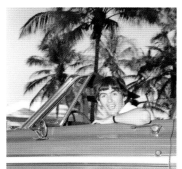
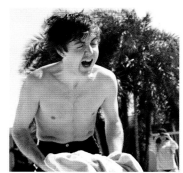
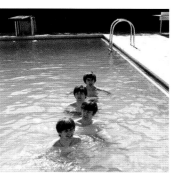

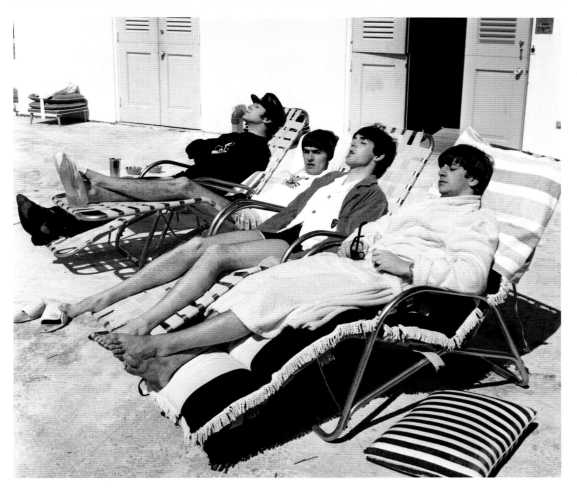

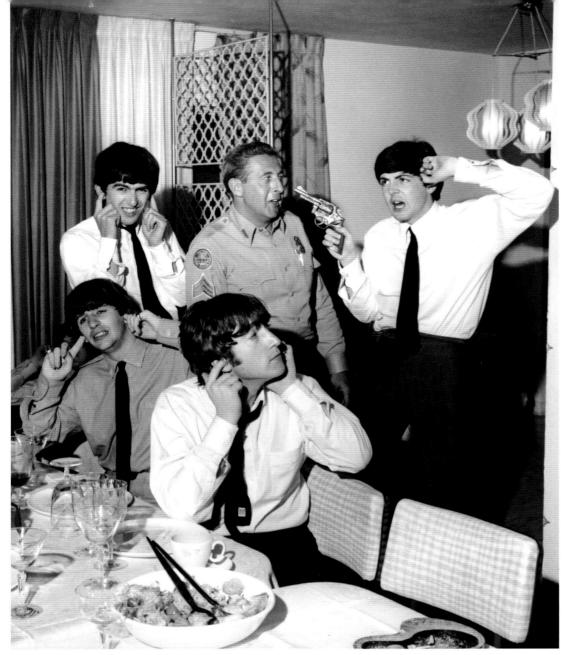

MIAMI BEACH, FLORIDA
FEBRUARY 14, 1964

On Valentine's Day evening, The Beatles and their immediate entourage accepted an invitation from Sgt. Buddy Dresner, the head of their personal police security detail, to sample a typical home-cooked American roast dinner. The photos show The Beatles and Brian Sommerville kicking back at the Dresner residence with Buddy, wife Dottie and children Barry, Andy and Jeri.

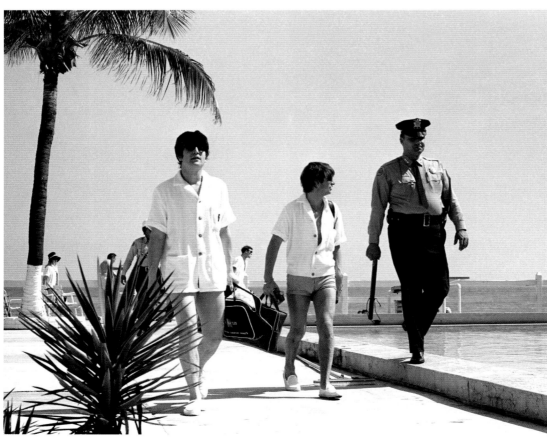

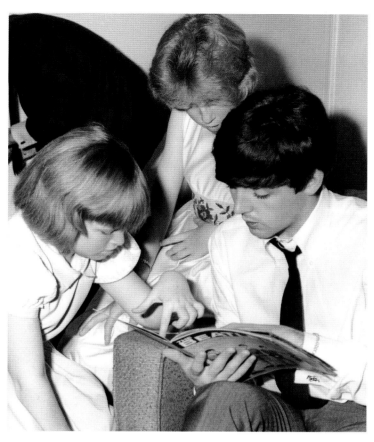

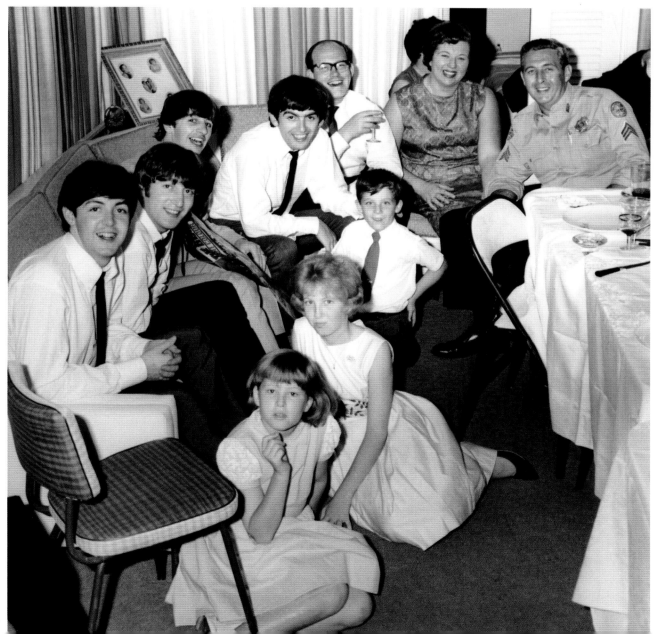

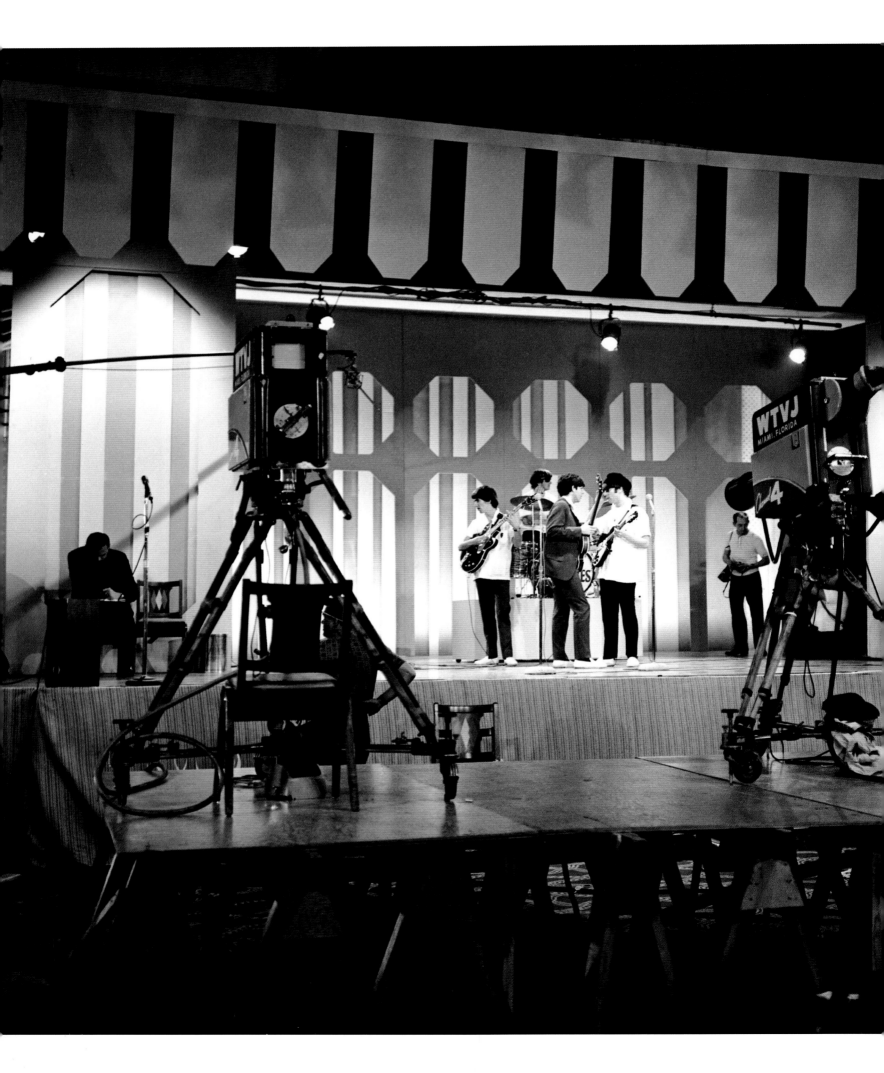

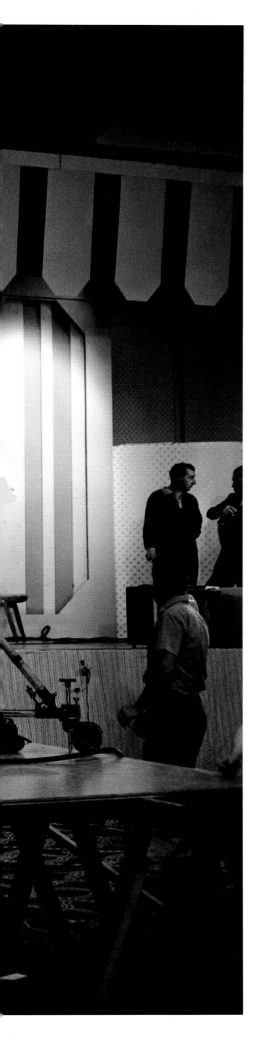

DEAUVILLE HOTEL, MIAMI BEACH
FEBRUARY 15–16, 1964

The Beatles spent most of the weekend rehearsing for *The Ed Sullivan Show* which went out live the evening of Sunday the 16th. The audience that night included champion boxers Joe Louis and Cassius Clay (soon to fight Sonny Liston in the World Heavyweight Championship) whom The Beatles met at his Miami gym during their stay. John had just taken delivery of his new black model Rickenbacker 325 and back in New York George had been presented with a Rickenbacker 360 12-string. The influential sound of these guitars would distinguish the next set of Beatles recordings for the soundtrack of *A Hard Day's Night*.

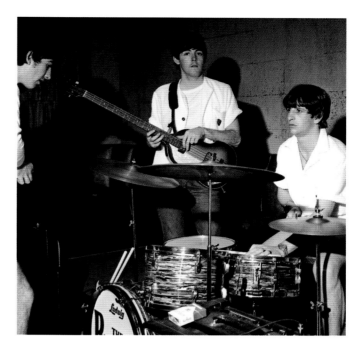

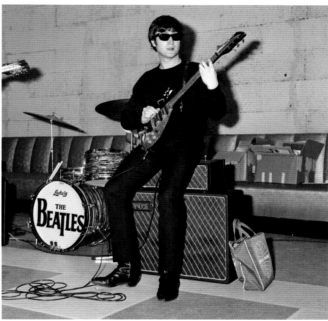

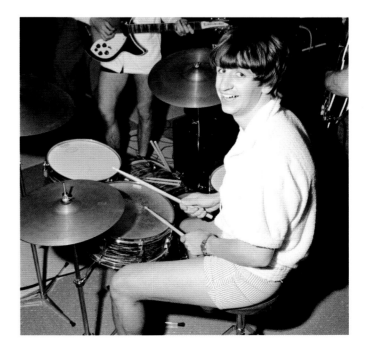

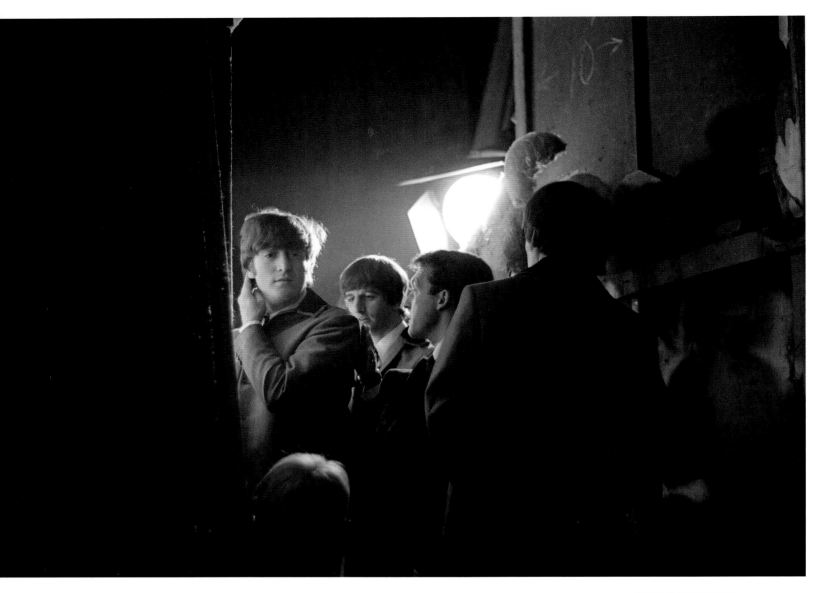

SCALA THEATRE, LONDON
MARCH 1964

Shooting of *A Hard Day's Night*, The Beatles' first venture into celluloid, started on March 2 when a specially chartered British Rail train pulled out of Paddington station heading for Minehead in the West Country. On March 23, the action moved from Twickenham Film Studios to the Scala Theatre in central London for the television concert sequence in front of a specially-invited audience of fans and extras. In these pictures The Beatles pose with director Richard Lester, his wife Deirdre and young son Dominic, with whom George shares his cuppa. John indulges in a test of iron strength with Norman Rossington (who played Norm, their fictional road manager) and among the showgirl extras was a former Miss United Kingdom and Miss World, Rosemarie Frankland, seen with Paul and George.

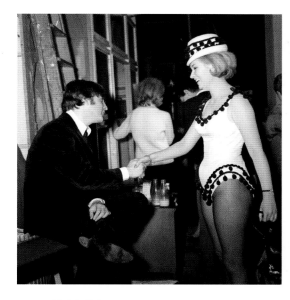

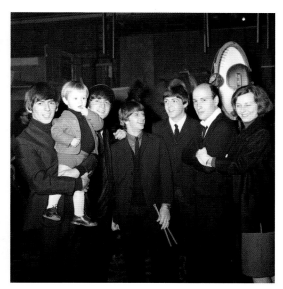

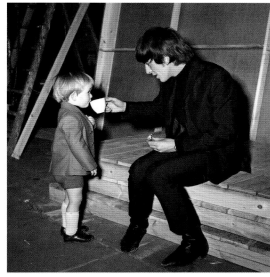

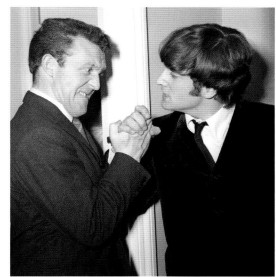

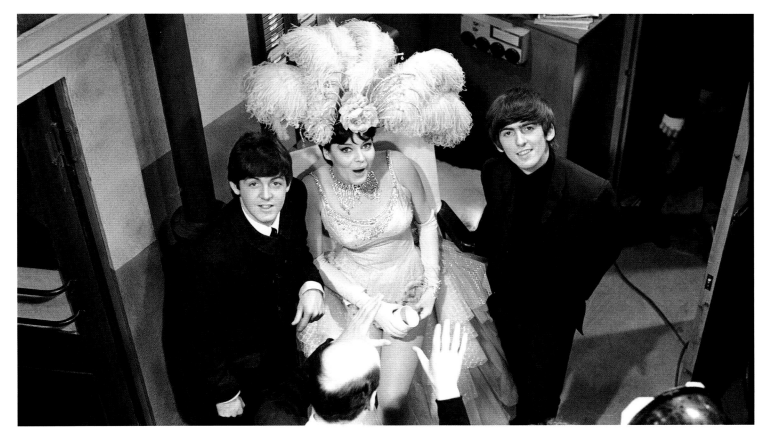

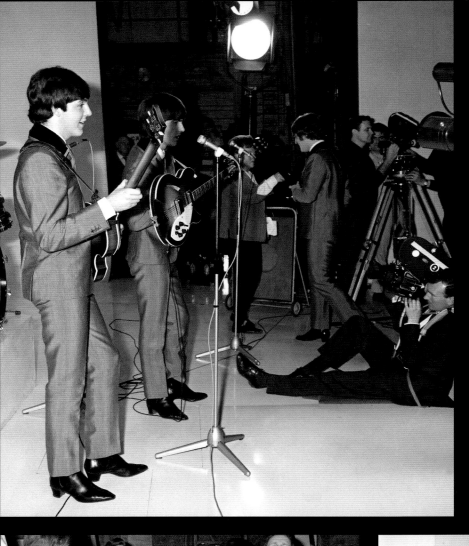
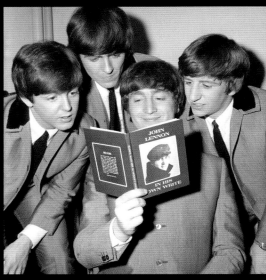
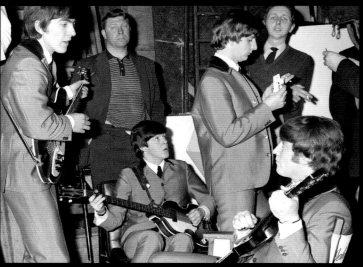
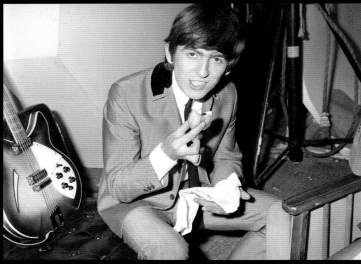
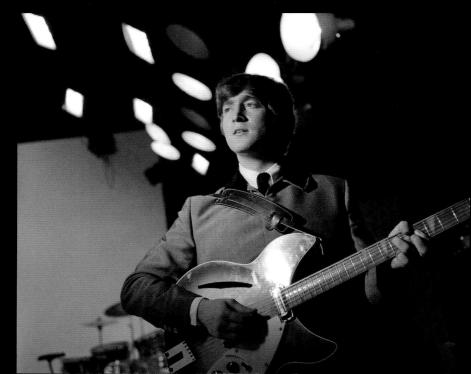

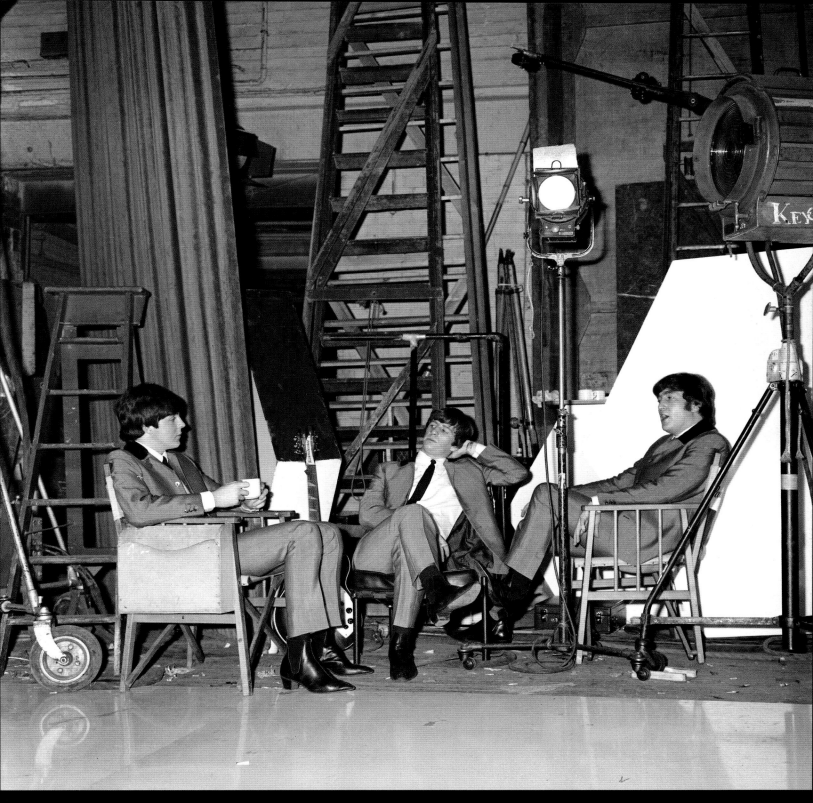

SCALA THEATRE, LONDON MARCH 1964

The Beatles approached the task of filming with gusto although, being night birds, having to be roused at six am by Neil Aspinall for an eight am start on set was not to their liking; neither was the endless waiting around between takes. John took every opportunity to plug *In His Own Write* – his "most wonderfoul correction of short writtys" – which had just been published by Jonathan Cape. (A copy of the book can be spotted by the eagle-eyed on a shelf during the film's scene with Douglas Millings, The Beatles' tailor.)

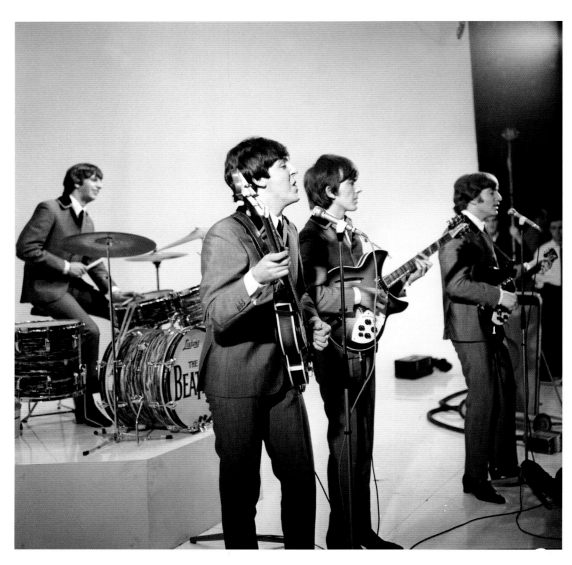

SCALA THEATRE, LONDON
MARCH 1964

Shooting the climactic television concert sequence which included 'Tell Me Why', 'If I Fell', 'I Should Have Known Better' (featuring John on harmonica), 'You Can't Do That' (which was cut from the finished film) and 'She Loves You'. Started and completed in a mere eight weeks, like so many of the new media The Beatles ventured into, *A Hard Day's Night* was an instant success – not only with Beatle fans but film critics as well. "...It fizzles with the kind of heedless gaiety that has made The Beatles a draughty gust in pompous ante-rooms," wrote Robert Ottoway in *The Daily Sketch*. "It makes other British musicals relics from a stiff-jointed past... A pell-mell string of zany happenings... crackles with imagination."

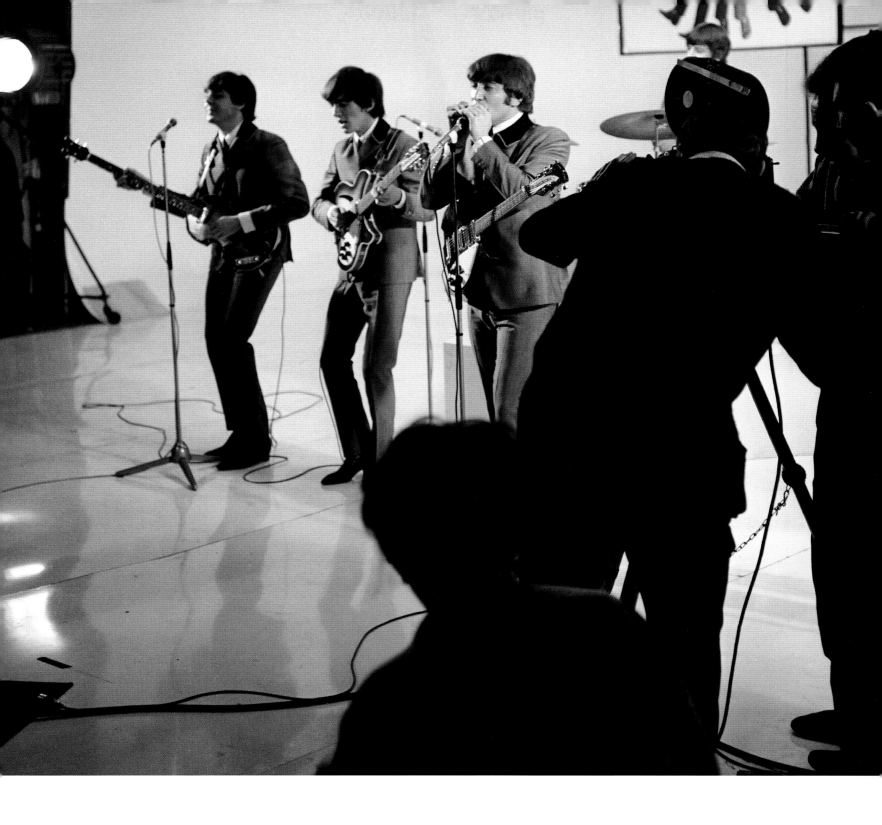

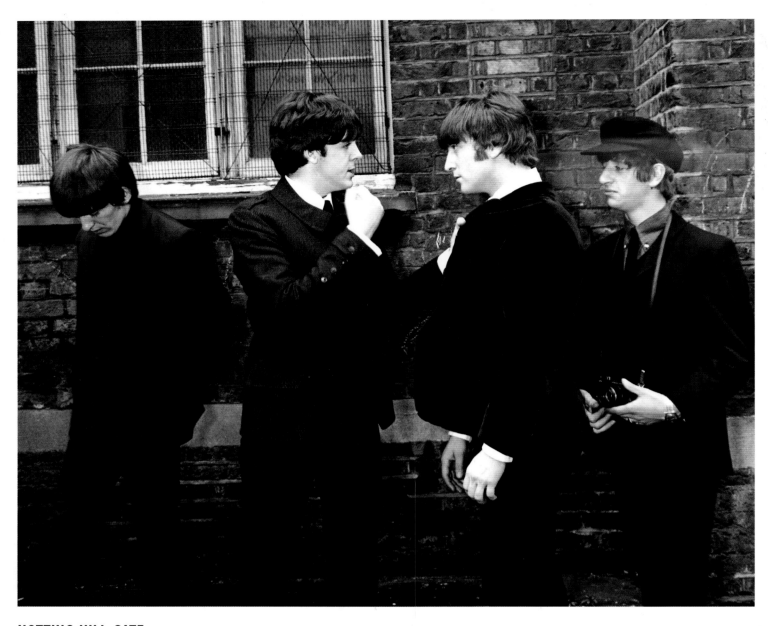

NOTTING HILL GATE, LONDON
APRIL 16, 1964

Location filming for *A Hard Day's Night* in west London. The 'peeking round brick wall' scene –deleted from the final cut – was shot in a cul-de-sac on Heathfield Street while a "mock" police station was installed at St. John's Secondary School, 83 Clarendon Road. However, real-life police had to be constantly on hand to control the crowds that soon materialised wherever The Beatles appeared. "What baffles me is how they know so promptly exactly where The Beatles are likely to appear," Richard Lester told *The Beatles Book*. "We tried hard to keep actual locations a secret between just the people most concerned… but it always leaks out." The scene showing The Beatles running through one entrance into The Portland Arms pub and immediately out the other was also left on the cutting room floor but Lester revived the sight gag for his next film, *The Knack (And How To Get It)*.

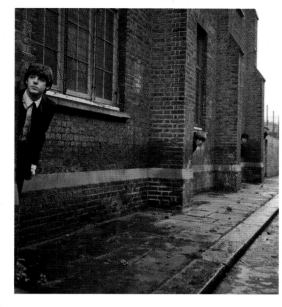

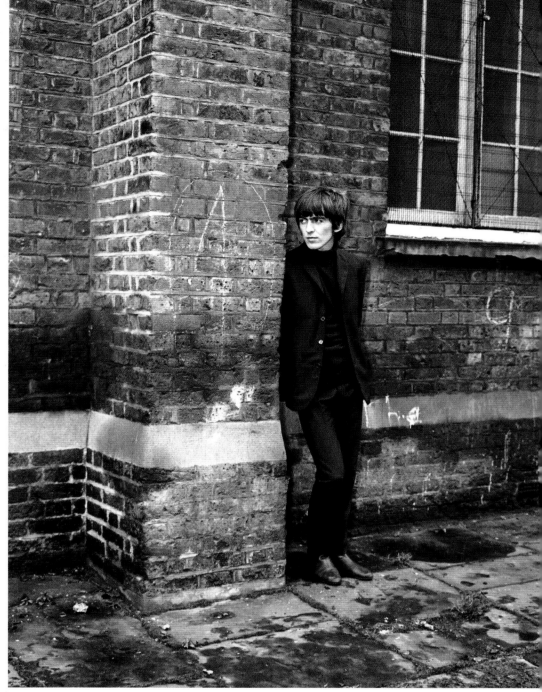

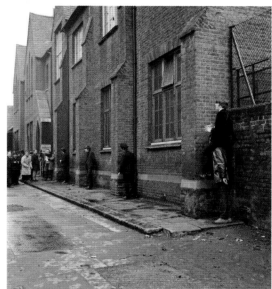

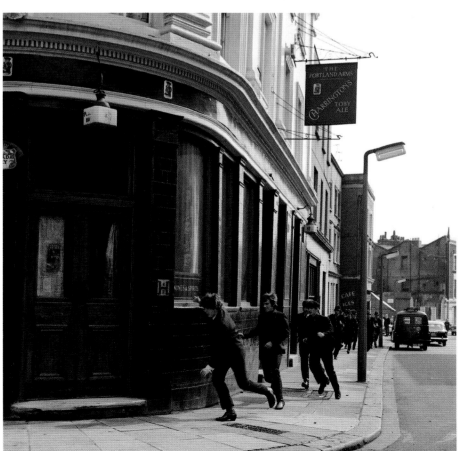

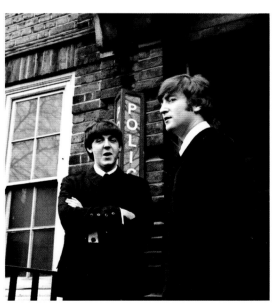

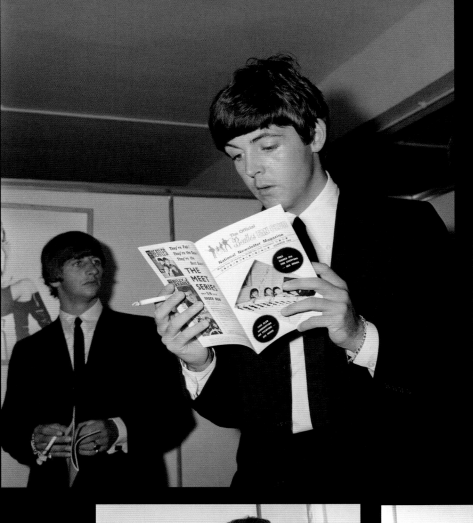
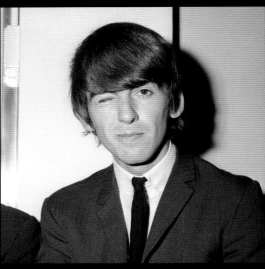
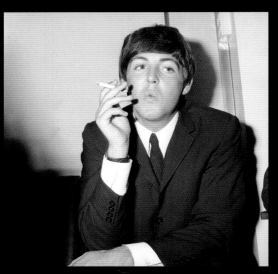
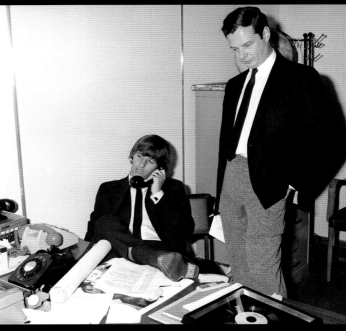
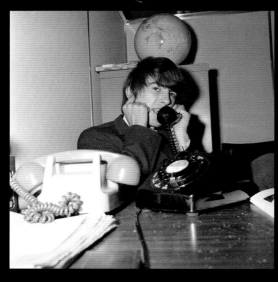
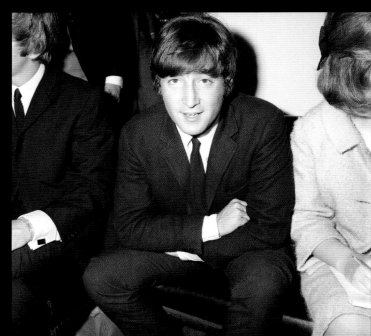

NEMS OFFICE, ARGYLL STREET, LONDON MAY 30, 1964

The Beatles had enjoyed a much-deserved holiday throughout the month of May; John and Cynthia with George and model girlfriend Pattie Boyd went to Honolulu and on to Tahiti; Paul and Ringo with girlfriends Jane Asher and Maureen Cox travelled to the Virgin Islands via Lisbon and Puerto Rico. On their return, a press conference for the world's media was held at Brian Epstein's new NEMS offices at 5-6 Argyll Street, next door to the London Palladium. As well as being interviewed in person, individual Beatles took calls from around the world; Brian Epstein seems unperturbed that Ringo has his foot up on the boss' desk. Paul had a chance to preview *The Beatles Book* Fan Club special that was about to be sent out to Fan Club members while each picked the winning cards of a *Beatles Book* competition for which the prizes were four EMI portable record players.

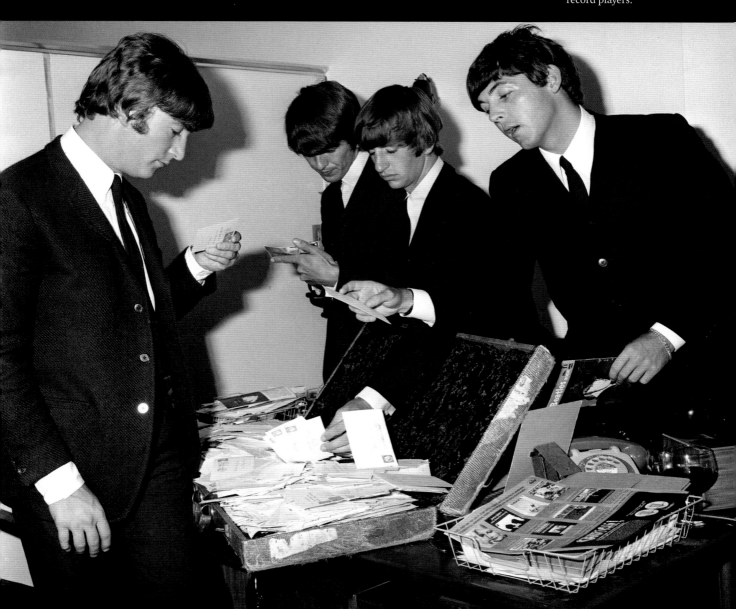

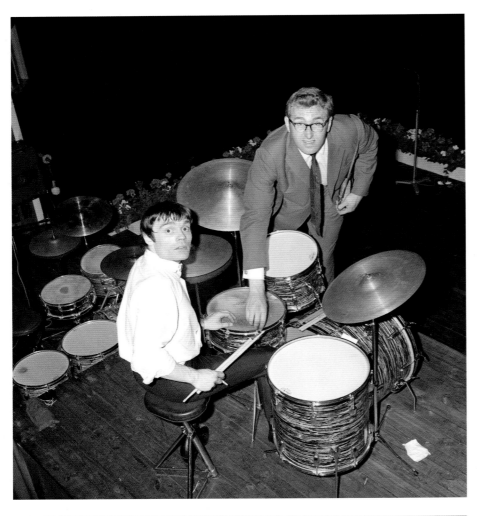

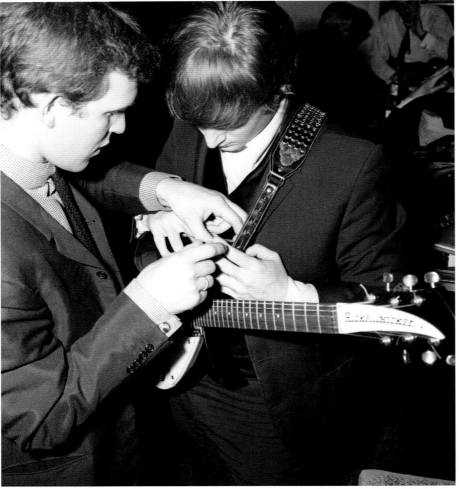

K.B. HALLEN, COPENHAGEN, DENMARK JUNE 4, 1964

On June 4, the Fab Three and Jimmie Nicol departed London Airport for Copenhagen to commence The Beatles' world tour. Ringo had collapsed with tonsillitis during a photo session the day before so session drummer Nicol was hastily recruited as his deputy. According to an on-the-spot *Beatles Book* report, an autograph-hunting member of the flight crew refused to accept that Ringo wasn't aboard, prompting George to urge Paul "Go on, Ringo, give him your signature." A last-minute rehearsal was arranged at the K.B. Hallen for Nicol to get into his groove as a Beatle – no easy task as Leslie Bryce commented: "I didn't realise how difficult it was to be a Beatle until you see a new man among them." As well as playing Ringo's kit, Jimmie wore his stage suits – finding the trousers were too short for him. Mal and Neil had come up with a practical solution to remembering the set-list by taping a copy to each Beatle's instrument.

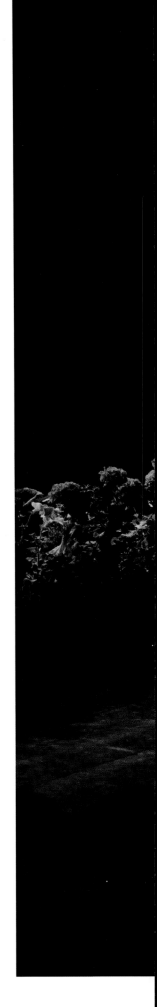

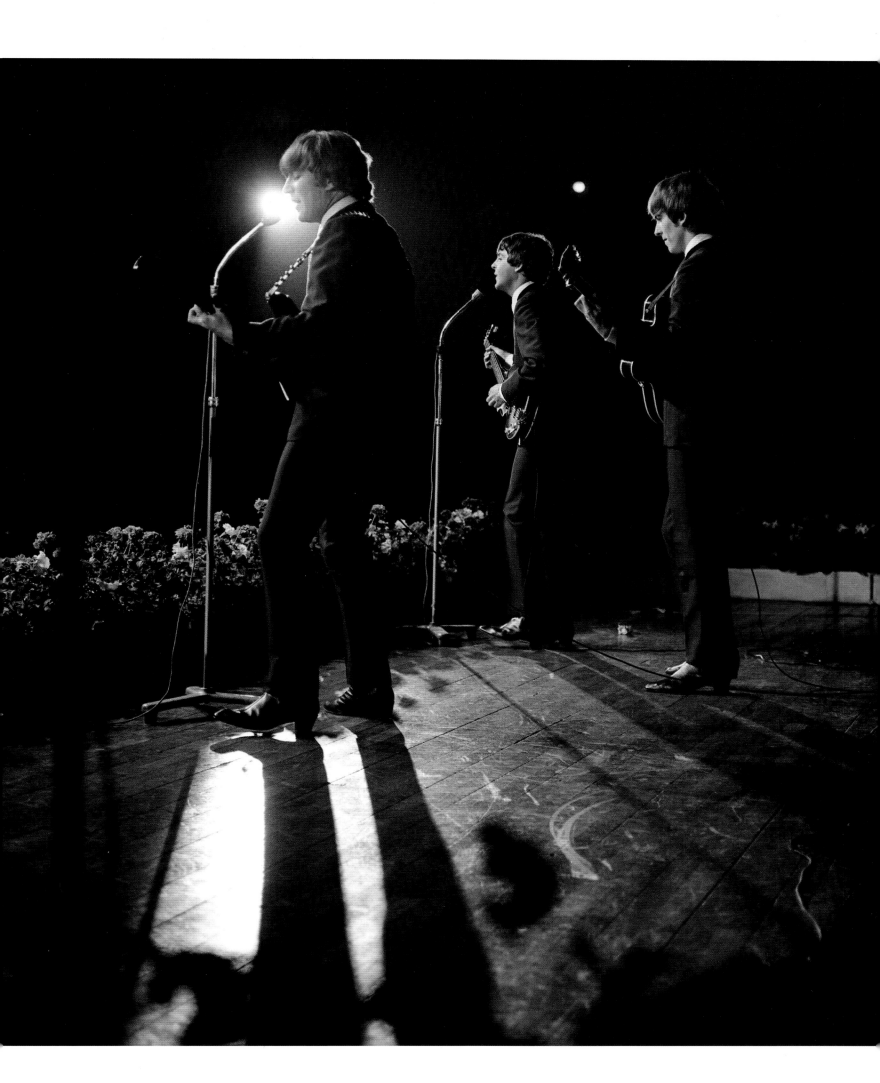

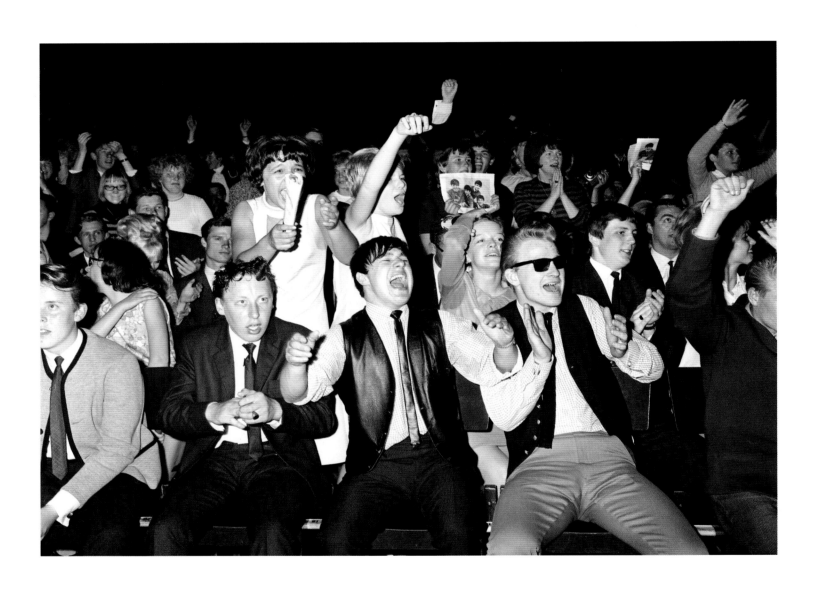

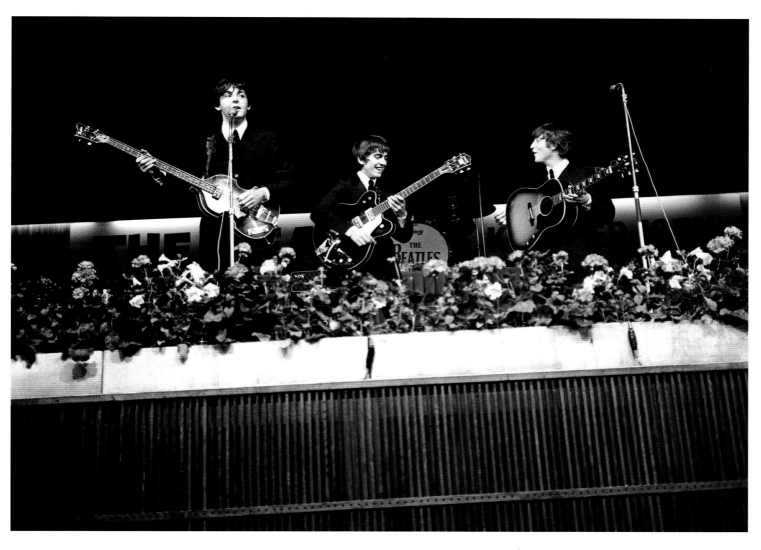

K.B. HALLEN,
COPENHAGEN, DENMARK
JUNE 4, 1964

Paul makes a stage announcement while George and John (playing his Gibson electric-acoustic) share a joke. Obscured in this photo, The Beatles were playing in front of a large United Artists backdrop advertising their imminent film release. As indicated in the picture opposite, the excitable element of the audiences at these European concerts was largely male. At the end of the second Copenhagen show, when the MC announced The Beatles would not be returning for an encore, one disgruntled Dane picked up a pot of delphiniums and threw it at him!

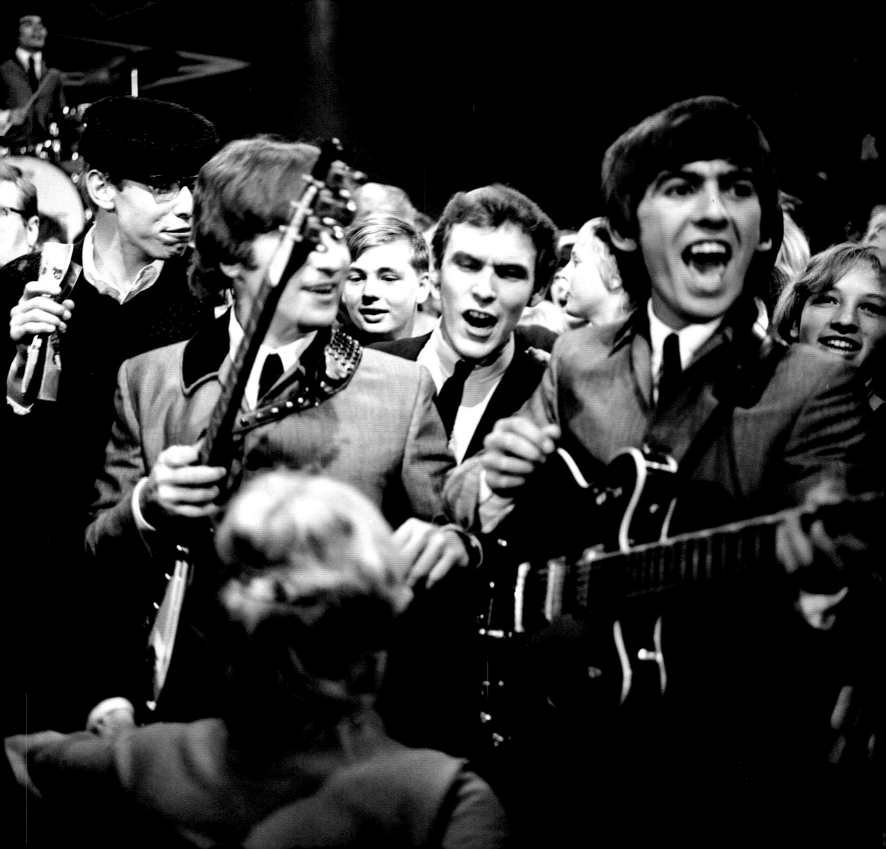

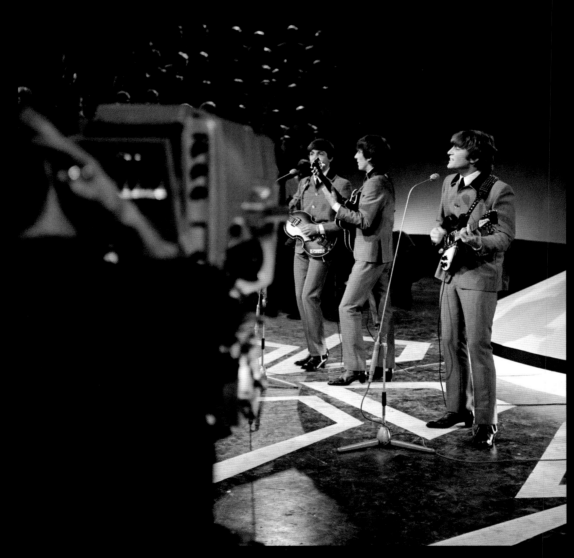

CAFÉ-RESTAURANT TRESLONG, HILLEGOM, THE NETHERLANDS JUNE 5, 1964

The Beatles first duty in Holland was to rehearse and tape a VARA television special in their honour at Treslong, 26 miles south of Amsterdam. The four were interviewed in the restaurant bar and then emerged to mime several songs before an enthusiastic Dutch crowd that ended up swamping the musicians: only Jimmie Nicol was left on his podium as Neil and Mal hustled John, George and Paul to the safety of the dressing room.

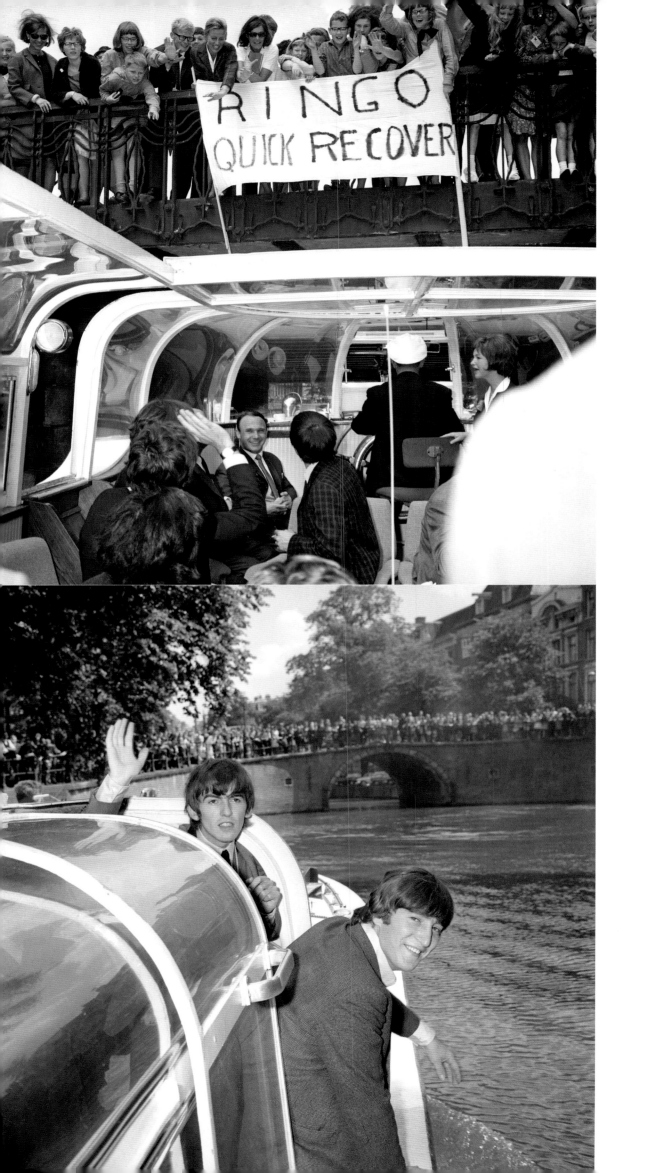

AMSTERDAM,
THE NETHERLANDS
JUNE 6, 1964

The following morning, The Beatles took an hour-long, glass-topped boat trip along Amsterdam's canal system. Fans hung banners wishing Ringo a speedy recovery while those wanting a closer look actually dived into the water to swim to the boat, only to be roughly manhandled on board by Dutch police, which annoyed John Lennon in particular. Jimmie Nicol, seen here with John and Paul checking out Danish newspaper reports of their reception, was slowly being accepted into The Beatles circle, while George attends to his instrument.

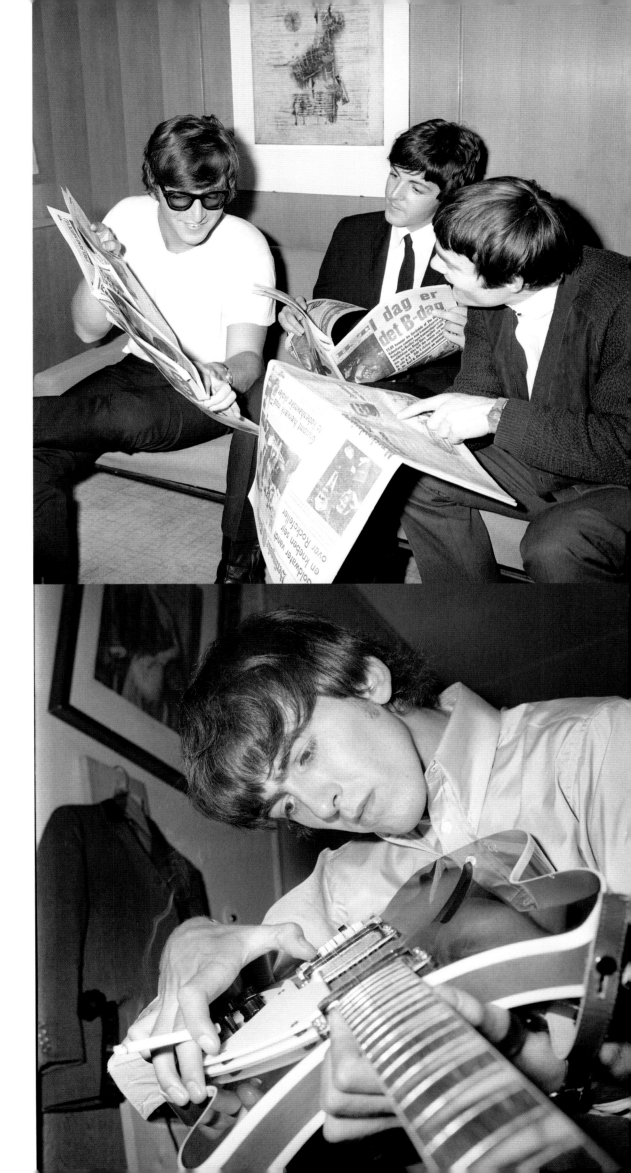

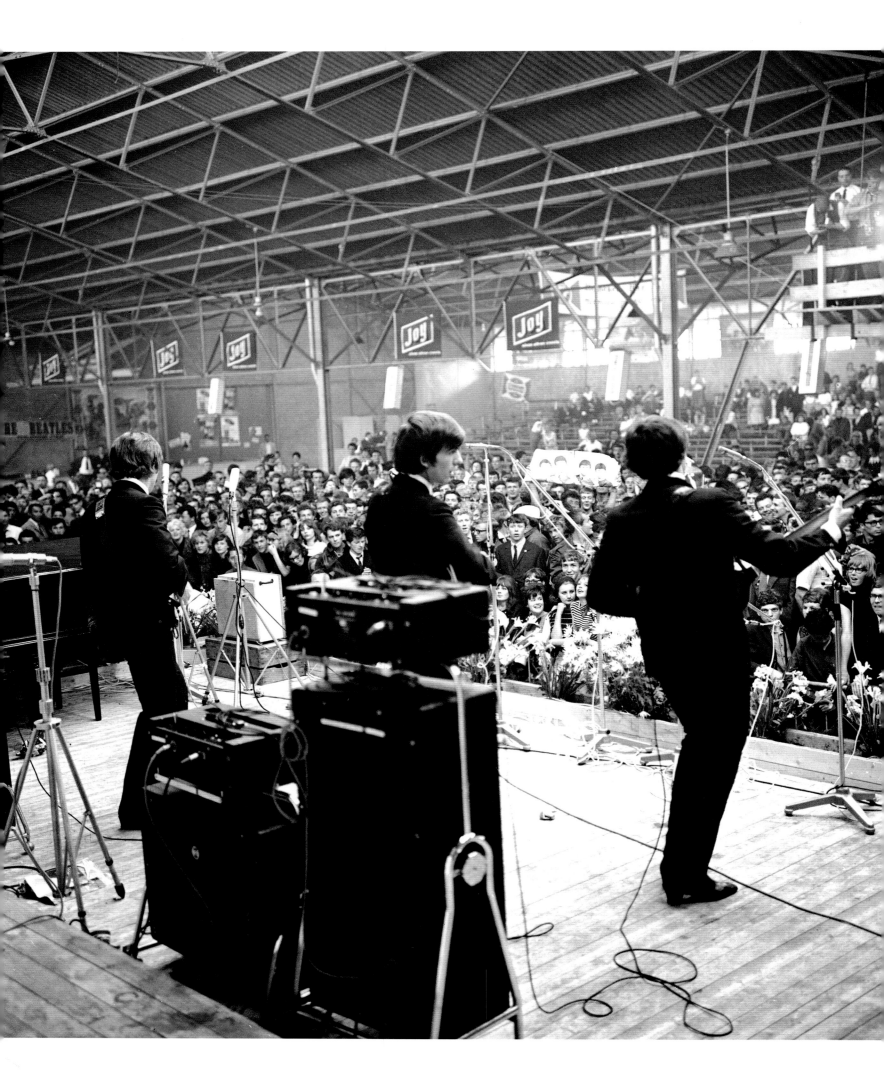

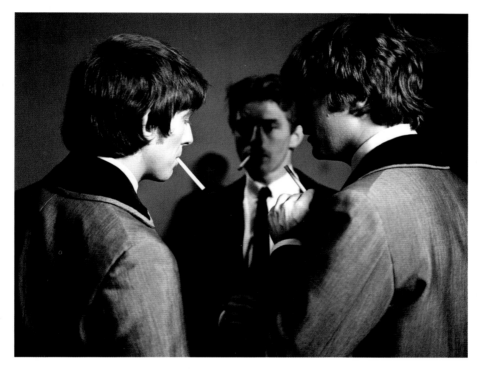

VEILINGHAL OP HOOP VAN ZEGEN, BLOKKER, THE NETHERLANDS JUNE 6, 1964

The Beatles played afternoon and evening shows at an auction hall in Blokker, north of Amsterdam, with scenes from the concerts filmed for a British-Pathe newsreel. Seen talking to John and George is newly-appointed Beatles press officer Derek Taylor, who was thrown in at the deep end as far as trying to handle the constant clamour surrounding The Beatles was concerned. The following day, The Beatles flew back to London and changed planes, flying on to Hong Kong to start their memorable tour of the Far East and Australasia. For Leslie Bryce, this was a junket beyond the budget; he remained in London to have his exclusive European shots and report ready for the next issue of *The Beatles Book*.

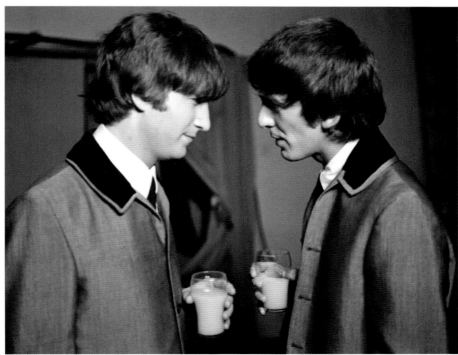

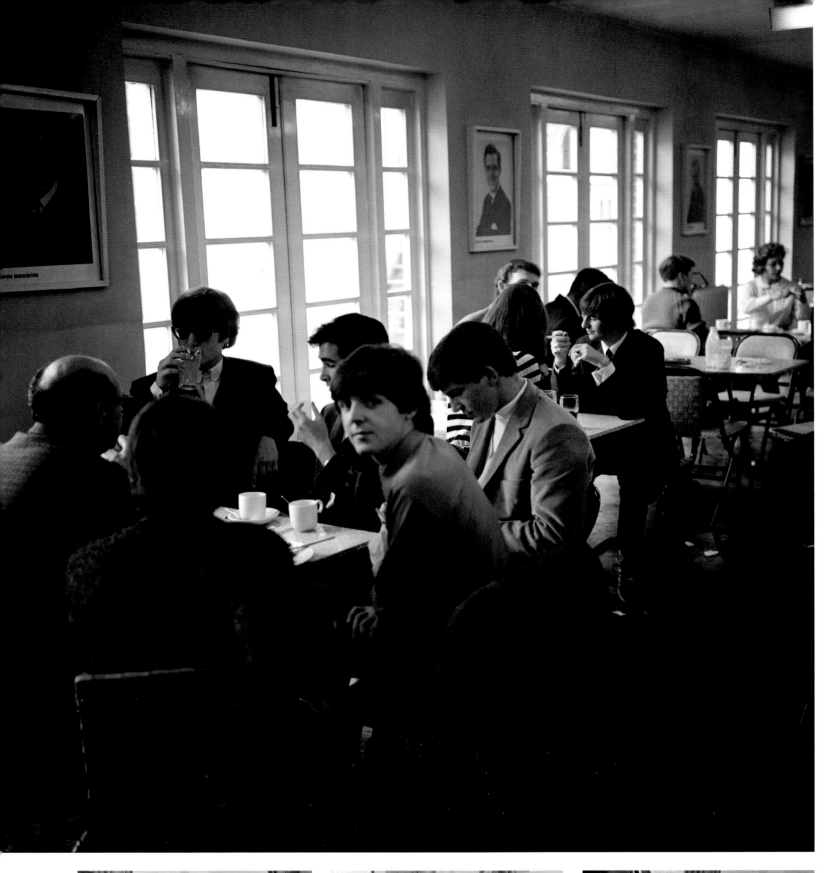

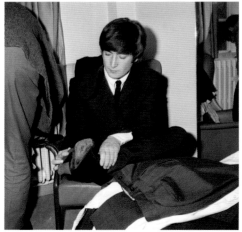

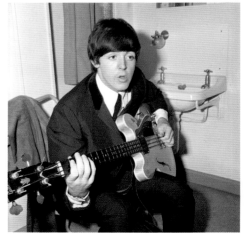

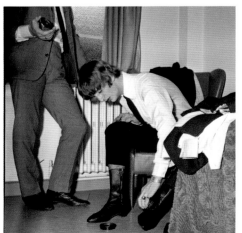

ABC TV STUDIOS, TEDDINGTON
JULY 11, 1964

Beatles Book #9 (April 1964) reported that The Beatles disliked miming on television and would insist on playing live in future "because that's the way their fans want it." This appearance on the *Summer Spin* model of top-rated Saturday teatime variety show *Thank Your Lucky Stars* went only halfway to fulfilling this intention. Because of an ITV technicians strike, The Beatles had to fly back to London after the Northern premiere of *A Hard Day's Night* in Liverpool the night before to appear live on the programme (which was normally pre-recorded the preceding Sunday). However their instruments remained unplugged during mimed performances of 'A Hard Day's Night', 'Long Tall Sally', 'Things We Said Today' and 'You Can't Do That'. Other artistes that week included guest host Dusty Springfield (seen with her own personal Beatle hairdresser), Manfred Mann and Sounds Incorporated – Paul is seen having a vamp on bass player Wes Hunter's blonde Gibson EB2. A break from dress rehearsals provided an opportunity for a business briefing with Dick James, The Beatles' music publisher, in the restaurant – the walls featuring framed images of ABC Television staff announcers – before The Beatles got suited and booted for the live slot.

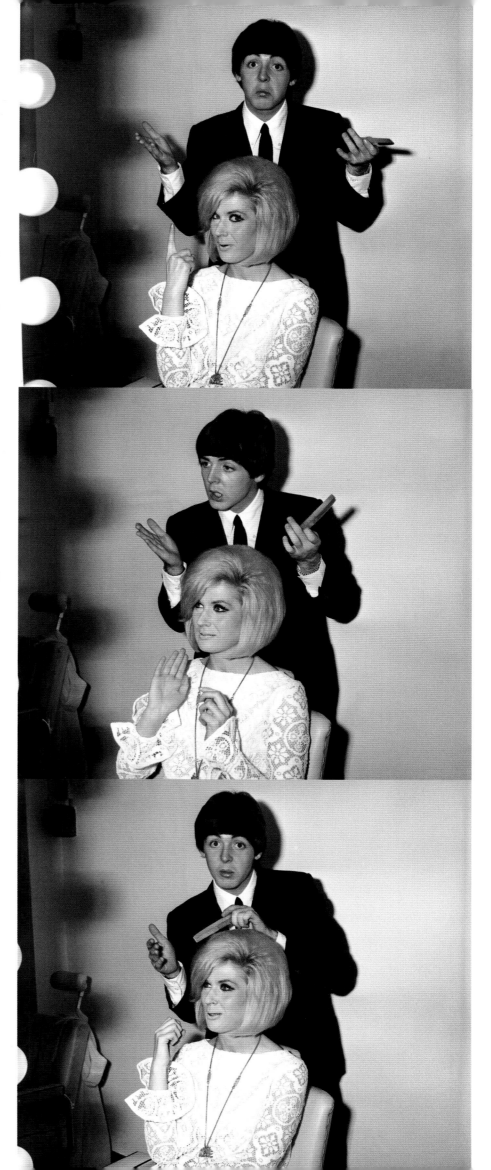

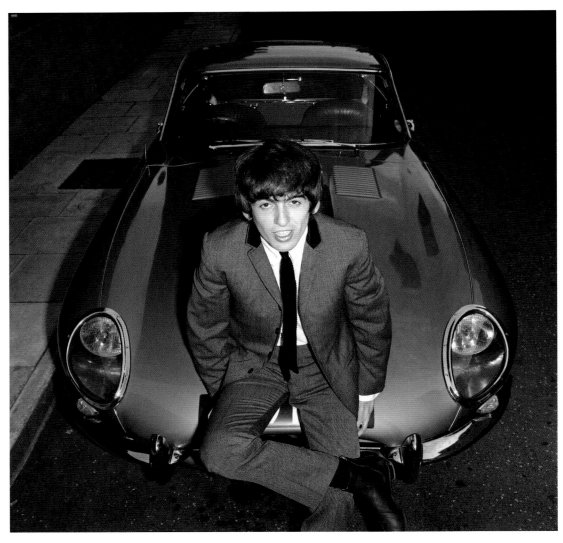

WHADDON MEWS, KNIGHTSBRIDGE, LONDON JULY 11, 1964

Now that the fruits of their worldwide endeavours were rolling in, The Beatles started indulging themselves accordingly. John and George moved to expansive and expensive houses in Surrey; Paul bought a steel blue 1964 Aston Martin DB5 while George plumbed for a grey E-Type Jaguar, complete with all the trimmings including portable record player. He had only just taken possession of the vehicle when these pictures were taken by Leslie Bryce after returning from The Beatles' *Thank Your Lucky Stars* appearance in Teddington. Unfortunately, his pride and joy was involved in a minor collision with another vehicle in Fulham on the way to a Beatles show in Brighton the following day. If contemporary news reports are to be believed, passing pedestrians collected bits of broken glass as souvenirs. Of all The Beatles, Harrison was the most obsessed with motor vehicles ever since being taken to see Juan Fangio in the 1955 British Grand Prix by his brother as a youngster in Liverpool, and he would continue to drive classy cars and include Formula One racers among his closest friends throughout his life.

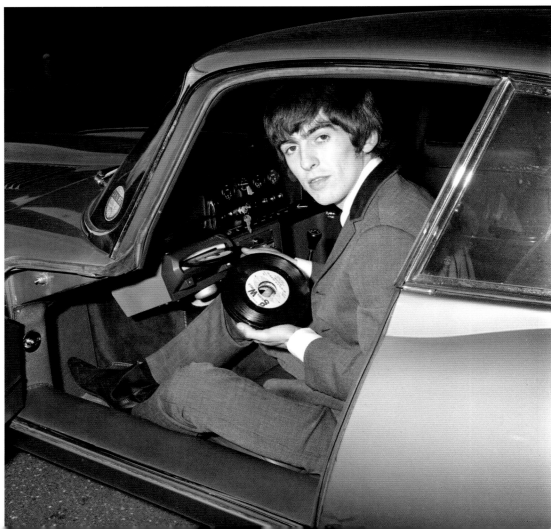

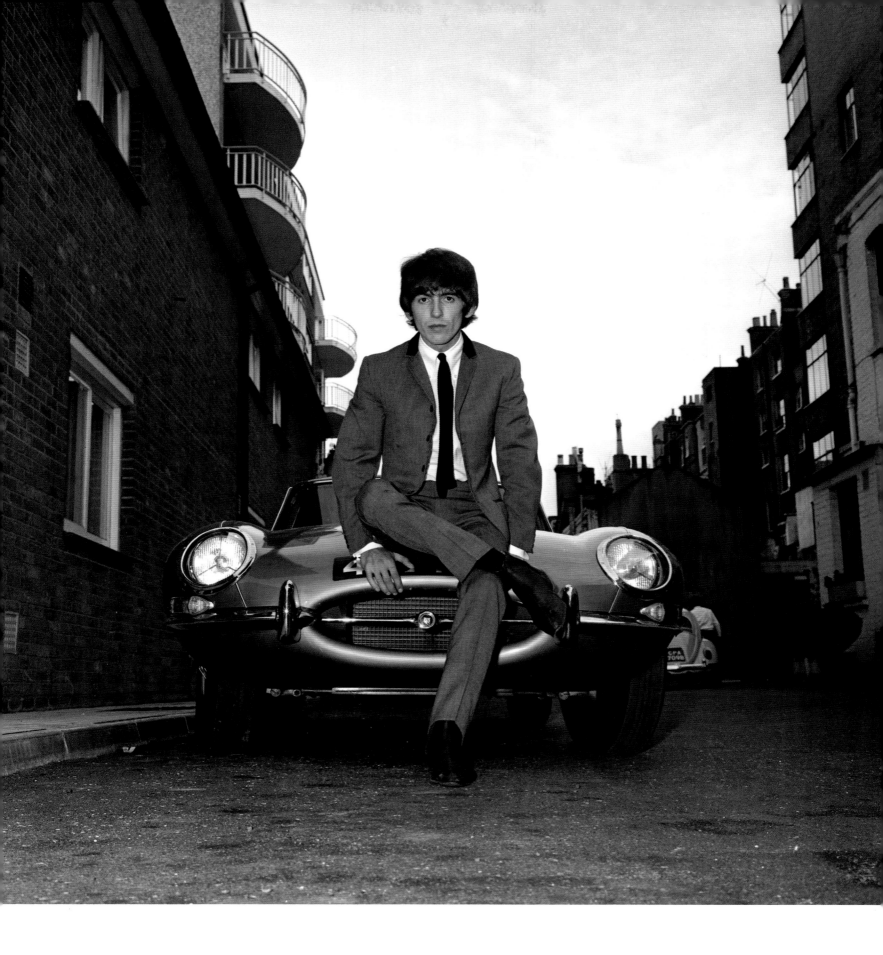

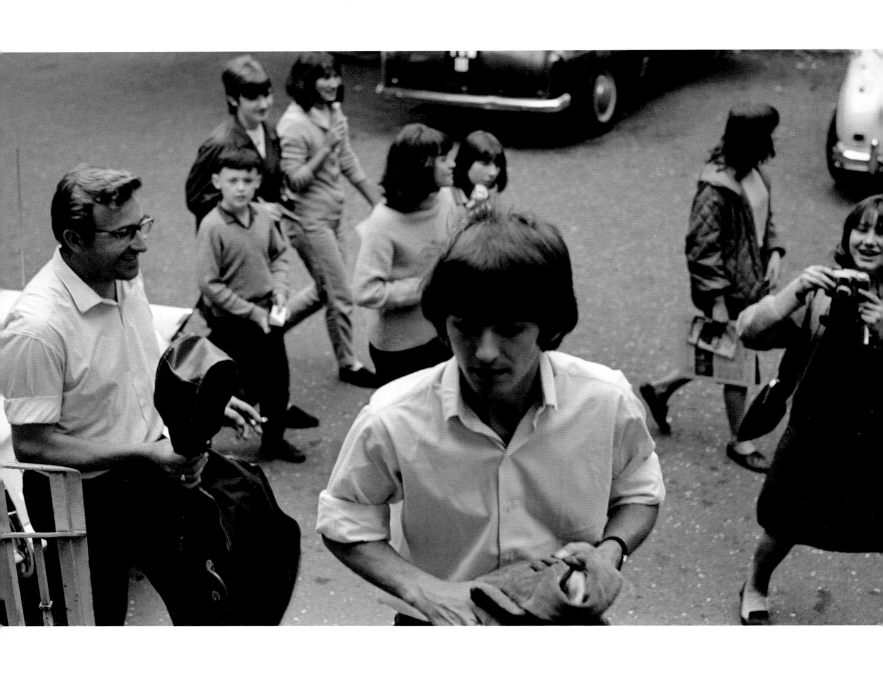

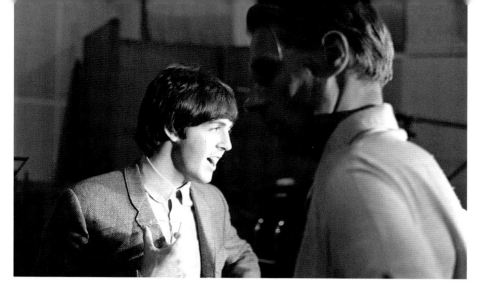

EMI STUDIOS, LONDON
AUGUST 11, 1964

The pressure to keep up with EMI's desired Beatles output of three singles and two albums per year amid the onslaught of worldwide Beatlemania meant George Martin had to snatch whatever studio time he could. Just days before leaving for their first major concert tour of America and Canada, the group spent time at Abbey Road stockpiling tracks for either a single or LP. This particular evening session was the first devoted to what would become their fourth album, *Beatles For Sale*; John and Paul's lament in waltz time, 'Baby's In Black' being taped. The lyrics that John and Paul read from were written on the back of a fan letter. As ever, fans with a sixth sense about the boys' movements were lying in wait as George arrived in his Jaguar. Visitors to the recording in No. 2 studio included Brian Epstein, Cynthia Lennon and Peter Asher, the brother of Paul's actress girlfriend Jane and one half of pop duo Peter & Gordon, who were gifted several Lennon-McCartney compositions.

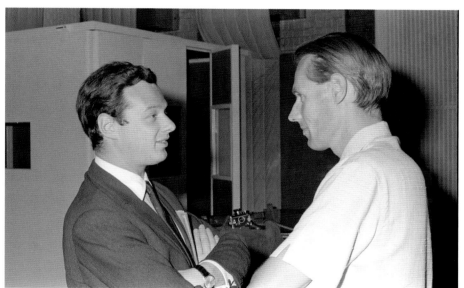

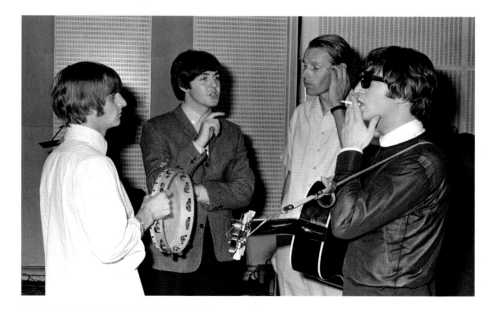

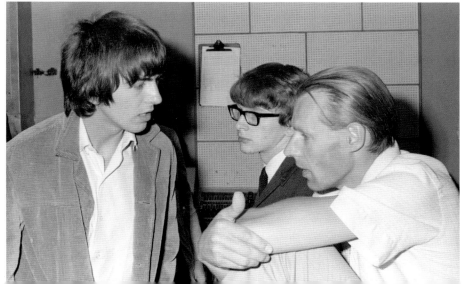

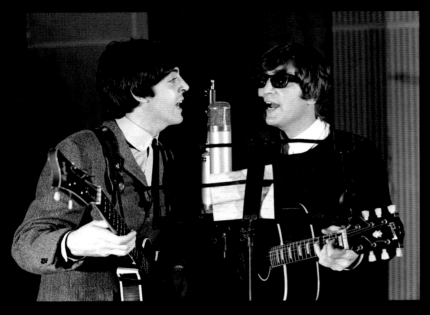
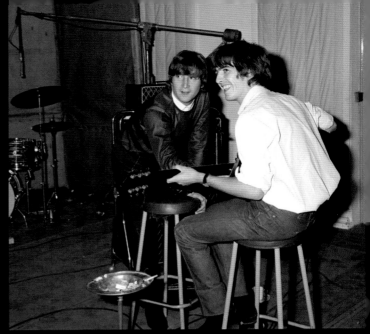
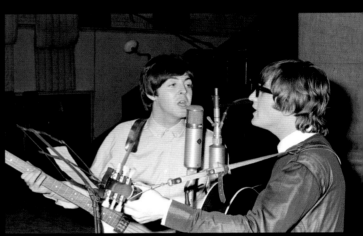
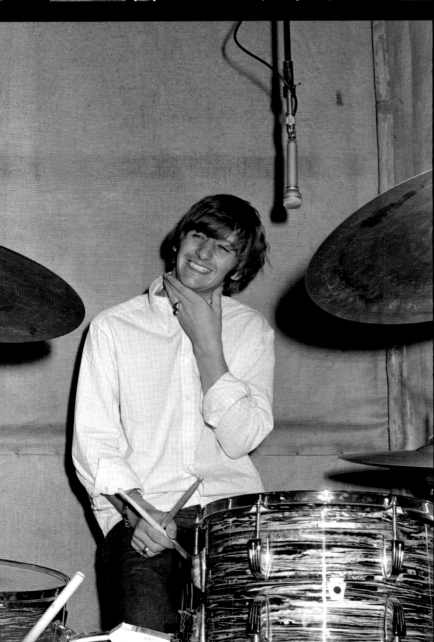
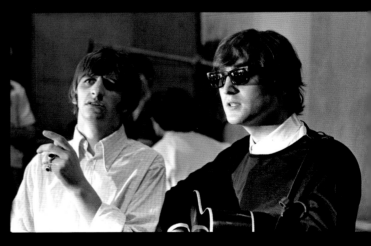

'Baby's In Black' featured a distinctive guitar sound and much effort was spent on trying to perfect the song's opening twanging note involving John manipulating the volume tone knob on George's Gretsch Tennessean. After numerous attempts, according to Mark Lewisohn's detailed *Beatles Recording Sessions*, the results were not used. 'Baby's In Black' took 14 takes to complete; Paul is seen through the window of the control room listening to a playback with studio engineer Ken Townsend (who later went on to become Abbey Road Studios general manager) in the background. Ringo leans against Paul's Vox AC-100 bass rig. By now John and George had upgraded to Vox AC-50 amps and before long these would be further improved to AC-100s, the 'Super Beatle' amps capable of blasting out into the vast arenas the group were booked into. Even then, they were virtually inaudible thanks to the shrieking power of thousands of pubescent females.

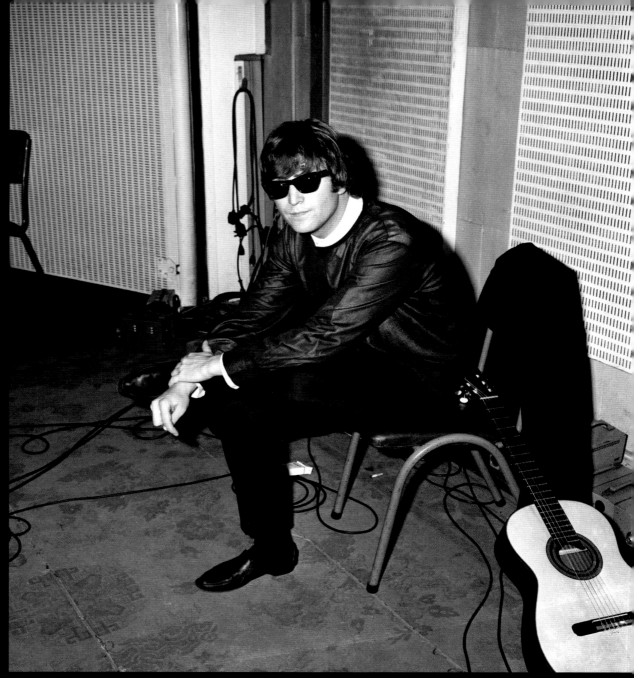

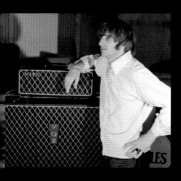

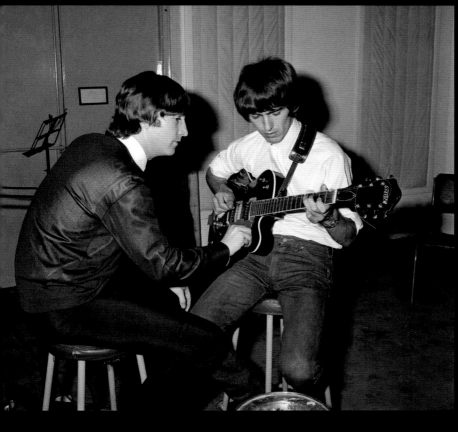

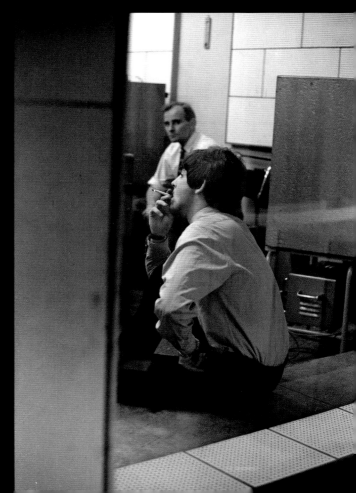

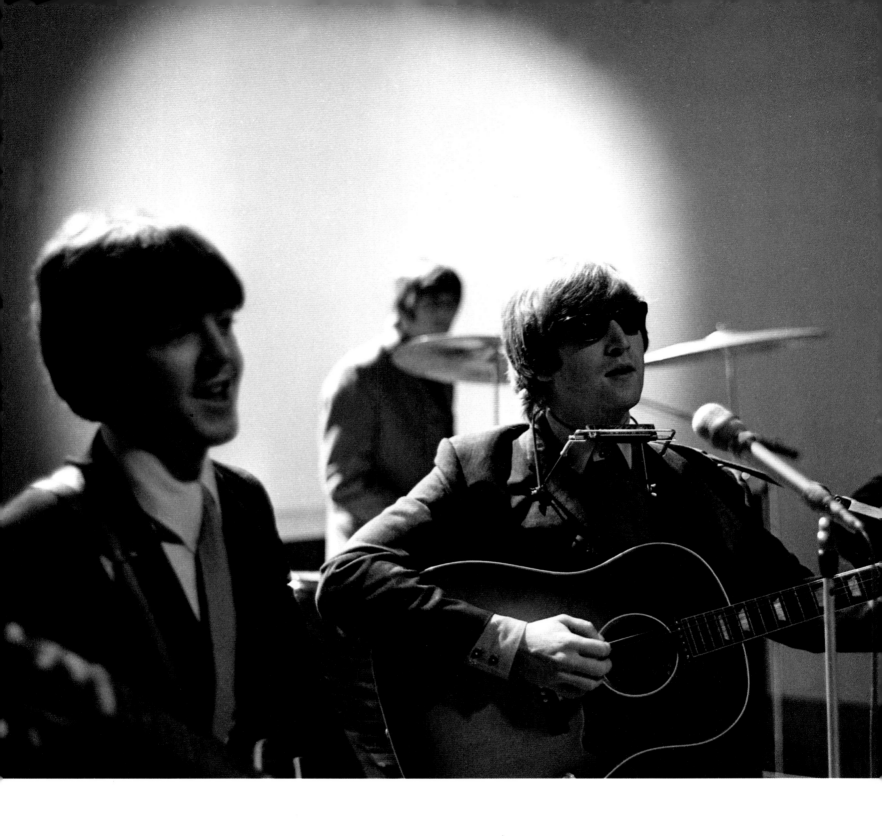

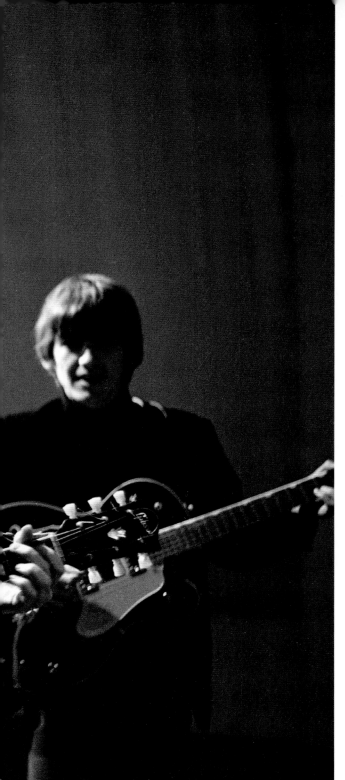

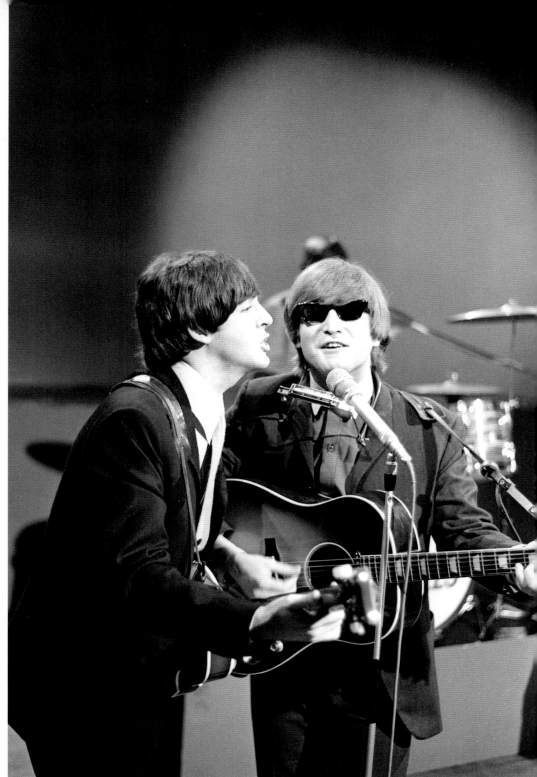

GRANVILLE THEATRE, FULHAM, LONDON OCTOBER 3, 1964

In the wake of The Beatles and other British Invasion acts' success in the United States, American television was ready for a showcase that would feature the new 'fave rave' groups from across the Atlantic as well as home-grown talent. ABC's *Shindig!* was the first and best of the new shows to plug that gap and naturally The Beatles' services were sought. Having only just returned from an exhaustive, coast-to-coast tour of America and with a British tour imminent, there was no way they would consent to a return trip just to appear on a TV show. Hence the mountain came to Mohamed. The *Shindig!* producers got an unexpected bonus with the public premiere of a new Beatles song, 'I'm A Loser', not released until December on *Beatles For Sale*. Written mainly by John, its Bob Dylan influence was clearly evident – right down to the acoustic guitar and wire holster Lennon used for the harmonica part.

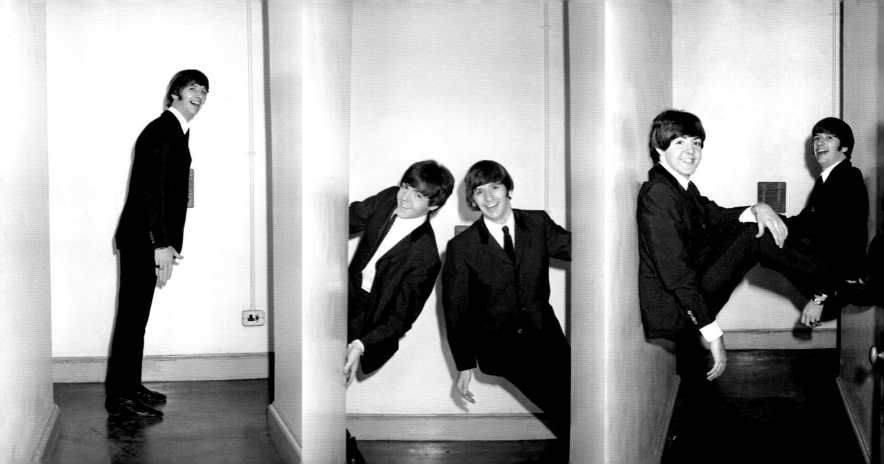

FULHAM, LONDON
OCTOBER 3, 1964

During breaks in the show taping, Paul and Ringo were the two Beatles seemingly willing to fall into ham-like poses for the benefit of Bryce's camera. "Paul was a dream for someone in my position. If I'd been with them for a day and hadn't got any good photos I'd ask him for ten minutes and we'd go off and he'd do something for me." By this juncture, and thanks to the influence that incredible fame and a certain verdant herb was having on them, John and George were less amenable to "being Fab" although George appears in a happy mood as he prepares to leave the Granville. The special British edition of *Shindig!* – taped before an enthusiastic audience comprising 150 randomly-selected London-area members of the Beatles Fan Club – also included fellow NEMS artistes Tommy Quickly and Sounds Incorporated as well as newcomers PJ Proby and Sandie Shaw, but was never shown in Britain.

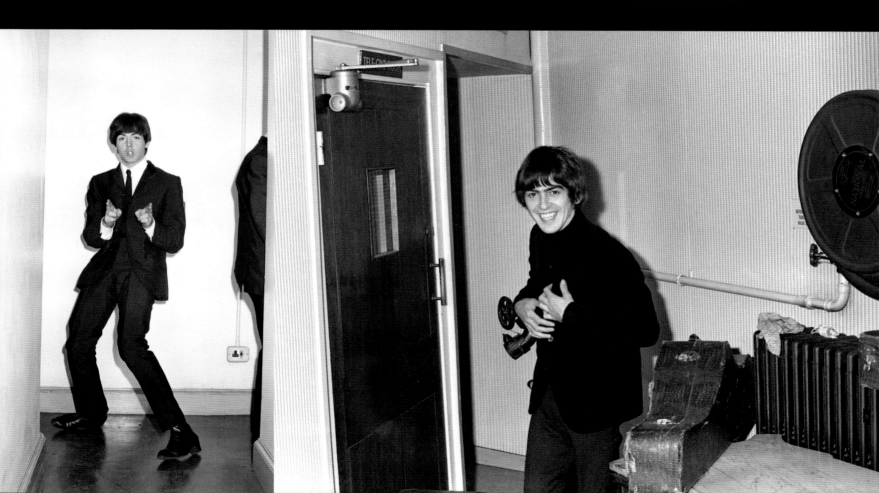

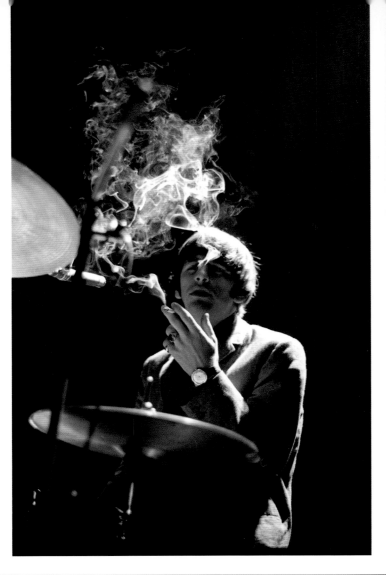
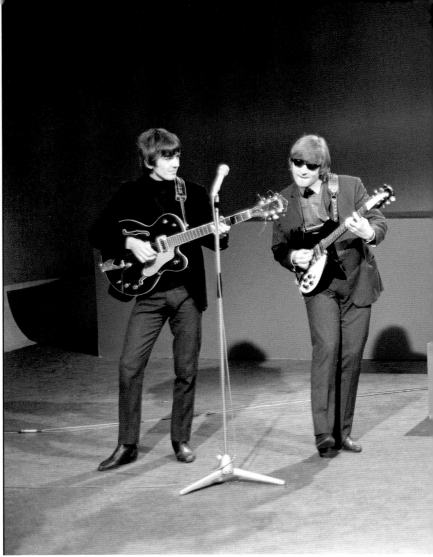
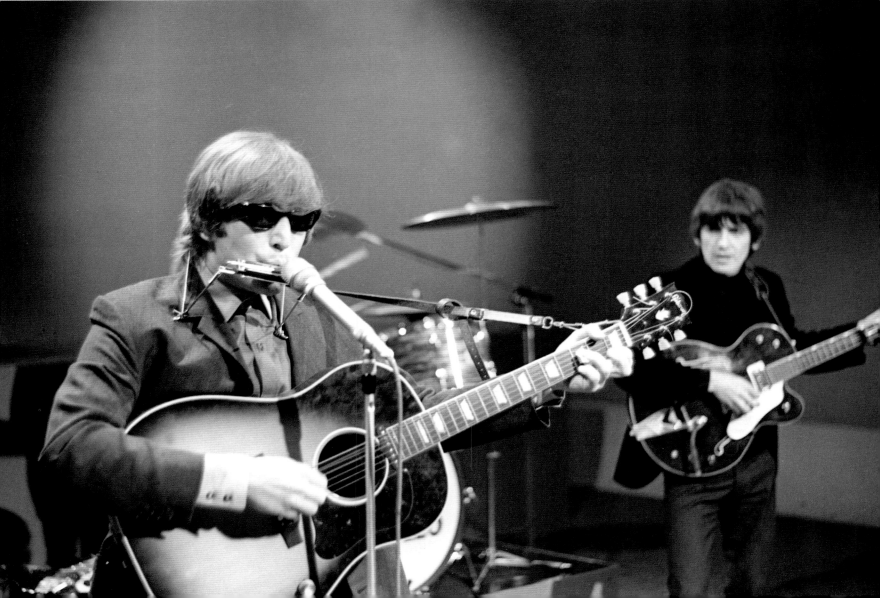

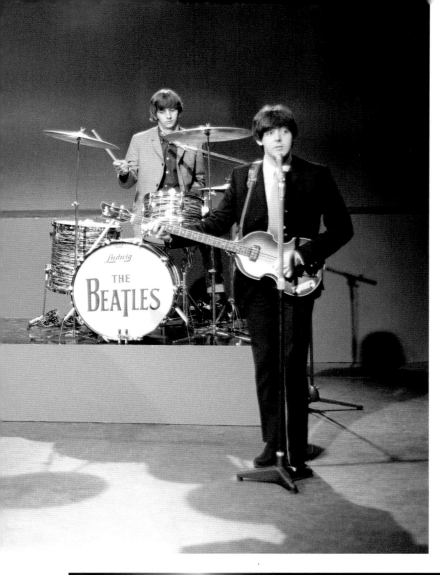

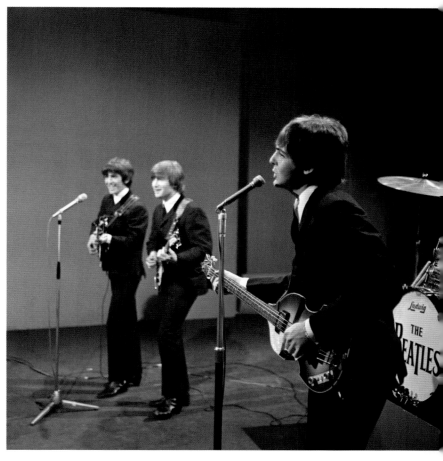

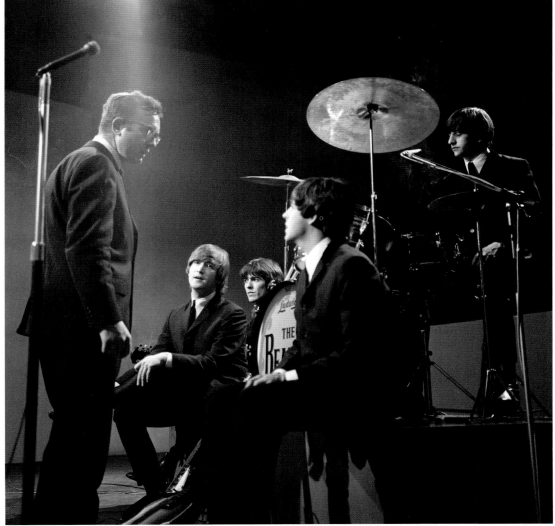

GRANVILLE THEATRE, FULHAM, LONDON OCTOBER 3, 1964

British television producer Jack Good (seen talking to the four), who had worked on the *Around The Beatles* special earlier in the year, was the driving force behind *Shindig!* The Beatles appreciated his work – not only for introducing rock 'n' roll to British television in the '50s with *6.5 Special* and *Oh Boy!* but for his astute taste as a former columnist for the music paper *Disc Weekly*. As well as 'I'm A Loser' and Ringo's spotlight on 'Boys', The Beatles dug back to their Cavern and Hamburg days, performing a medley of Little Richard's 'Kansas City' and 'Hey, Hey, Hey,Hey!' with Paul belting out the lead vocal. This arrangement was also recorded and released on *Beatles For Sale*.

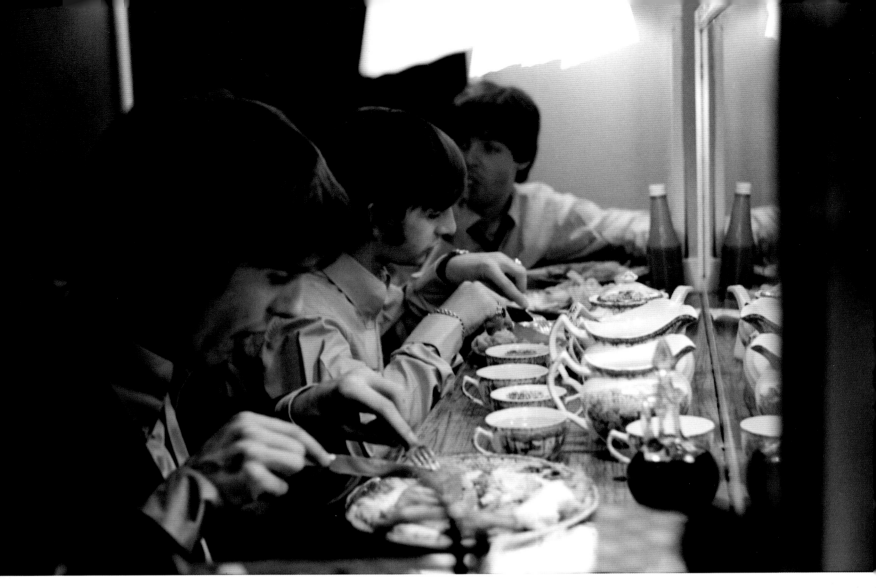

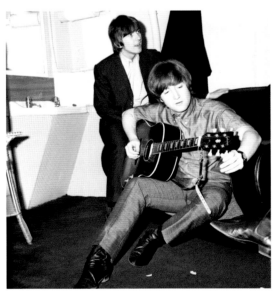

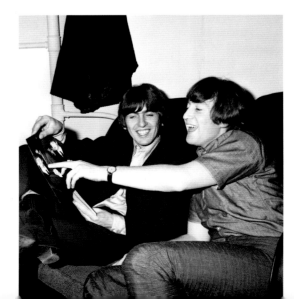

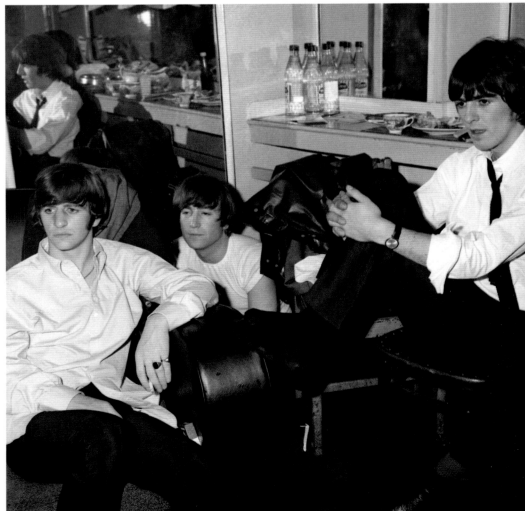

HIPPODROME THEATRE, BRIGHTON
OCTOBER 25, 1964

The closing months of 1964 were to see no respite for the Fab Four. Just a break of almost three weeks separated The Beatles' return from a five-week concert tour of America and Canada and the commencement of a month-long series of British one-nighters starting in Bradford on October 9, John Lennon's 24th birthday. Packed into free days were photographic assignments and recording sessions. Sean O'Mahony explains that he and Leslie Bryce decided to avoid the frantic atmosphere surrounding the group in London and travelled south to Brighton for their next *Beatles Book* encounter. As with Bryce's Bournemouth backstage shots, the cramped dressing room conditions are a far cry from the lavish backstage areas that modern day stars demand as a matter of course. All four Beatles bunched up on a narrow bench in front of the large mirror to eat a between-shows dinner of fish, chips and peas, washed down with tea and arranged themselves as best they could for Bryce's camera. Among the other backstage visitors were Annie Nightingale, later the first female broadcaster on BBC Radio 1, then an entertainment columnist for the *Brighton Evening Argus*, a local Romany clairvoyant Eva Petulengro who offered to read their palms – only George taking up the offer – and actor Richard Harris (star of *This Sporting Life*) and his wife Elizabeth Rees-Williams who wanted an audience with the famous musicians. As Sean recalled, Paul and Ringo were agreeable but George pretended to be asleep on the sofa while John hid behind it, covering himself with a green plastic mac. Having obtained autographs for their children the couple took the hint and made a tactical exit, allowing John and George to resume their places watching telly.

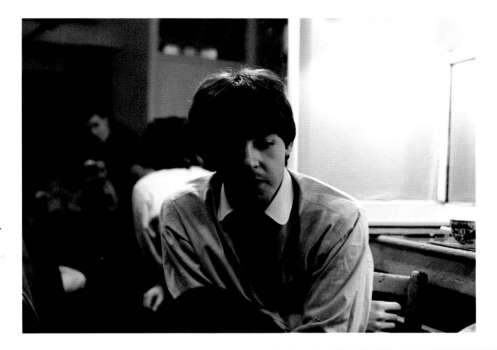

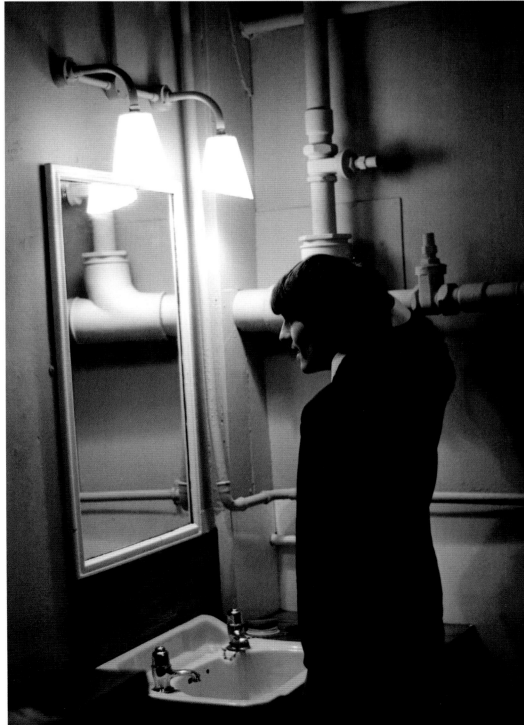

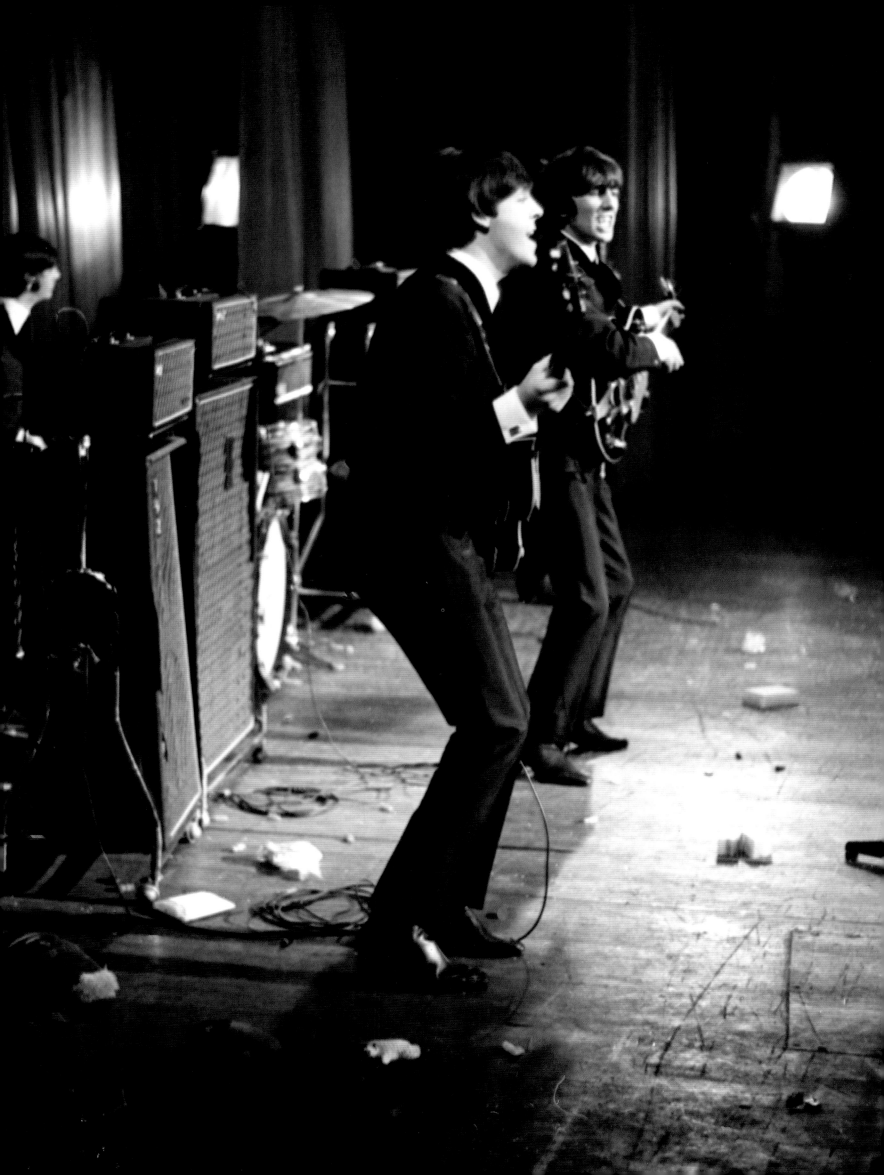

HIPPODROME THEATRE, BRIGHTON
OCTOBER 25, 1964

The Beatles caught from the wings at the 2,000-capacity Hippodrome. Their set-list comprised 'Twist And Shout', 'Can't Buy Me Love', 'Things We Said Today', 'I'm Happy Just To Dance With You', 'I Should Have Known Better' (featuring John on harmonica), 'If I Fell', 'I Wanna Be Your Man', 'A Hard Day's Night' and 'Long Tall Sally'. Backstage Sean and Leslie were treated to a unique preview of The Beatles' forthcoming single but as Sean revealed, "For once they were unusually reticent and I began to realise they were just that little bit worried about their next release... Paul eventually picked up a guitar and played 'I Feel Fine'. Despite my assurances that their fans would love it, the boys still seemed strangely doubtful... Every star has doubts from time to time but I never thought The Beatles had any until that day."

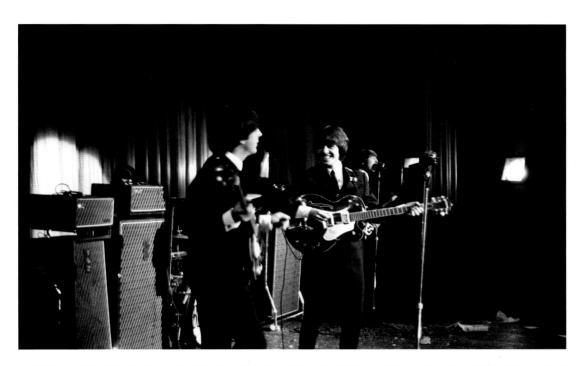

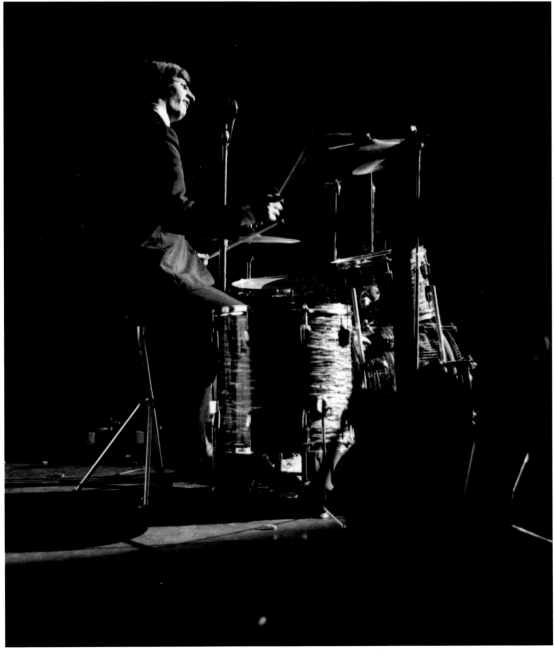

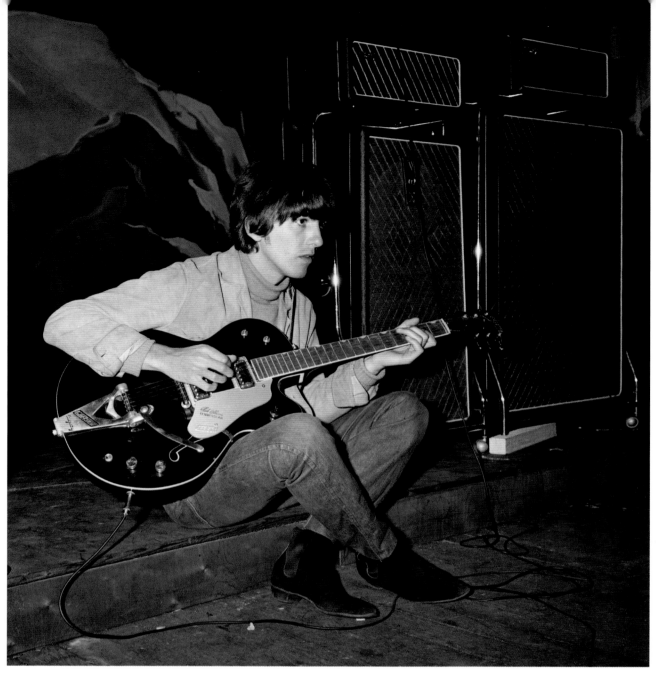

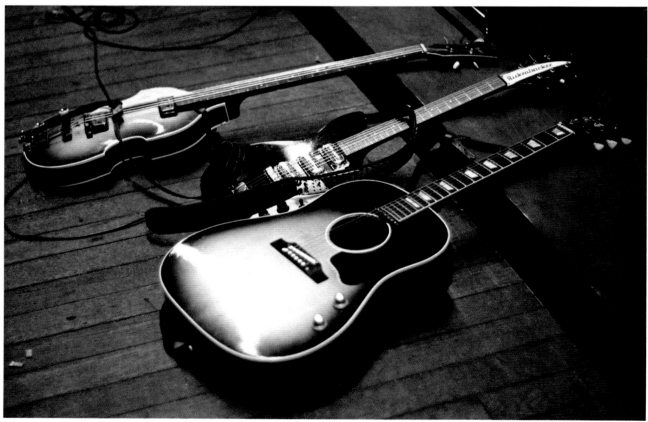

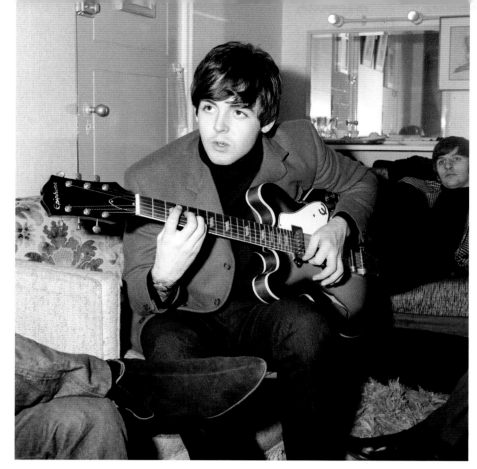

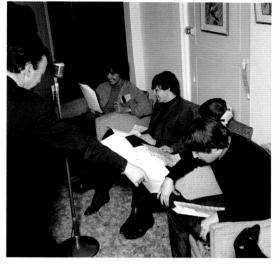

ODEON THEATRE, HAMMERSMITH, LONDON DECEMBER 21, 1964

During a three-week break before regrouping for 'Another Beatles Christmas Show', John and Paul spent most of their time with family – Paul at 'Rembrandt', the house he bought for his father on the Wirral peninsula in Cheshire; George and Pattie went on holiday to the Bahamas and poor Ringo spent time at London's University College Hospital getting his troublesome tonsils removed. It was a hectic time for producer Peter Yolland (the man behind the previous year's festive run at the Finsbury Park Astoria). As well as the Fab Four's three-week extravaganza, he was busy staging 'Gerry's Christmas Cracker', starring Gerry & The Pacemakers, in Liverpool, Leeds and Glasgow for Brian Epstein.

During rehearsals, George sits on the Odeon's revered stage, while John exorcises his inner drummer. In the dressing room, overseen by Yolland, The Beatles record their scripted dialogue to be played over the PA. Paul tries out his new Epiphone Casino guitar. The position of the scratch plate and control knobs indicate it was a right-handed model so he may well have been pondering how it could be altered to play left-handed. John and George, too, later bought Casinos and their metallic sound would be heard on many important Beatles recordings, most notably *Revolver*.

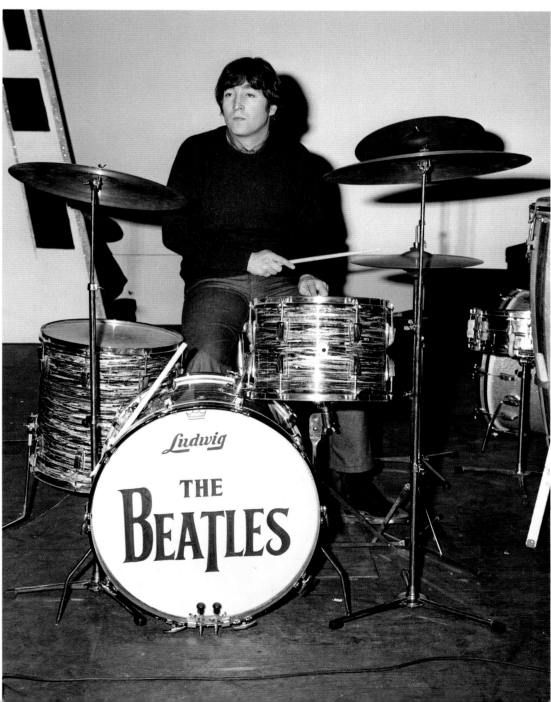

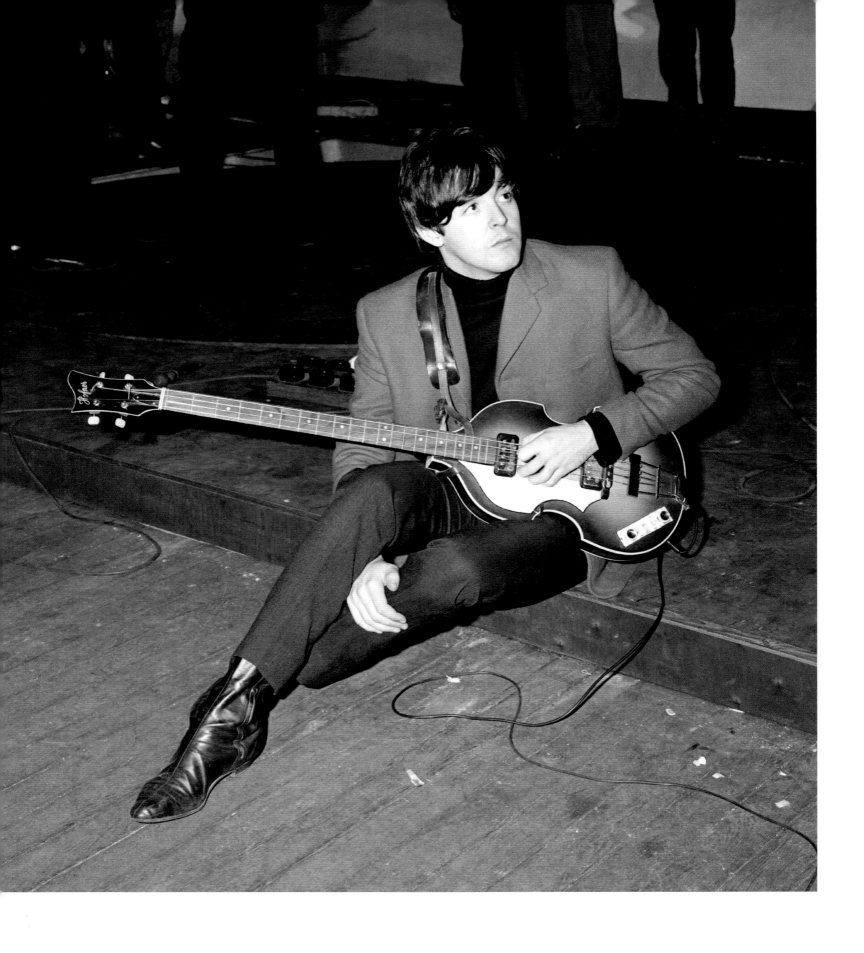

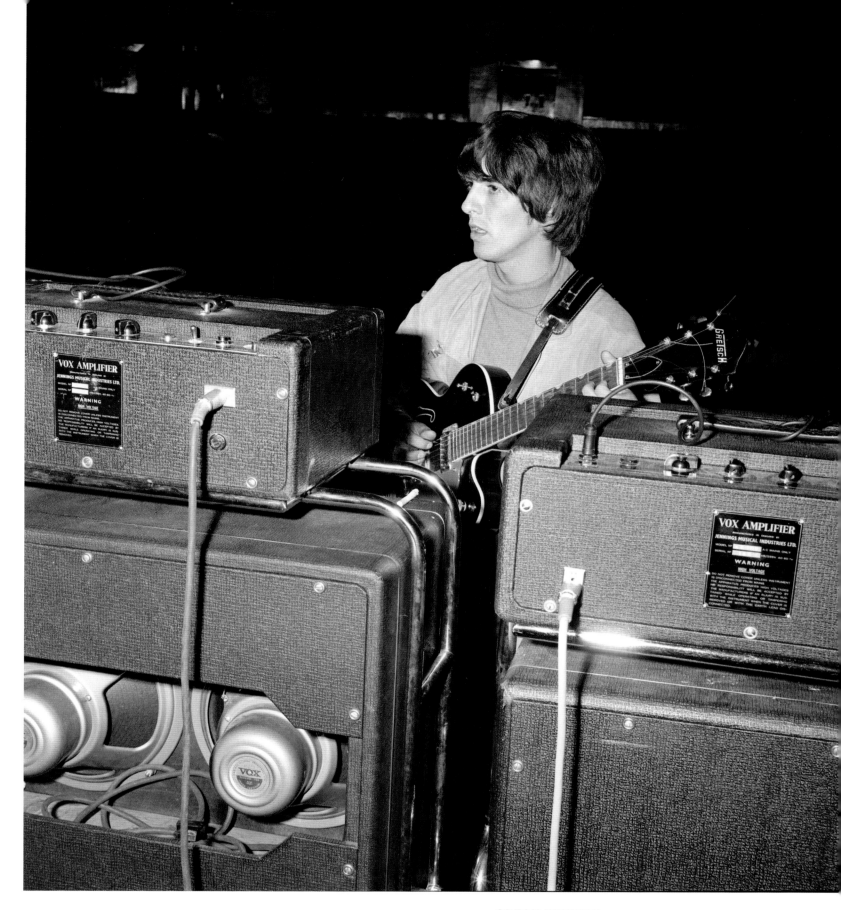

ODEON THEATRE, HAMMERSMITH, LONDON DECEMBER 21, 1964

The box office for the seasonal run had opened on September 7 and all 132,240 tickets sold. On the last night (January 16), Sean O'Mahony acquired a supply of the souvenir programme – which featured a typically Lennon Yuletide line drawing on the covers and a spread of Leslie Bryce photos inside – as a bonus for *Beatles Book* readers and Fan Club members unable to get to the shows. As further evidence of The Beatles' unassailable popularity, both 'I Feel Fine' and *Beatles For Sale* held respective pole positions on the singles and album charts well into the New Year.

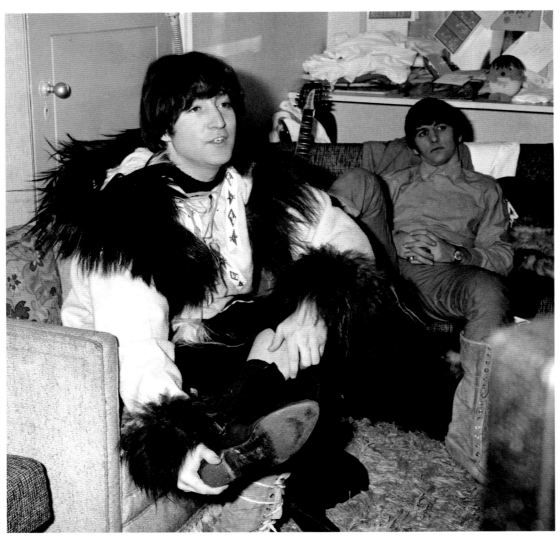

ODEON THEATRE, HAMMERSMITH, LONDON DECEMBER 30, 1964 AND JANUARY 15, 1965

The million-dollar cupboard. It's amusing in retrospect to see here (and on page 92) how The Beatles' guitars, now worth many kings' ransoms, were casually stored during rehearsals for 'Another Beatles Christmas Show'. Like last year's pantomime, the group appeared in sketches – one featuring them dressed as Eskimos. Never inclined to repeat themselves The Beatles were less than pleased with the presentation and, having turned down numerous requests to reappear at the London Palladium and the annual Royal Variety Performance, they made it clear to Brian Epstein that this was to be the last time such an outmoded production would involve them.

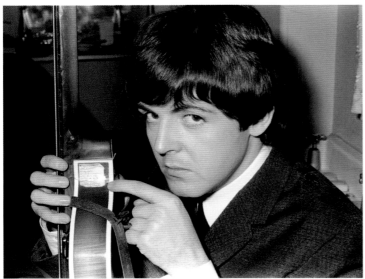

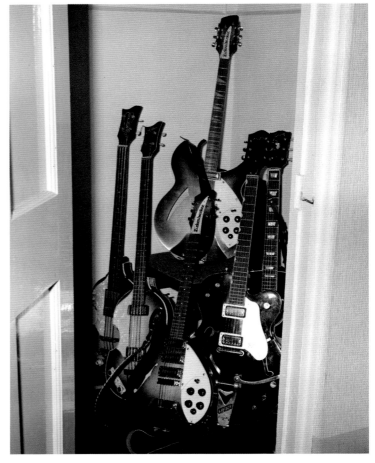

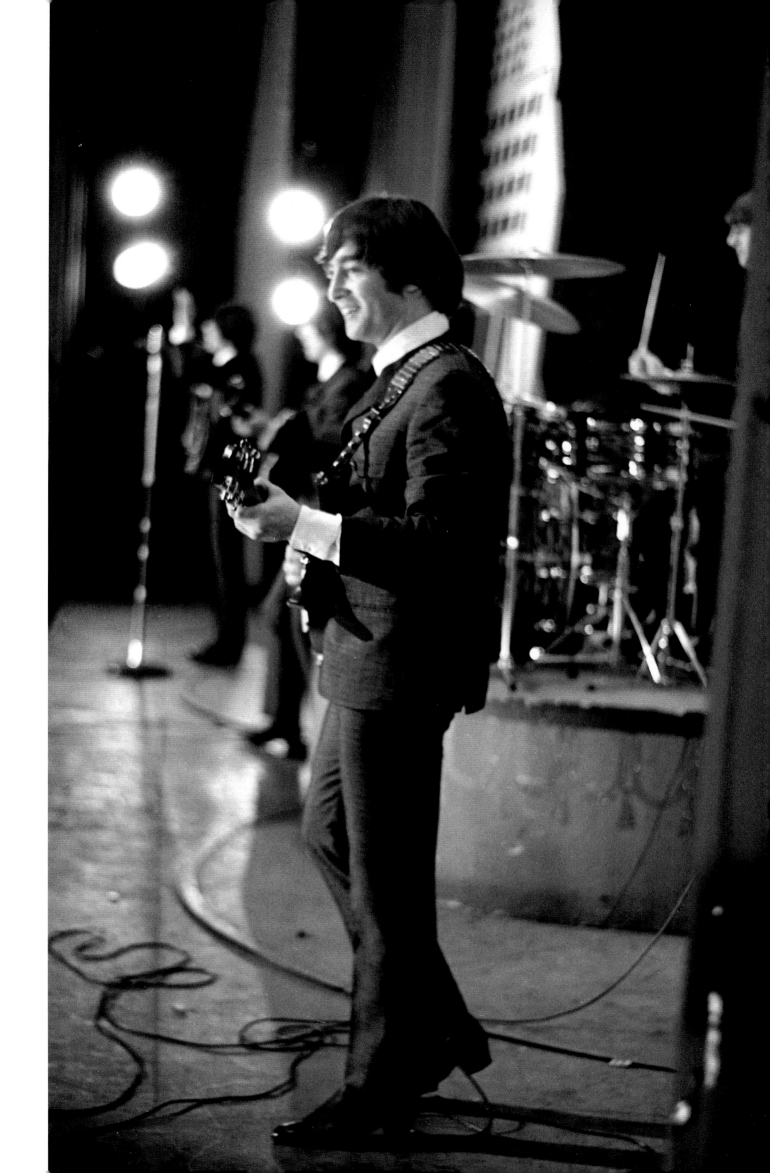

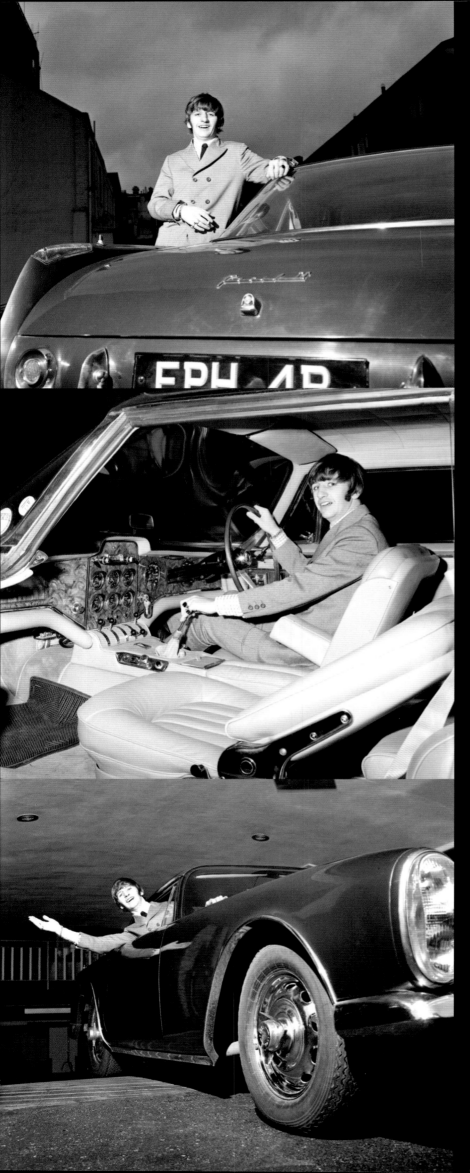

WHADDON MEWS, KNIGHTSBRIDGE, LONDON JANUARY 10, 196█

As he had done a session with George and his new motor, Leslie Bryce returned to the same location to shoot Ringo and his new bright red Facel Vega sports car, widely promoted as the fastest in the world. It was quite a time for the drummer – after having his tonsils removed (his recovery being reported by the Beatles Fan Club to anxious fans worldwide in hourly updates via a phone answering service) he had proposed to Maureen Cox at the Ad Lib Club during the New Year and the couple were married amid great secrecy at Caxton Hall on February 11 and moved into a rented flat in Montagu Square. They only had time for a weekend's honeymoon at Beatles' lawyer David Jacobs' mansion at Hove on the Sussex coast before Ringo was back to work.

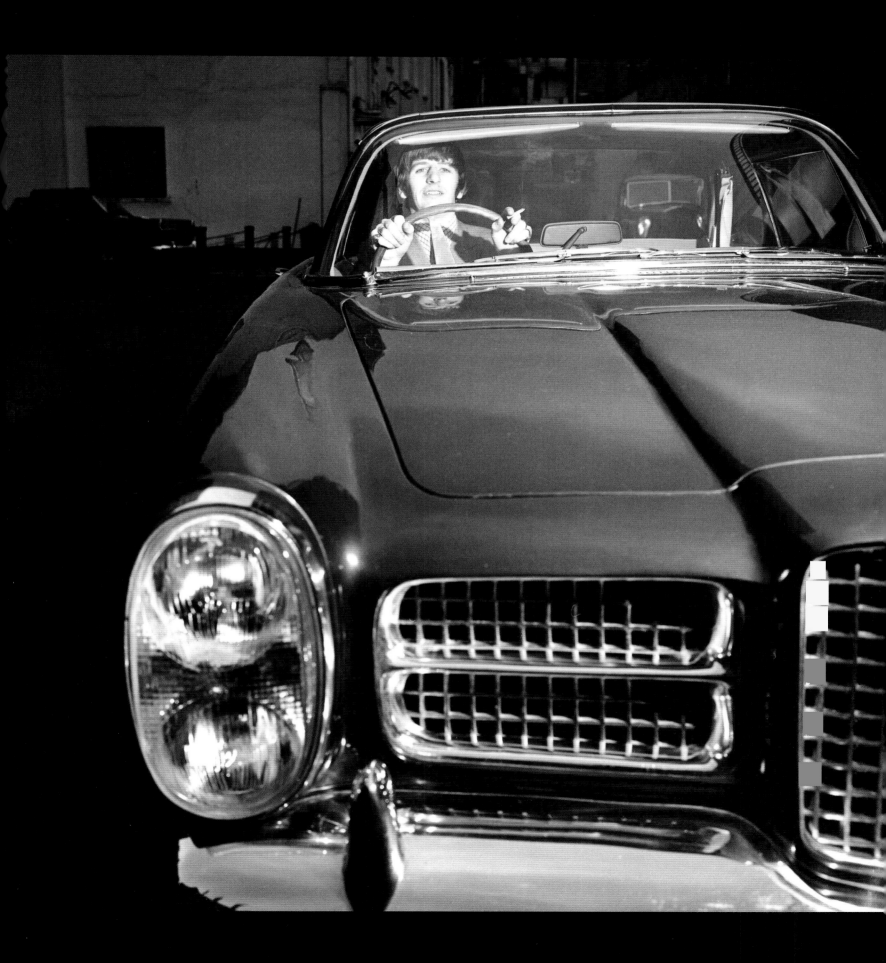

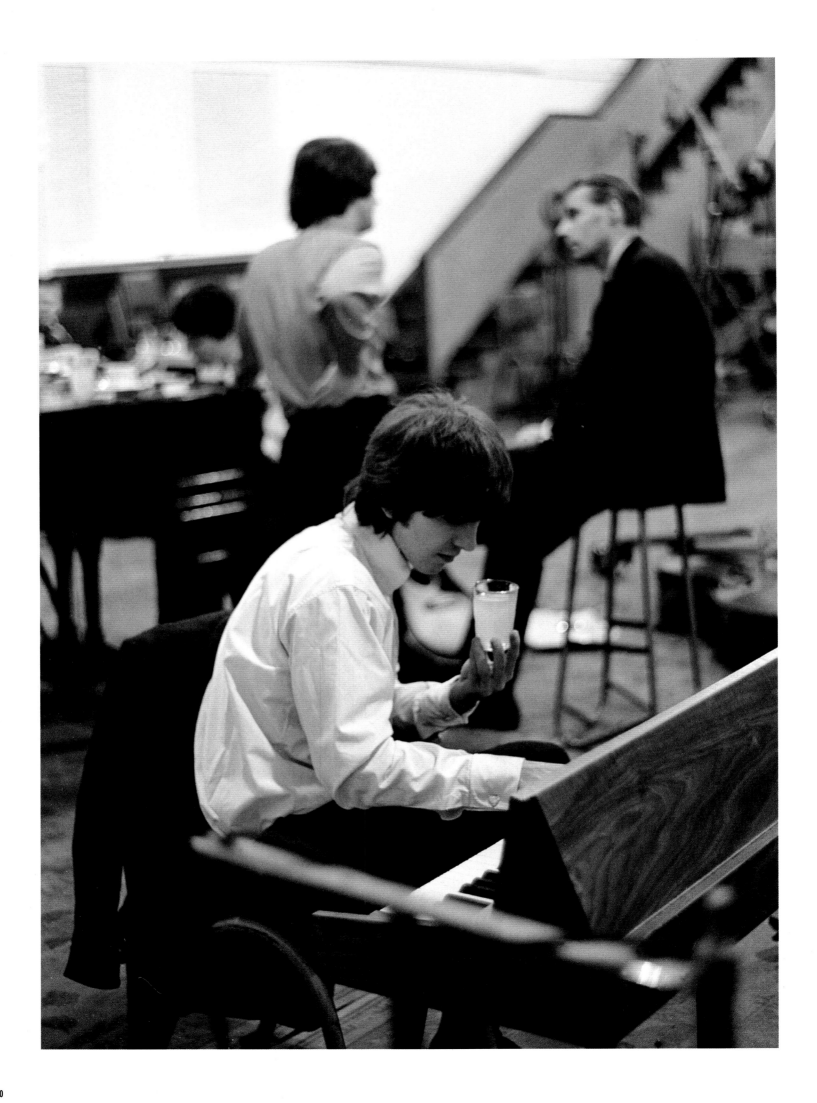

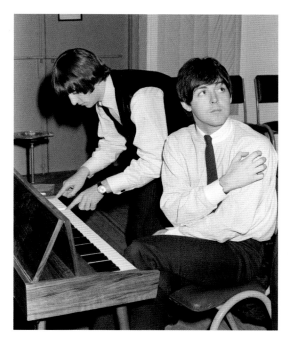

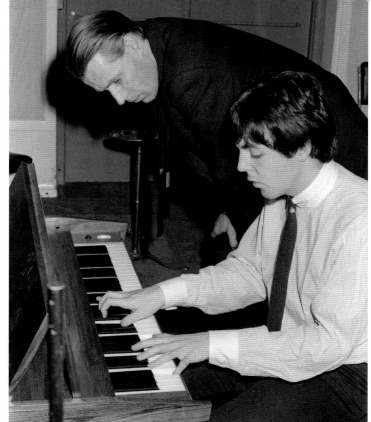

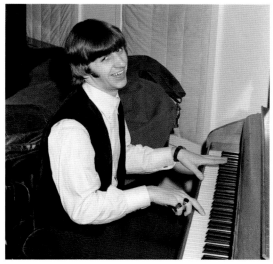

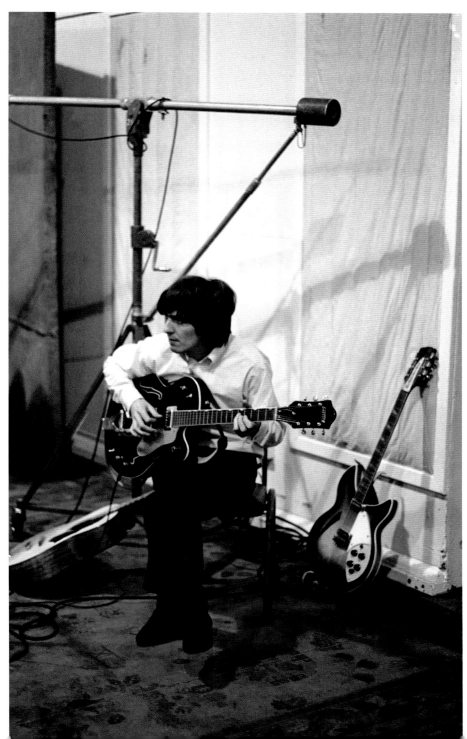

EMI STUDIOS, LONDON
FEBRUARY 19, 1965

The Beatles were heading for the Bahamas on February 22 to start shooting their second movie *Help!*, and before departure, had a busy week of sessions at EMI. They recorded 11 new songs, from which director Richard Lester had to select six or seven to film. These consisted of nine Lennon-McCartney compositions – 'Ticket To Ride', 'Another Girl', 'Yes It Is', 'The Night Before', 'You've Got To Hide Your Love Away', 'Tell Me What You See', 'You're Going To Lose That Girl', 'That Means A Lot' and 'If You've Got Trouble' (the latter two unreleased at the time) and two George Harrison songs, 'I Need You' and 'You Like Me Too Much'. Sean and Leslie's visit came towards the end of an industrious six days with George Martin. The photos show The Beatles trying out ideas for John's 'You're Going To Lose That Girl'. George, Ringo and Paul are seen tinkering on a Hohner Pianet electric piano whose sound can be heard on 'The Night Before', 'You Like Me Too Much' and 'Tell Me What You See'.

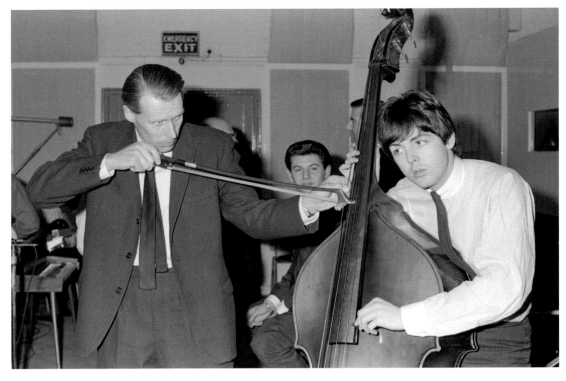

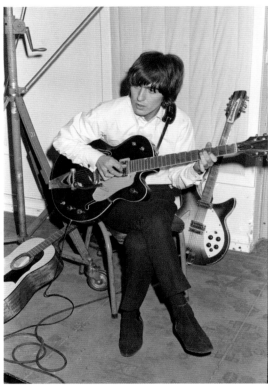

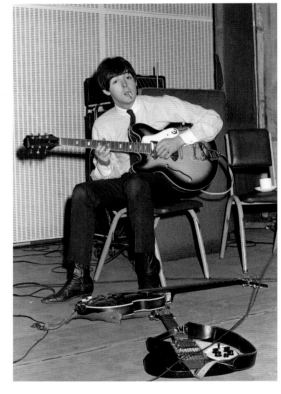

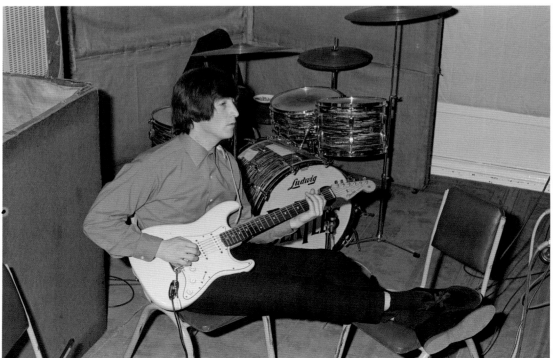

EMI STUDIOS, LONDON FEBRUARY 19, 1965

John, Paul and George lay down the vocal and harmony track for 'You're Going To Lose That Girl'. A panoply of Beatles instrumentation was on hand during the session. *Beatles Book #21*: "Apart from their usual line-up of drums, bass guitar and two lead guitars they also had a grand piano, an electric piano, a full-sized double bass and no fewer than six other guitars. Mal [Evans] was kept very busy changing broken strings!" John reclines with his new sonic blue Fender Stratocaster – George acquired an identical model, although the Strats would be heard more on The Beatles' next album *Rubber Soul*.

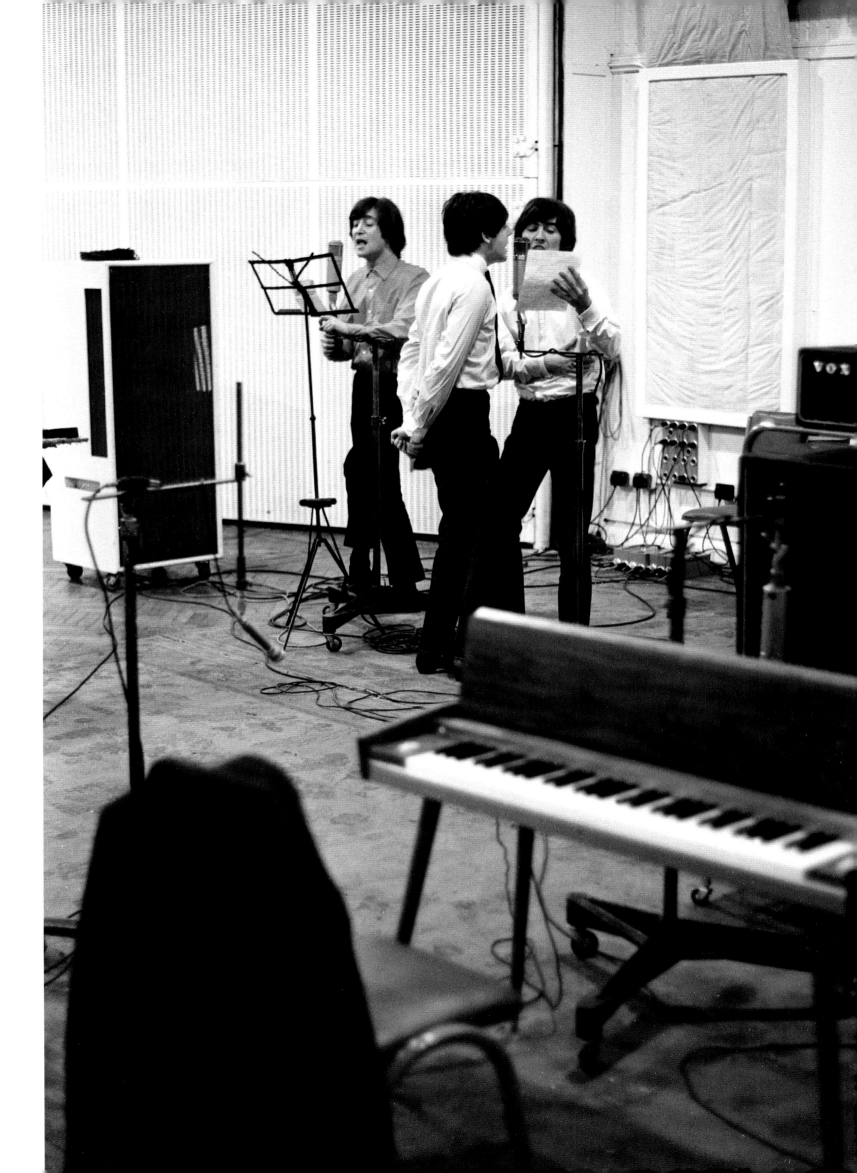

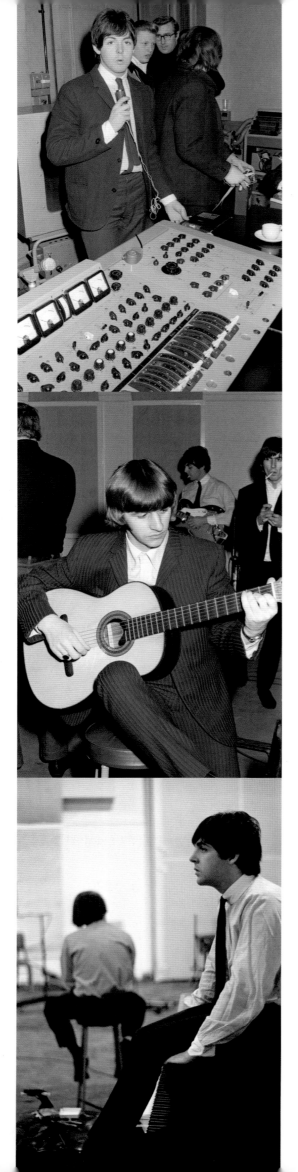

EMI STUDIOS, LONDON
FEBRUARY 19, 1965

'You're Going To Lose That Girl'
was recorded and completed in a
single afternoon session with just
two takes and overdubs. As the
session wound down, The Beatles
listened to another playback before
gathering around the control desk
to externally record the day's work;
a common practice before the days
of acetate cutting. Seen in front
of the console is Norman Smith,
principal engineer on The Beatles'
EMI sessions between 1962 and 1965.
John dubbed him 'Normal' and Paul,
'2dbs Smith' after the limit of extra
decibels Smith allowed during the
mixing process. Paul in particular
felt frustrated that the deep bass
presence on his favourite American
records could not be achieved by
EMI's technical boffins.

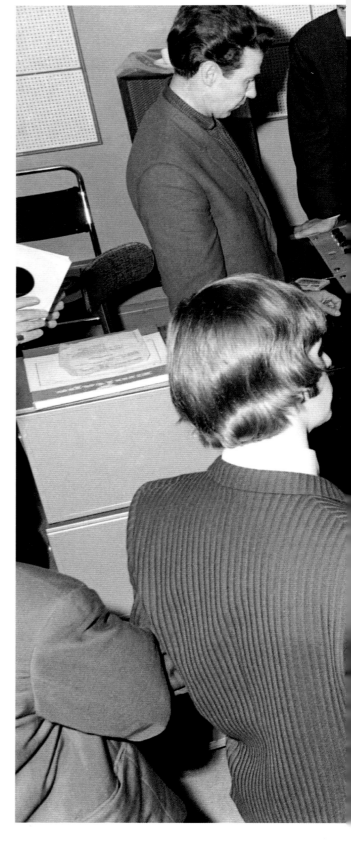

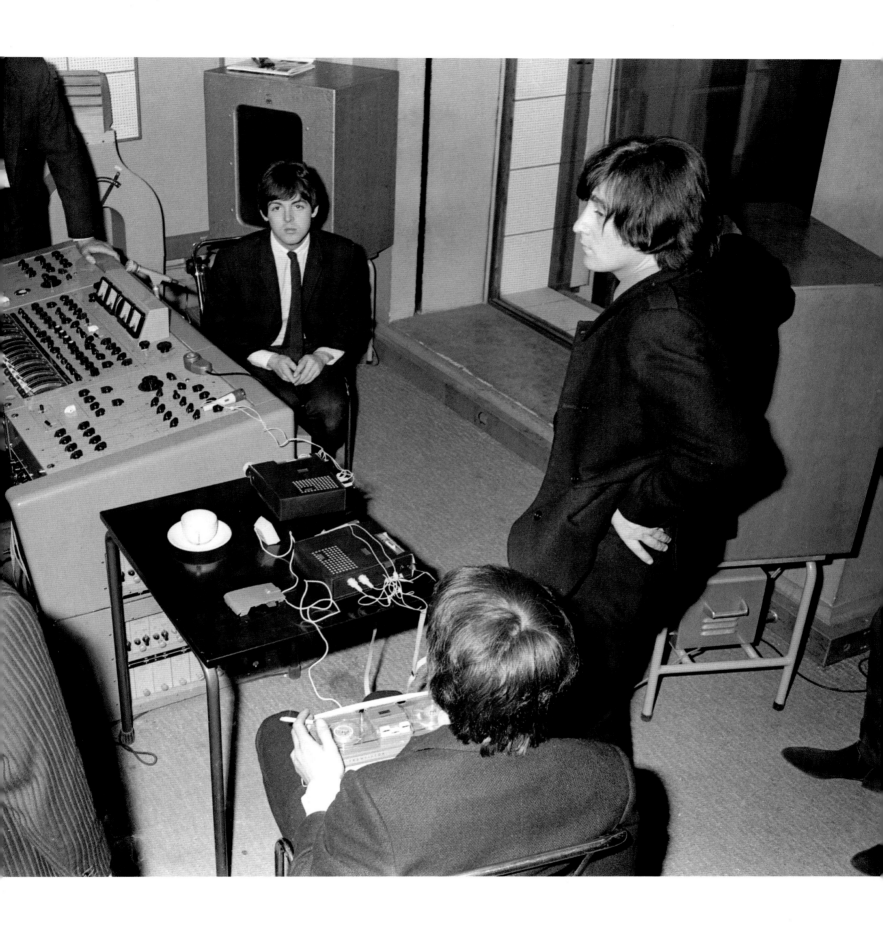

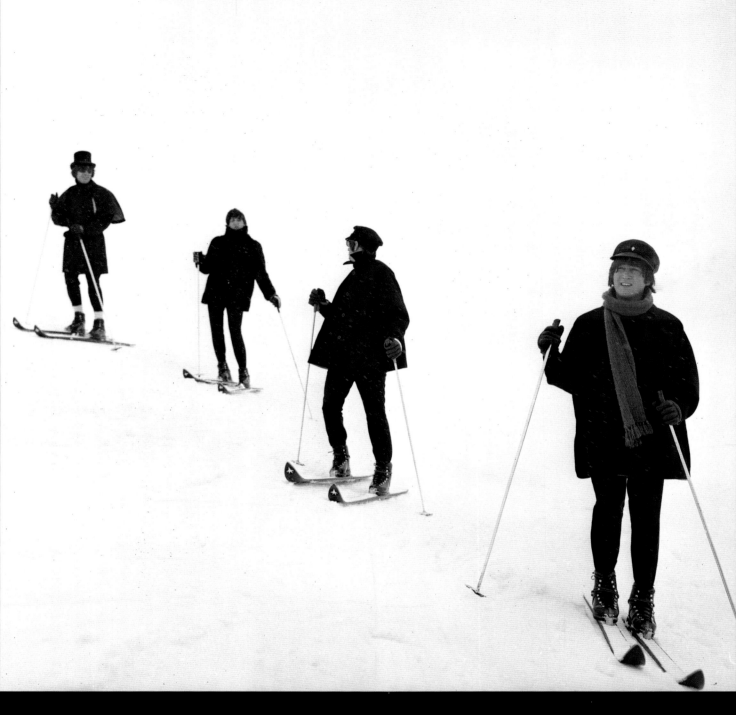

OBERTAUERN, AUSTRIA
MARCH 14-20, 1965

Having spent three weeks in the
Bahamian sun, location filming –
still under the working title *Eight
Arms To Hold You* – moved to the
chillier climes of the Austrian Alps.
The Beatles flew in to Salzburg on
March 13, an extended 'Beatles Go
Home' sign prominent among the
welcoming committee, staying at
the Hotel Edelweiss in Obertauern.
While John had taken a ski holiday
in St Moritz at the start of the
year, none of The Beatles were
experienced on the slopes, as the
memorable 'Ticket To Ride' sequence
in the film (from which these shots
were taken) clearly demonstrated.

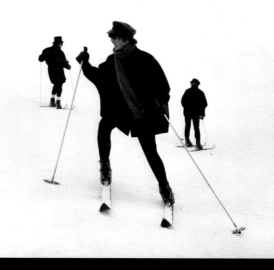

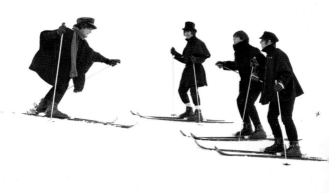

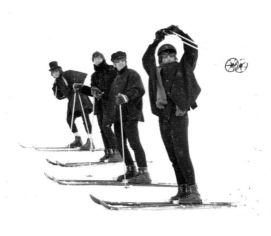

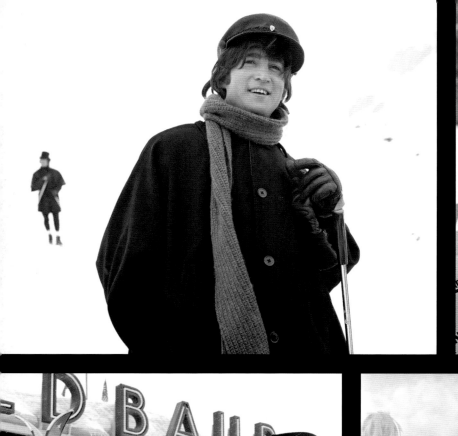
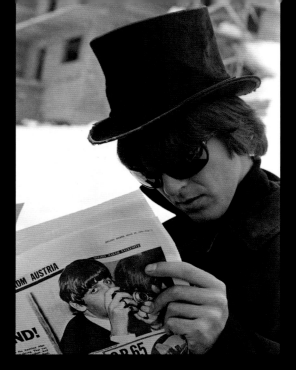
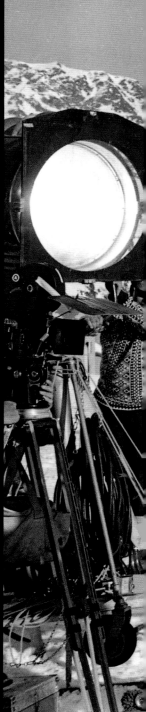
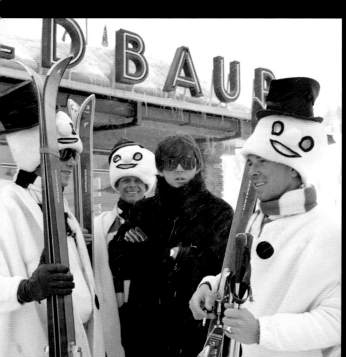
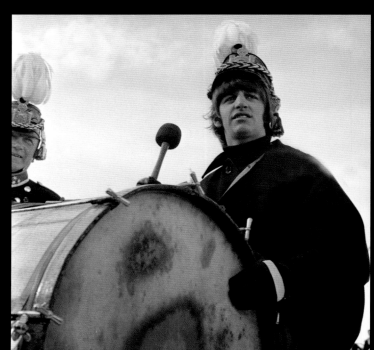

OBERTAUERN, AUSTRIA
MARCH 14–20, 1965

Even if a particular scene or shot required only one or two Beatles, all four made the dawn start on set. Because of the constant presence of spectators, fans and photographers threatening to spoil a take, director Richard Lester started using long-distance telephoto lenses to shoot the snow scenes. Between changeovers, George catches up with the latest pop news in *Melody Maker* while Paul chats to the ski-ing extras dressed as snowmen who play evil high priest Clang's henchmen. Ringo prepares for the scene where the group hide from their pursuers among a traditional Austrian band.

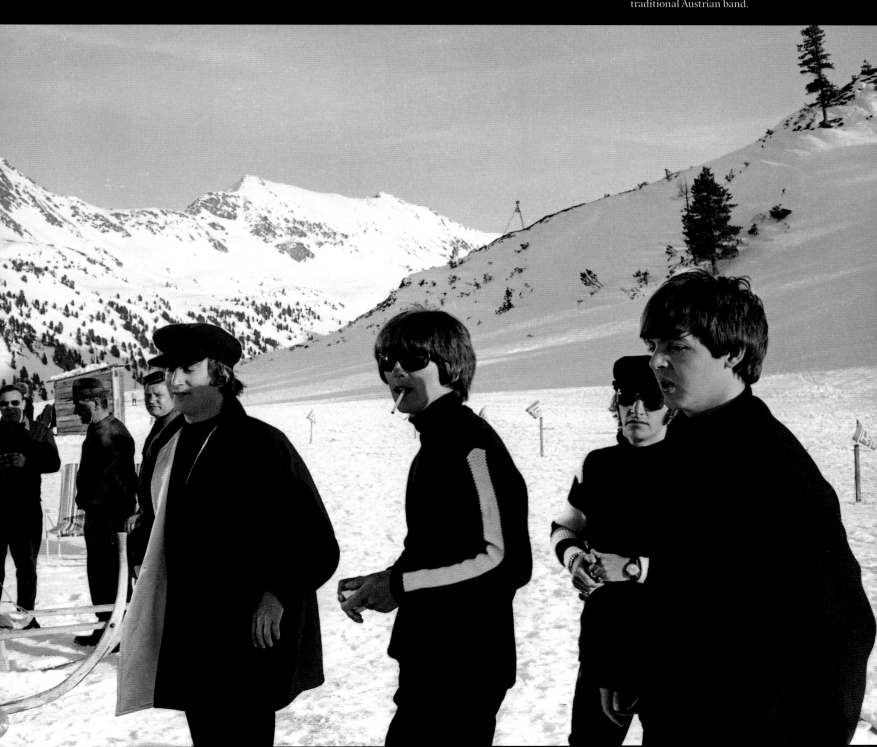

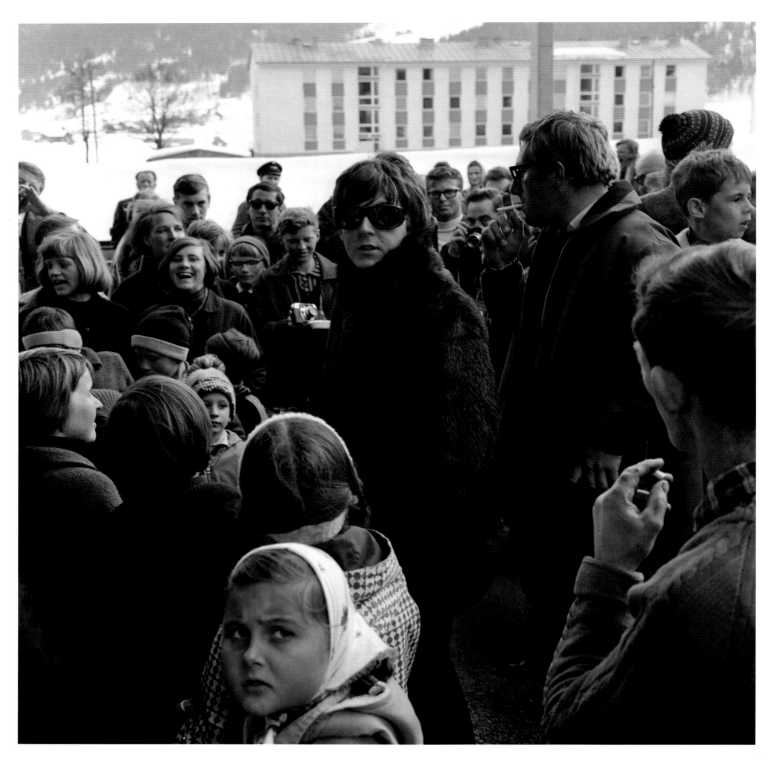

OBERTAUERN, AUSTRIA
MARCH 14–20, 1965

Paul meets some Austrian children
on the set, shadowed by Mal Evans
and Neil Aspinall. Both had minor
roles in the film; Neil told *Beatles
Book* his acting was so bad he hoped
it would end up on the cutting room
floor (it did) while Mal, greased
down, played a cross-channel
swimmer who pops up hopelessly
misdirected in the most unlikeliest
of places. For the trickier snow
scenes, stunt doubles – Cliff
Diggins, Mick Dillon, Peter
Cheeves and Joe Dunne, three
of whom are lined up with their
corresponding Beatle – were
pressed into service.

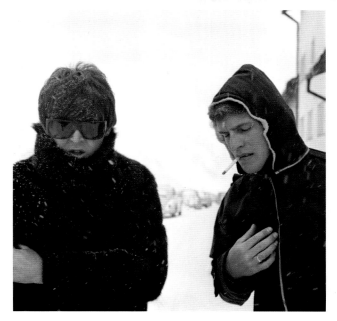

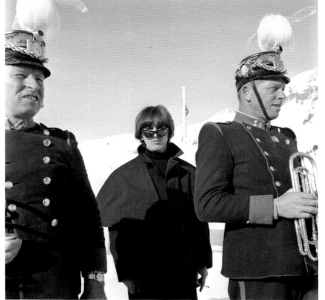

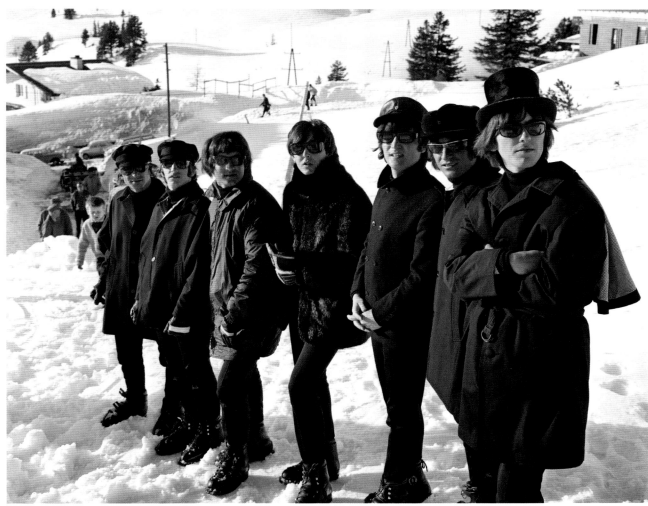

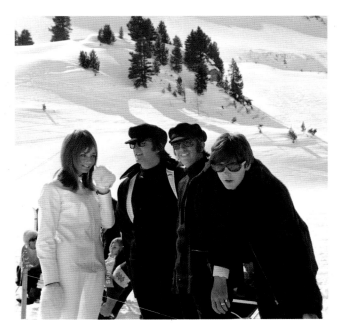

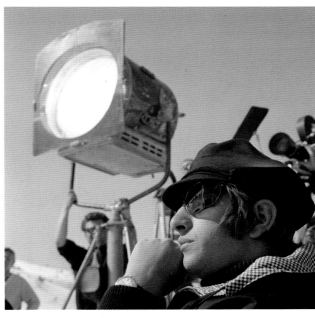

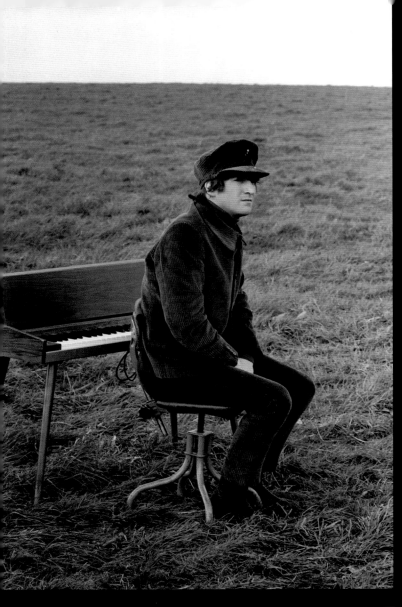
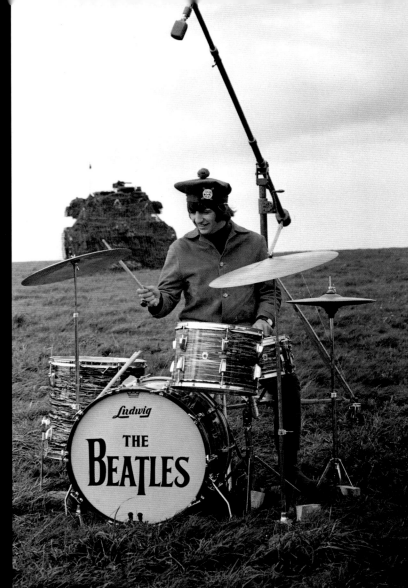
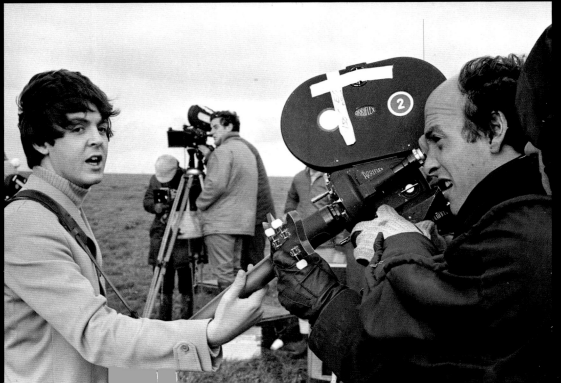
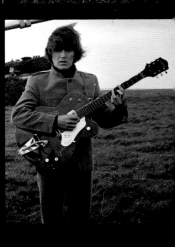

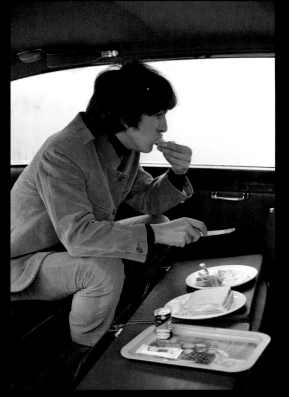

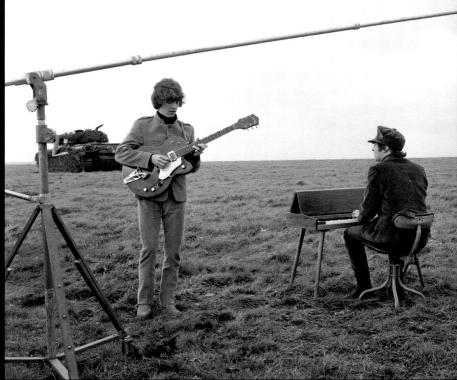

KNIGHTON DOWN, LARKHILL, WILTSHIRE MAY 4, 1965

Three days of filming occurred on
Salisbury Plain with Richard Lester
and tanks and troops on loan from 3
Division, who used the area for their
military manoeuvres. When not
needed on set, The Beatles retreated
from the cold wind and heavy rain
to a caravan or the shelter of their
Austin Princess where George is
seen grabbing lunch. Premiered at
the London Pavilion on July 29, *Help!*
was a commercial – if not critical –
success. With a supporting cast of
Leo McKern, Eleanor Bron, Victor
Spinetti, Roy Kinnear, Patrick Cargill
and Frankie Howerd (whose cameo
hit the cutting room floor), John
Lennon later grumbled that he felt
like an extra in his own film. It was a
prophetic comment. Plans for a third
United Artists' Beatles film included
a Western entitled *A Talent For Loving*.
A script was prepared and filming
was due to start in spring 1966
but The Beatles vetoed it. Further
Beatles film ideas ran in press stories
throughout 1966 and 1967 but
none reached fruition.

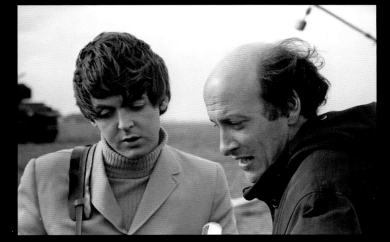

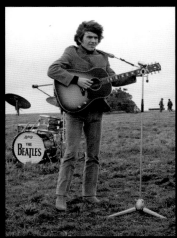

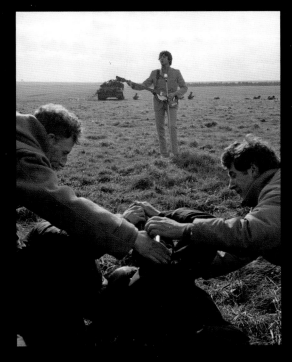

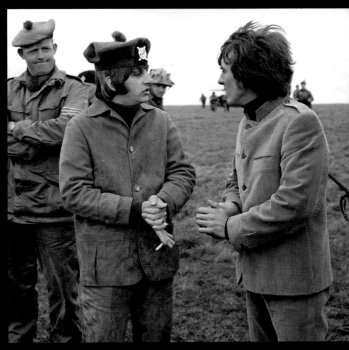

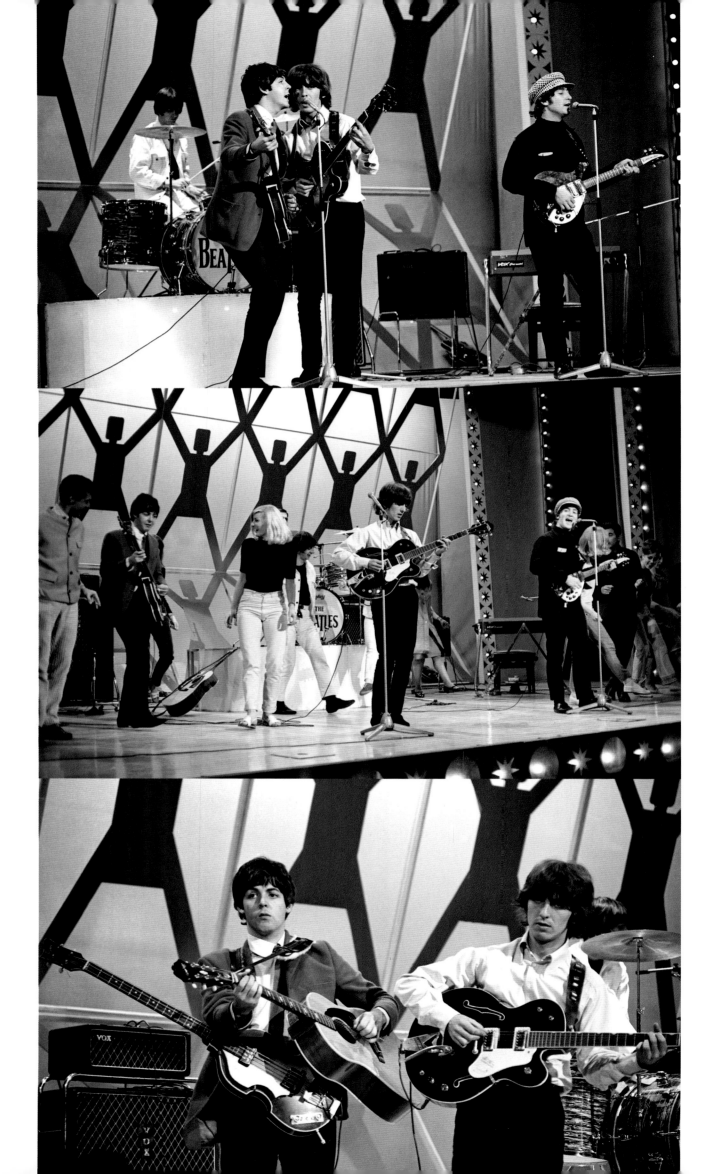

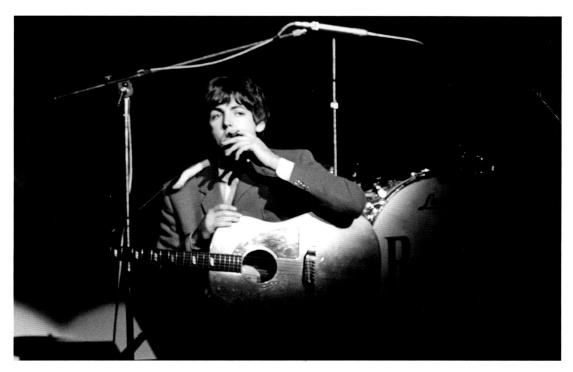

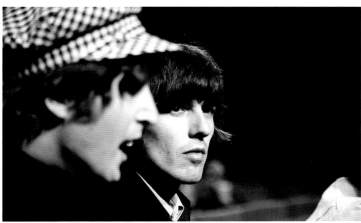

ABC THEATRE, BLACKPOOL
AUGUST 1, 1965

It had been just over a year since The Beatles' live appearance on comedian brothers Mike & Bernie Winters' popular weekend variety programme *Blackpool Night Out*. The Beatles had vastly cut down on television and radio appearances but because the show reached a large audience and realising the power of a good plug, Brian Epstein accepted the booking. As on their 1964 slot, the group rehearsed and performed several numbers, namely 'I Feel Fine', 'I'm Down' (the B-side of new single 'Help!'), 'Act Naturally' (Ringo's latest turn in the spotlight), 'Ticket To Ride', 'Yesterday' and 'Help', as well as rehearsing a basic chorus line for the show finale coached by Lionel Blair (seen in the middle photo) and dancers. It was the worldwide live debut of 'Yesterday', Paul's widely covered standard and he nervously performed it solo on acoustic backed by the house orchestra. As George jokingly introduced it "For Paul McCartney of Liverpool... Opportunity Knocks."

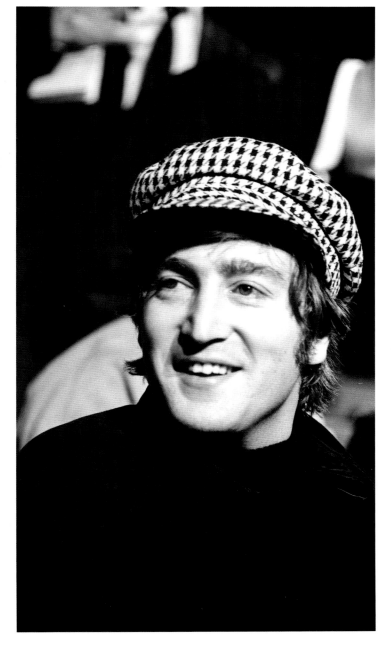

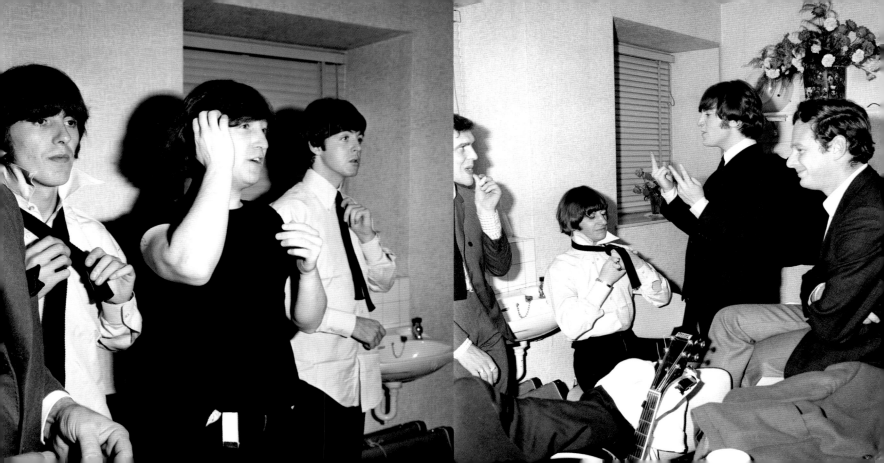

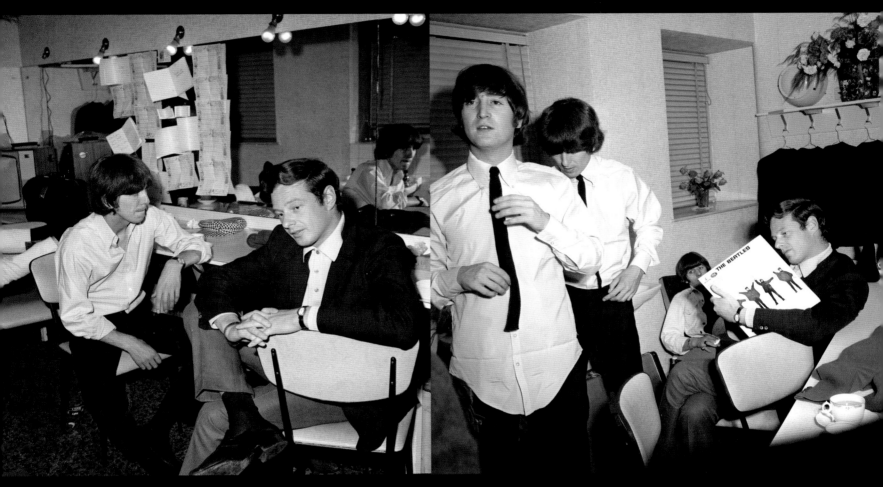

ABC THEATRE, BLACKPOOL
AUGUST 1, 1965

The Beatles get ready for the live broadcast with John making a point in inimitable Lennon fashion. 'Eppy', as the boys called Brian Epstein, was on hand to ensure all went well and is seen inspecting an advance copy of the *Help!* album which didn't (officially) reach British record shops until the following Friday.

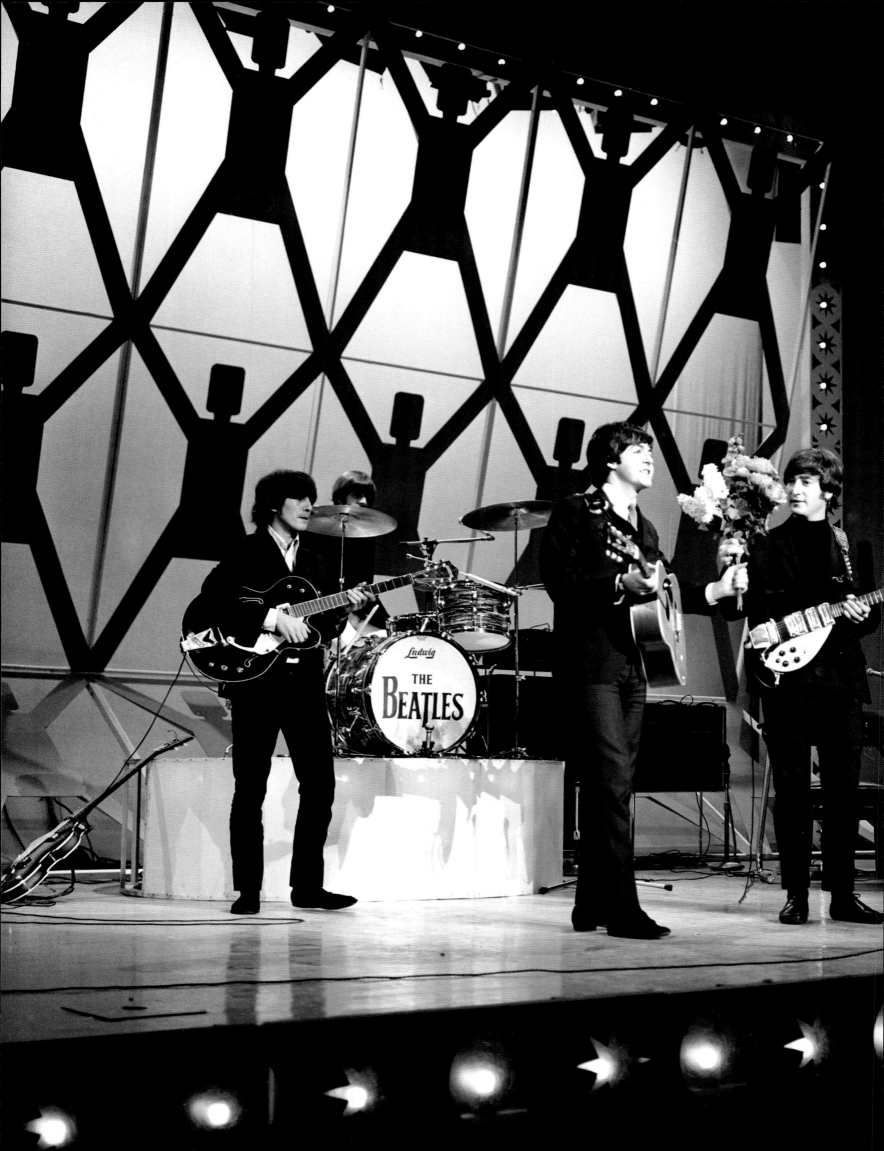

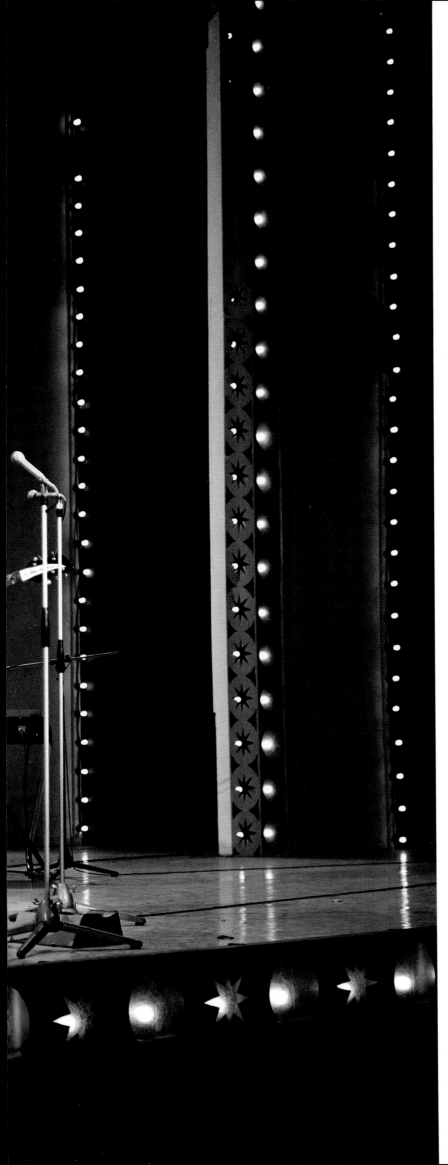

ABC THEATRE, BLACKPOOL
AUGUST 1, 1965

Following Paul's rendition of 'Yesterday', a comedy link
was rehearsed for when the others reappeared on stage;
John clutched a plastic bouquet of flowers which came
away as Paul accepted them, leaving him holding only
the bottom stems. As if to further puncture any pompous
formality, John announced "Thank you Ringo, that
was wonderful." "The Beatles were in a terrific mood..."
Sean O'Mahony wrote in his editorial (*Beatles Book #26*),
"laughing and gagging their way through rehearsals as
though they were preparing for a private Beatle People
Telly Show for the fan club rather than a national
networked performance to millions of viewers." However,
he now remembers a charged atmosphere at Blackpool
that day after Lennon sarcastically roared "Thank you,
Paul, that was bloody crap!" following McCartney's debut
of the song during the afternoon rehearsal. If there was
any tension it was swiftly diffused as Bryce's photographs
reveal the two relaxed and joking in each other's company.
Paul and John rode back to London together in comfort
that night in Lennon's new black Phantom V Rolls-Royce.

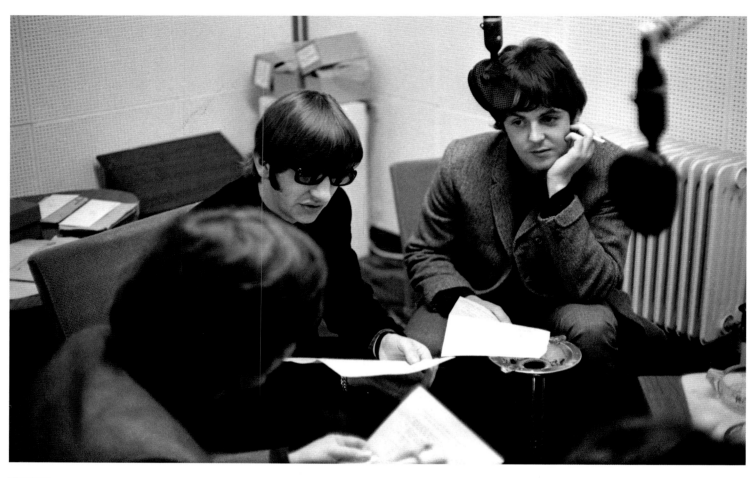

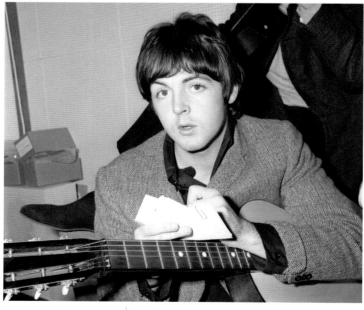

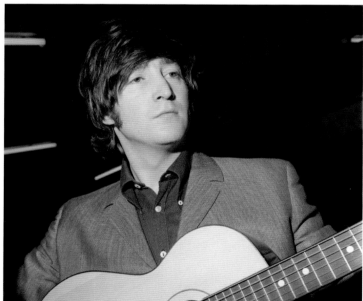

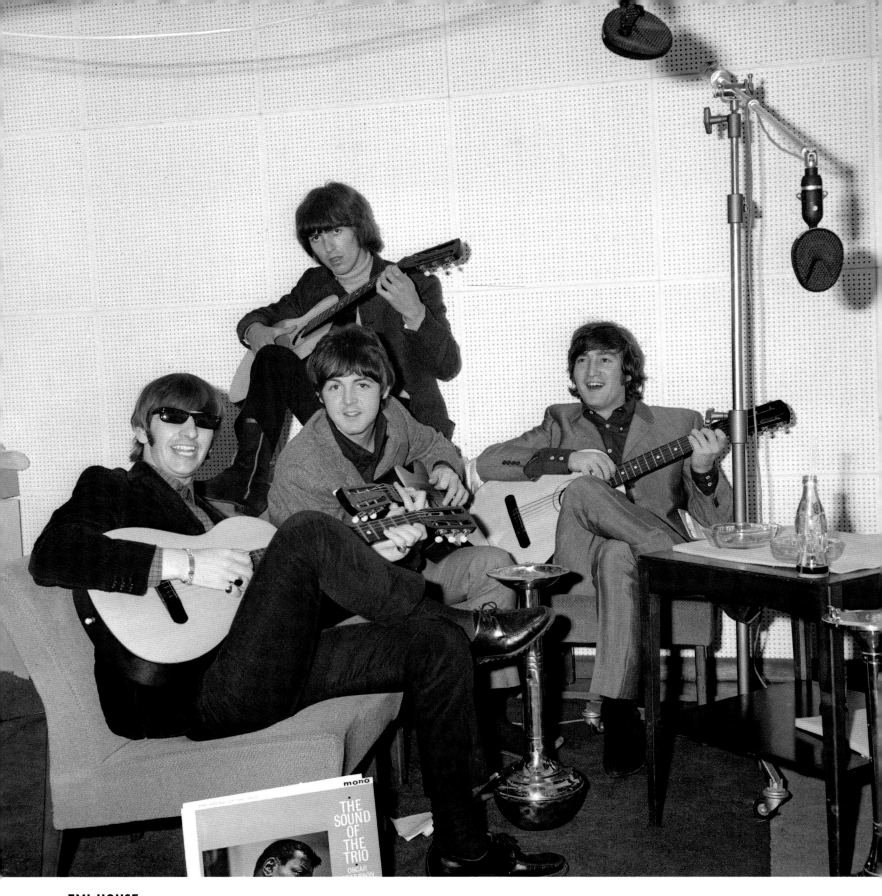

EMI HOUSE,
MANCHESTER SQUARE,
LONDON
OCTOBER 5, 1965

A *Beatles Book* session where details are scant.
According to *Beatles Book #28* the group went to
the West End headquarters of their record company
to collect four Russian-made acoustic guitars and
to be photographed playing them for the benefit of
the factory where they were made. The script session
and overhead microphones are intriguing; it may be
a read-through for their third Christmas record – an
unsuccessful attempt at recording it at the Marquee
studio, produced by Tony Barrow, occurred the
following week.

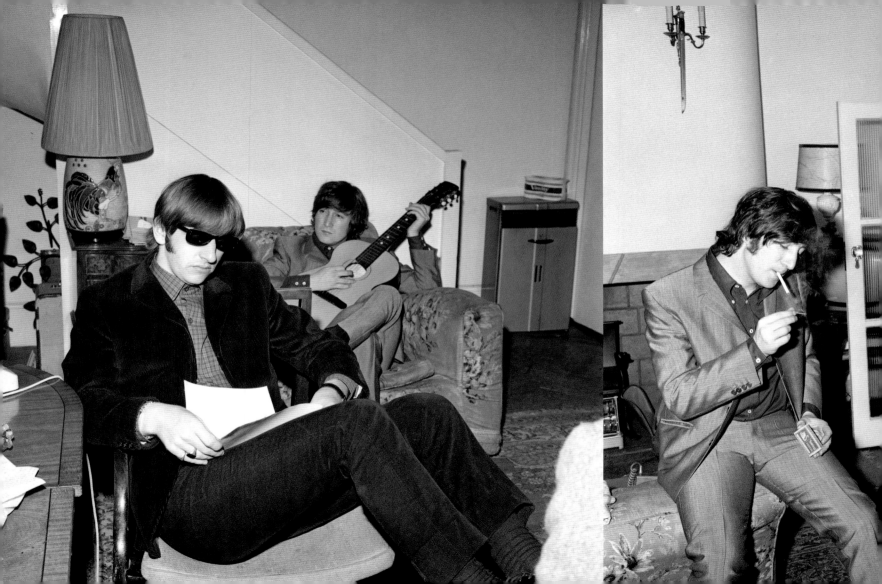

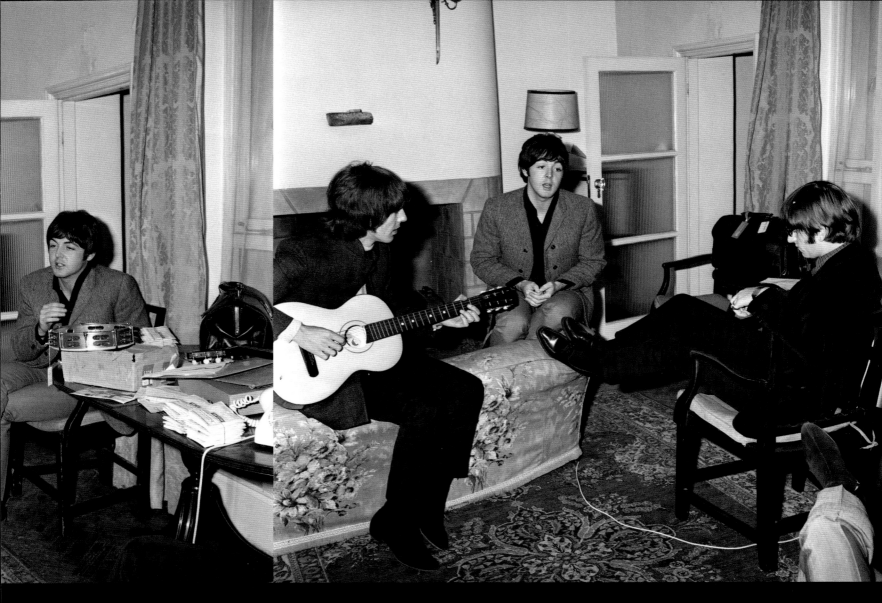

MONTAGU MEWS WEST, LONDON
OCTOBER 5, 1965

The Beatles were also photographed
at 16 Montagu Mews, the flat used
as a London base by Neil and Mal.
(Whether this occurred before or
after the session at EMI House is
unclear – but it was probably the
latter.) For some unknown reason,
the pictures were later mistakenly
captioned as an impromptu, last-
minute rehearsal before The Beatles

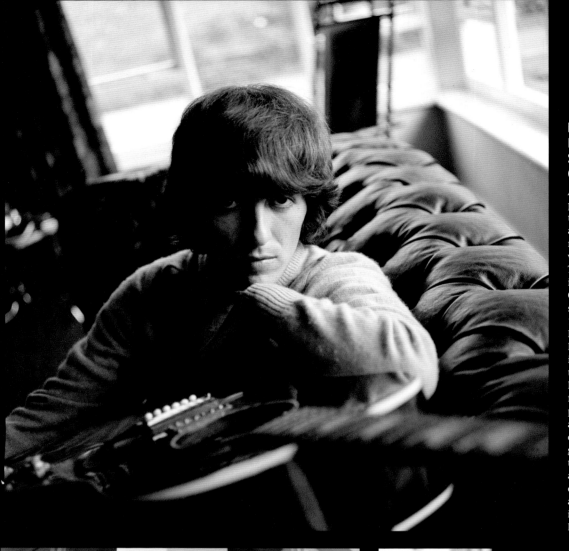

KINFAUNS, ESHER, SURREY OCTOBER 7, 1965

As the 'quiet' Beatle and the most private of the four, it's unsurprising to learn that George was the most ambivalent as regards The Beatles' monthly magazine. Ironically, he was nevertheless the first to allow *The Beatles Book* to document him in a series on the 'Beatles at home'. George had bought Kinfauns, a sprawling bungalow, back in July 1964 and he and girlfriend (later wife) Pattie Boyd moved in that month. Leslie Bryce photographed both inside and out while George swapped tops several times. He can be seen leaning against the changing rooms for the large outdoor swimming pool, the exterior wall decorated with a marble mosaic of a John Lennon drawing. The presence of the acoustic guitar and music box drew attention to George's blossoming ability as a songwriter; two strong Harrison compositions, 'Think For Yourself' and 'If I Needed Someone' would be included among the next series of Beatles recording sessions.

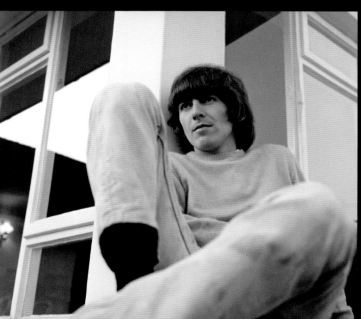

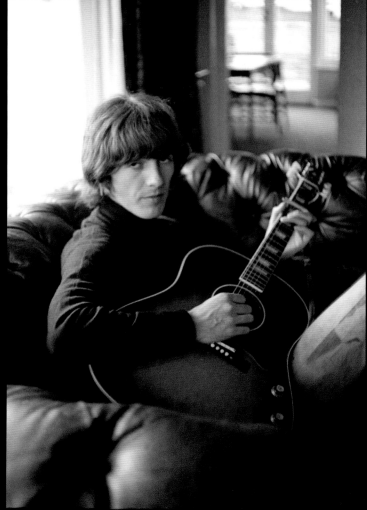

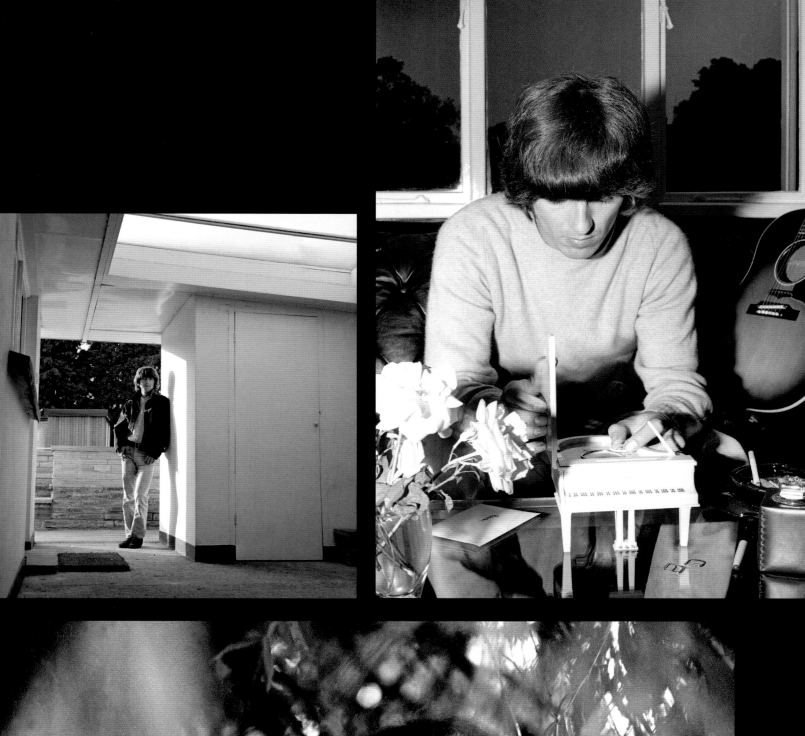
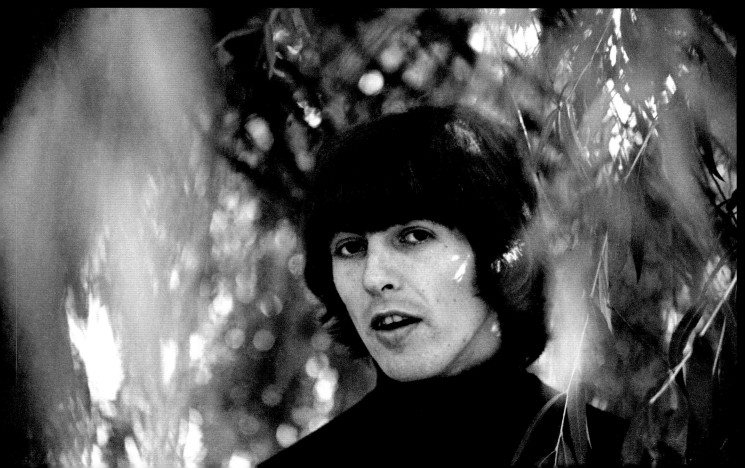

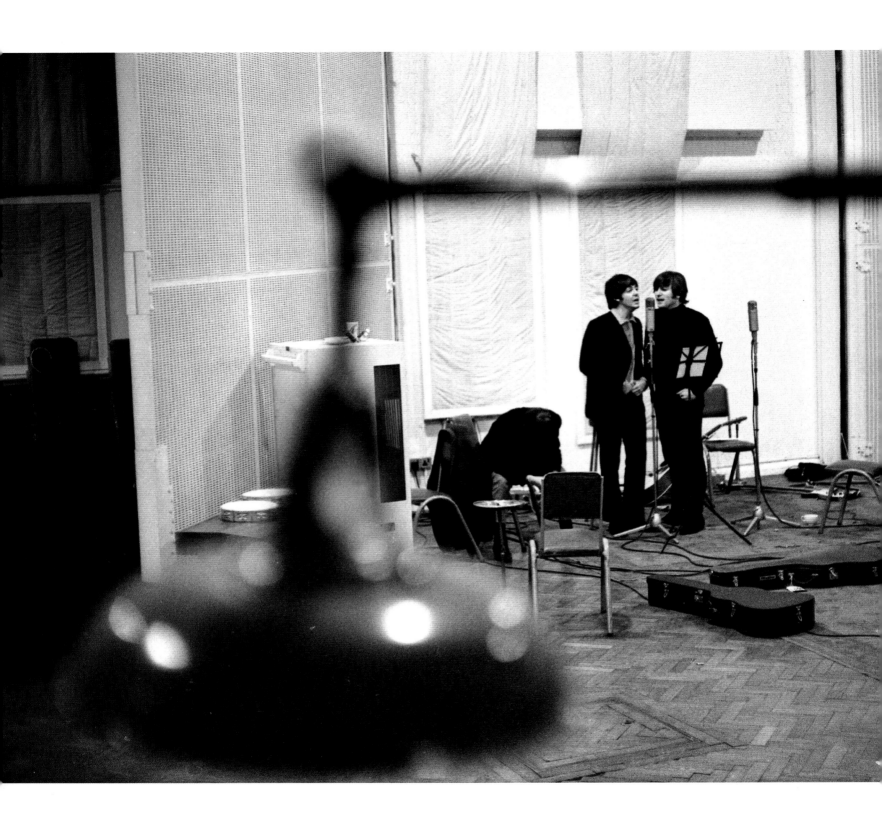

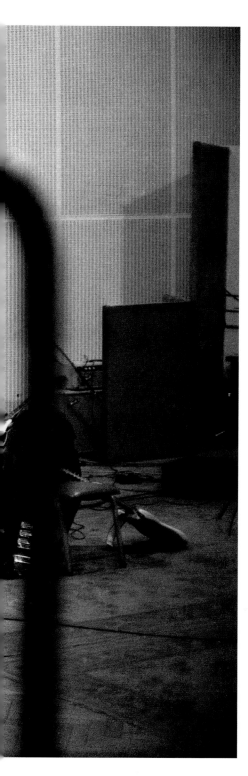

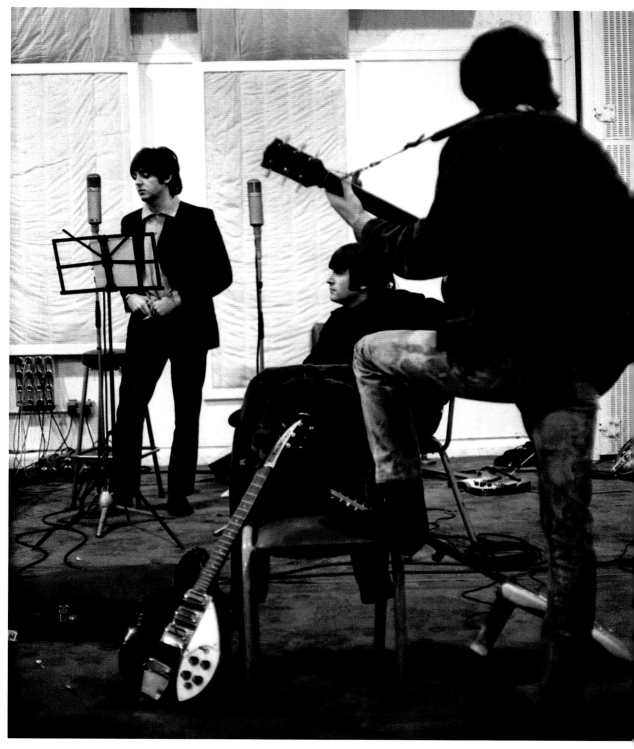

EMI STUDIOS, LONDON
NOVEMBER 3, 1965

The Beatles had an unprecedented six-week break after
returning on September 2 from their summer tour of the
United States and Canada where they played to record-
breaking crowds, including 55,600 at what was then
the biggest rock concert ever staged, at New York's Shea
Stadium on August 15. Ringo became a father with the
birth of his first son Zak on September 13, Paul's interest
in the creative art scene around 'swinging London'
increased and John and George generally took it easy.
On October 12, the four regrouped at Abbey Road to
commence recording their sixth album, the innovative
and inventive *Rubber Soul*. Leslie Bryce was privileged to
be granted access as no other photographs from these
watershed sessions are known to exist. This particular
afternoon was spent experimenting with the backing
track for Paul's ballad 'Michelle'.

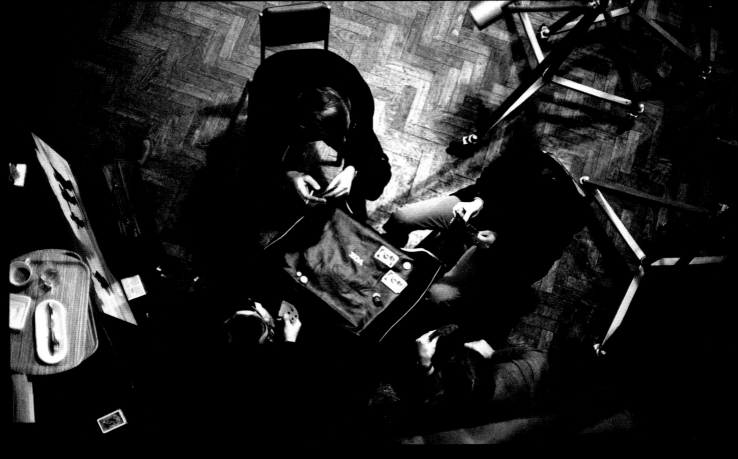

EMI STUDIOS, LONDON
NOVEMBER 3, 1965

Rubber Soul was notable for the prominent use of acoustic guitars on tracks such as 'Norwegian Wood', 'Girl' and, of course, 'Michelle'. Some commentators have described it as "The Beatles' folk-rock album", particularly the US version on which the track listing differed from its British counterpart. The sound of Paul's bass was changing, too. During their American tour, the head of Rickenbacker guitars gave each of The Beatles the company's latest instruments, and Paul's bass (seen here) was specially modified for left-handed playing. The 'Ricky' now took over as his main instrument of choice in the studio while on stage he continued to play his beloved Hofner. With the long hours spent working on ideas for song arrangements now a matter of course, Ringo was often left with time on his hands. Bryce's overhead shot from the stairs leading up to the control room shows yet another card game in progress involving (clockwise) Mal, Ringo, Neil and Alf Bicknell, The Beatles' driver.

Overleaf: A panoramic view of The Beatles at work in Studio 2.

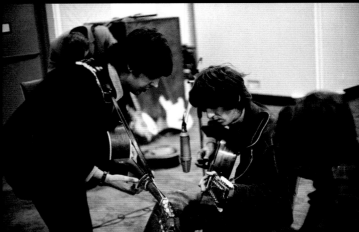

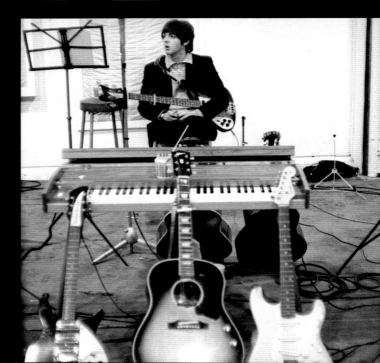

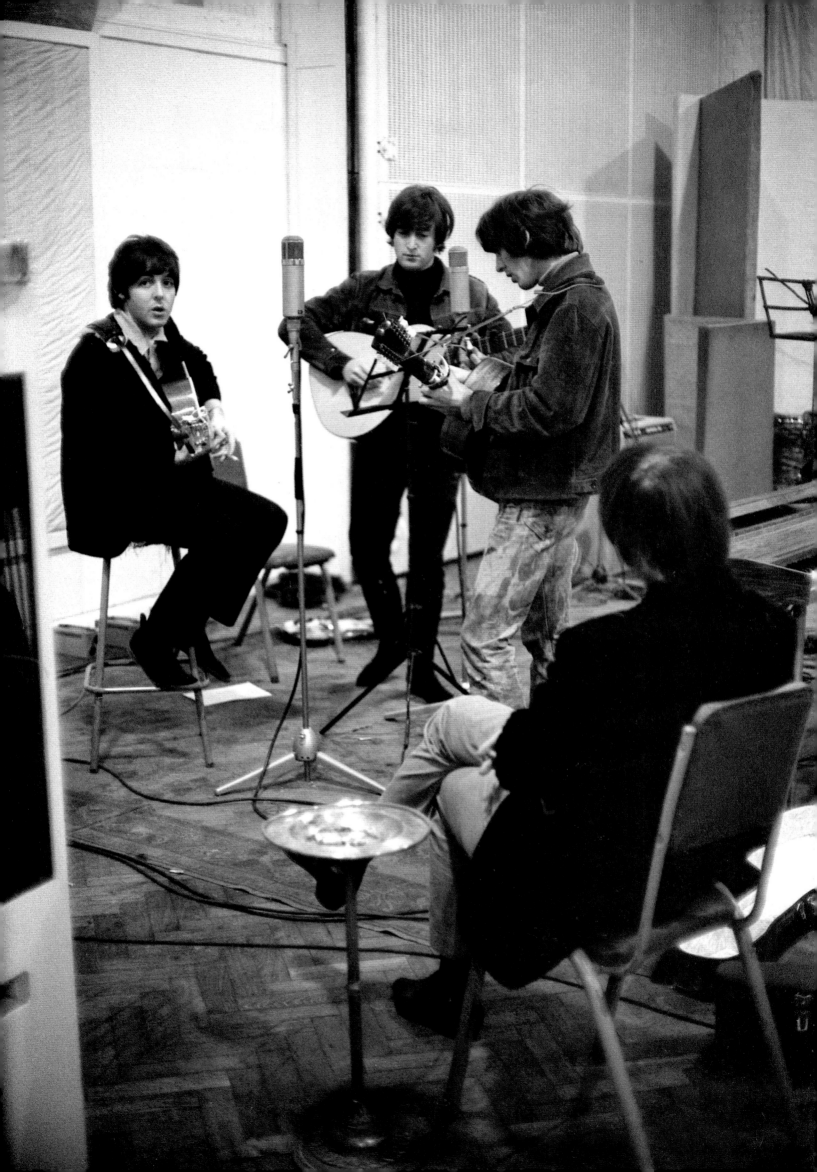

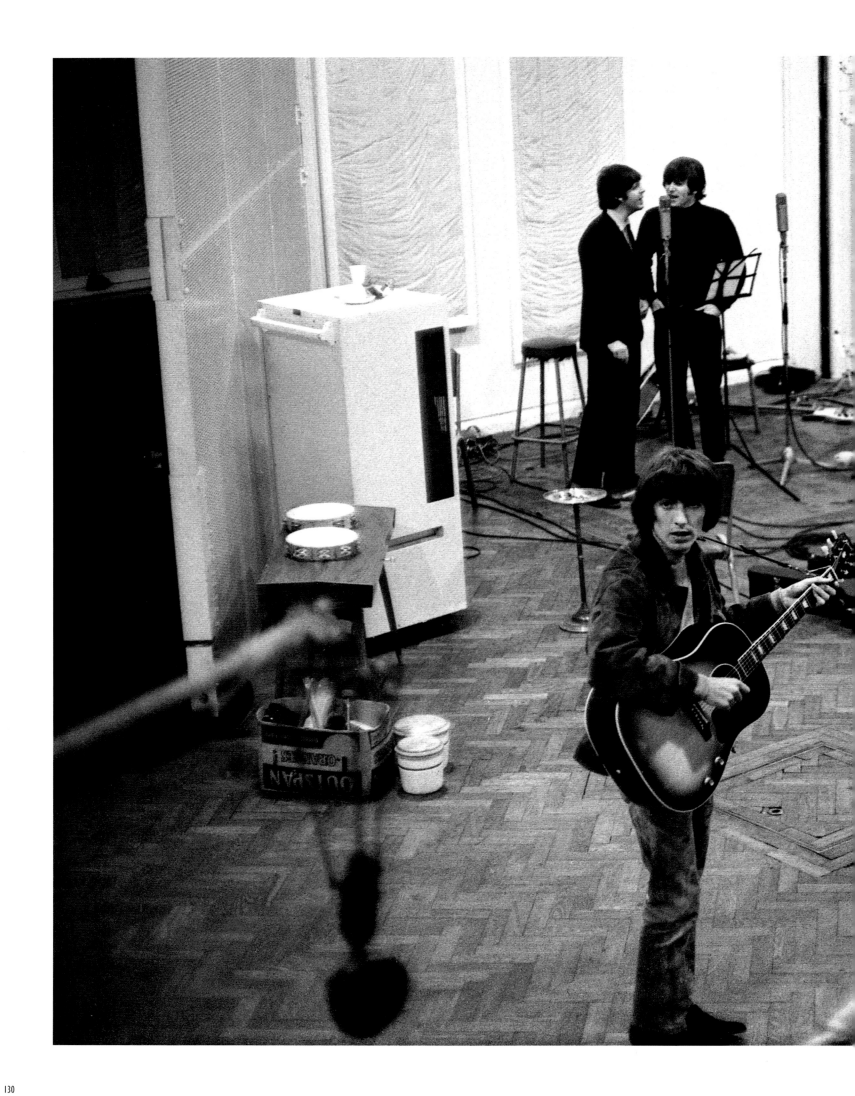

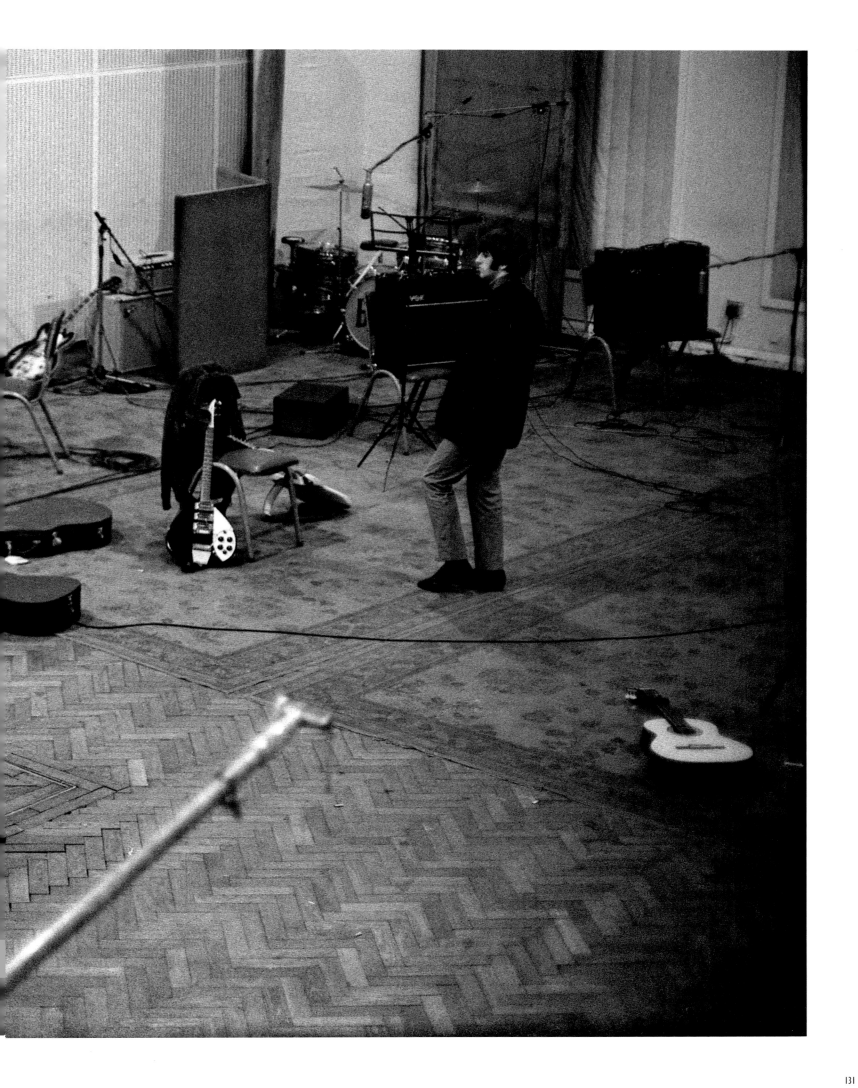

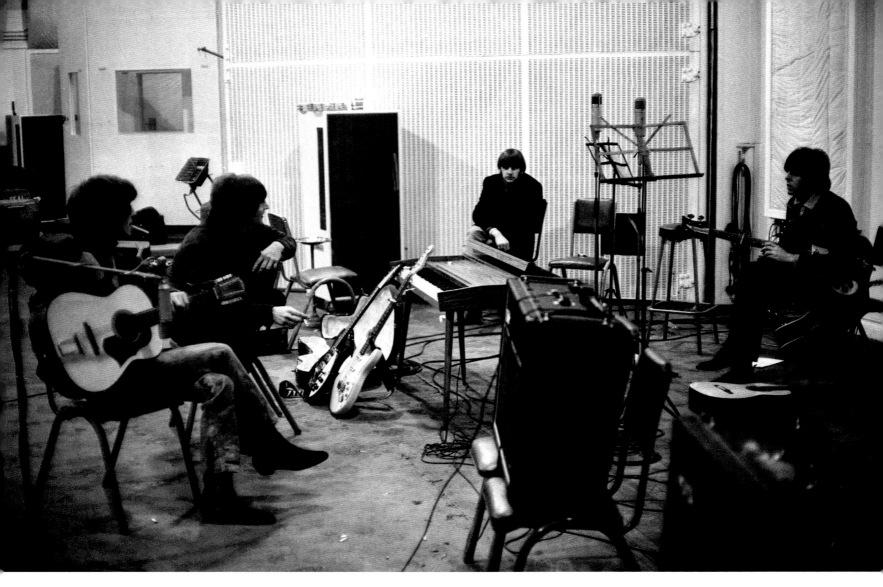

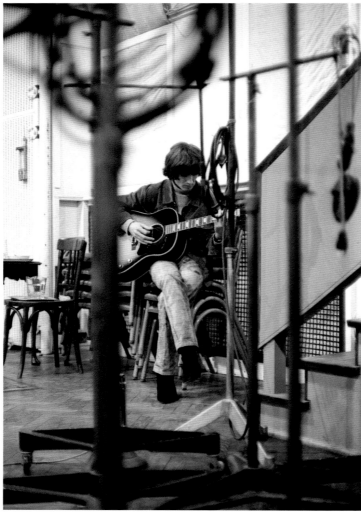

EMI STUDIOS, LONDON
NOVEMBER 3, 1965

In his editorial for *Beatles Book #28*, Sean O'Mahony waxed lyrical over Lennon and McCartney's work rate: "I heard them running through some of the numbers that they were going to record before they went into the studio, and they were really terrific... John and Paul have been working very hard on ideas and they told me they had written seven new songs in one week. Which is incredible when you think that many of the top songwriters consider themselves very clever if they manage to write just one good song per month."

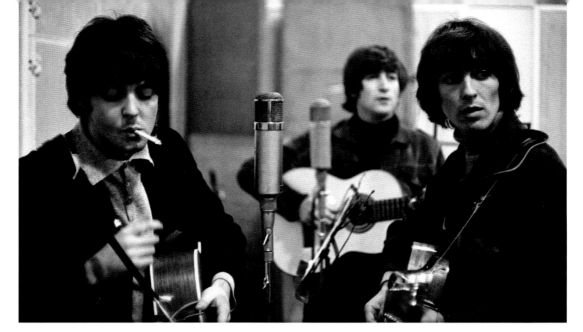

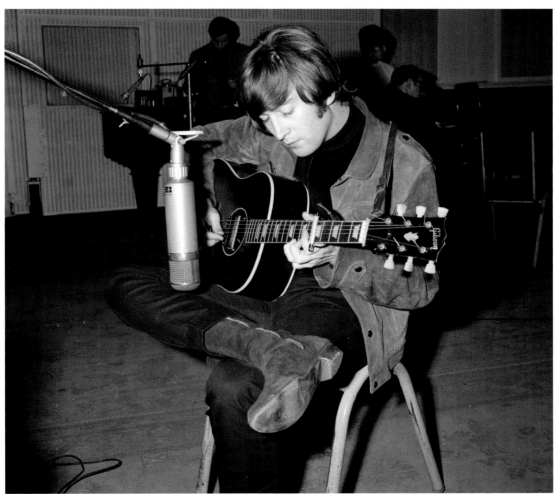

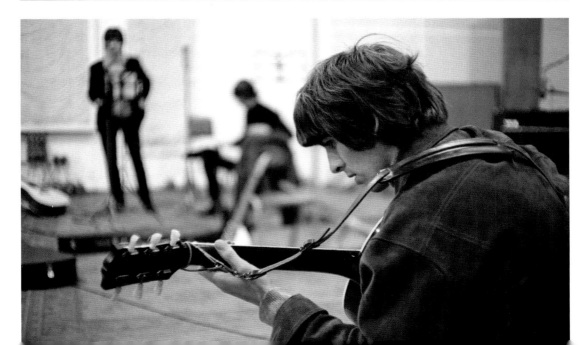

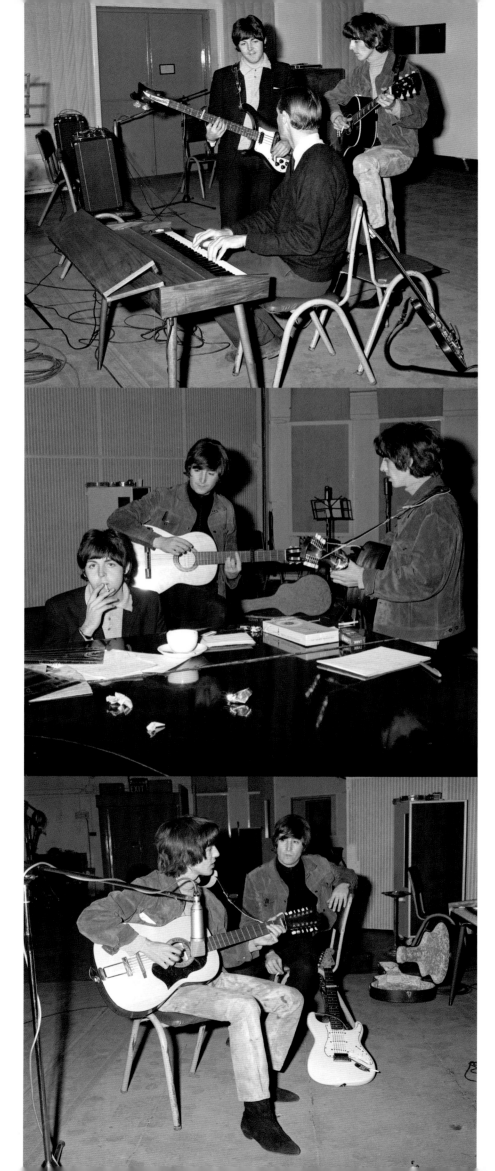

EMI STUDIOS, LONDON
NOVEMBER 3, 1965

The Beatles were doubly fortunate to have George Martin at the helm. Martin's grounding in comedy and the offbeat was the perfect foil for their creative aspirations, and his musical suggestions and input were invaluable. The recording studio provided not only a creative workshop atmosphere but a sanctuary against the outside pressures brought about by the intensity of Beatlemania. As work progressed on *Rubber Soul*, The Beatles continued to push the musical envelope with exotic instrumentation, unusual harmonies and experimental techniques. Even Robert Freeman's lopsided, distorted cover photo was a further artistic break from the norm.

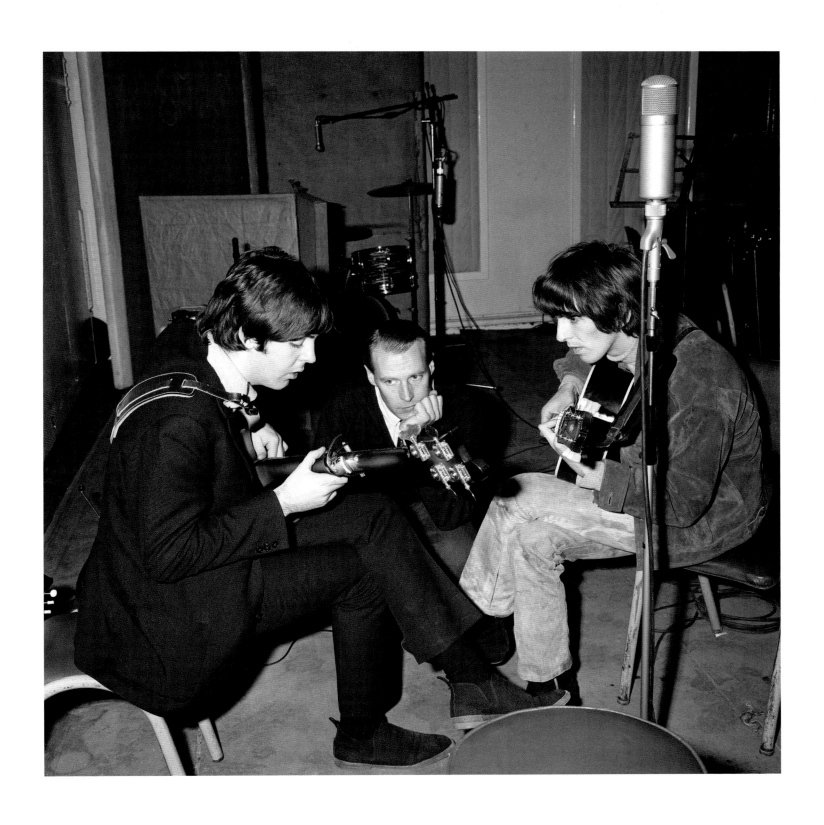

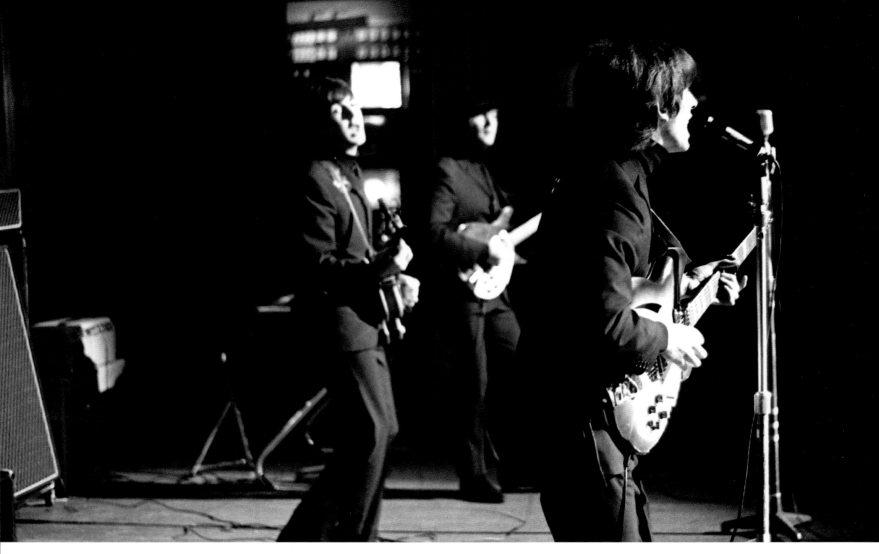

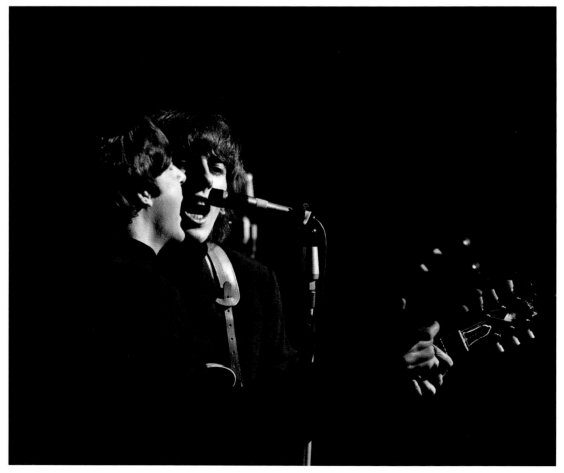

GAUMONT CINEMA, SHEFFIELD
DECEMBER 8, 1965

The Beatles increasing retreat into the recording studio was a reaction to the commotion that invariably surrounded their public appearances. As newly-anointed Members of the British Empire, the Fabs were now less agreeable to performing on stages where they couldn't be heard and the group's final eight-city UK trek covering England, Scotland and Wales owed much to Brian Epstein's powers of persuasion. *The Beatles Book* caught up with the tour five dates in at Sheffield. The set-list featured very little of The Beatles' new, forward-thinking music; just their latest single, the double A-sided 'Day Tripper' and 'We Can Work It Out' – the latter featuring John on Vox Continental organ – and only two tracks from just-released *Rubber Soul*, George's Byrds-like 'If I Needed Someone', for which he used his capoed Rickenbacker 360-12, and John's 'Nowhere Man'. For Ringo's spot on the tour, 'What Goes On' was briefly mooted but instead the familiar 'Act Naturally' was chosen. On 'Yesterday', Paul accompanied himself on the organ and John sat at the keys for the rocking finale of 'I'm Down'.

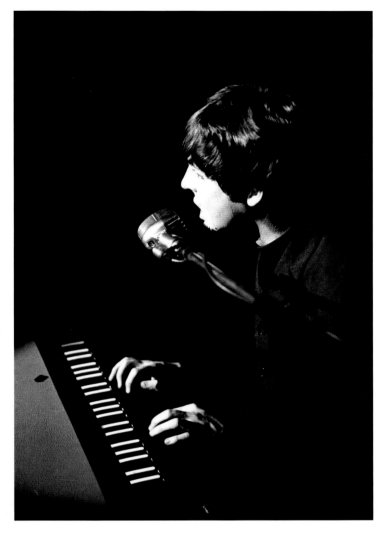

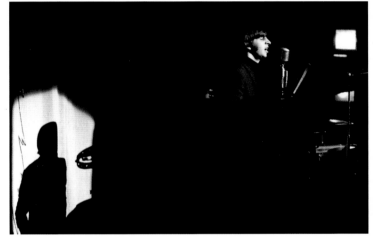

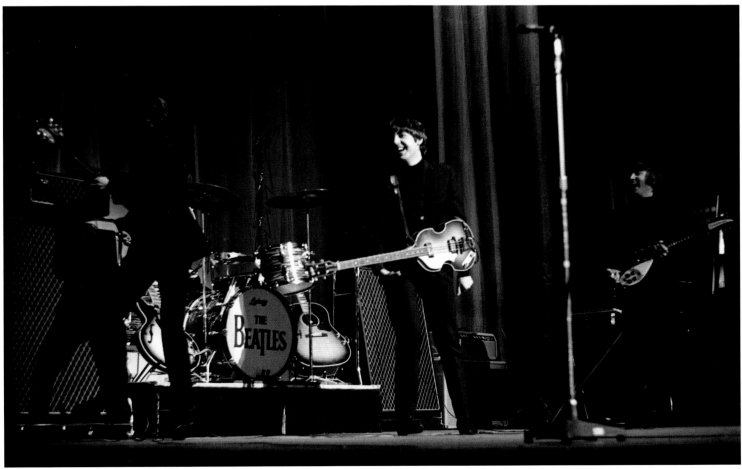

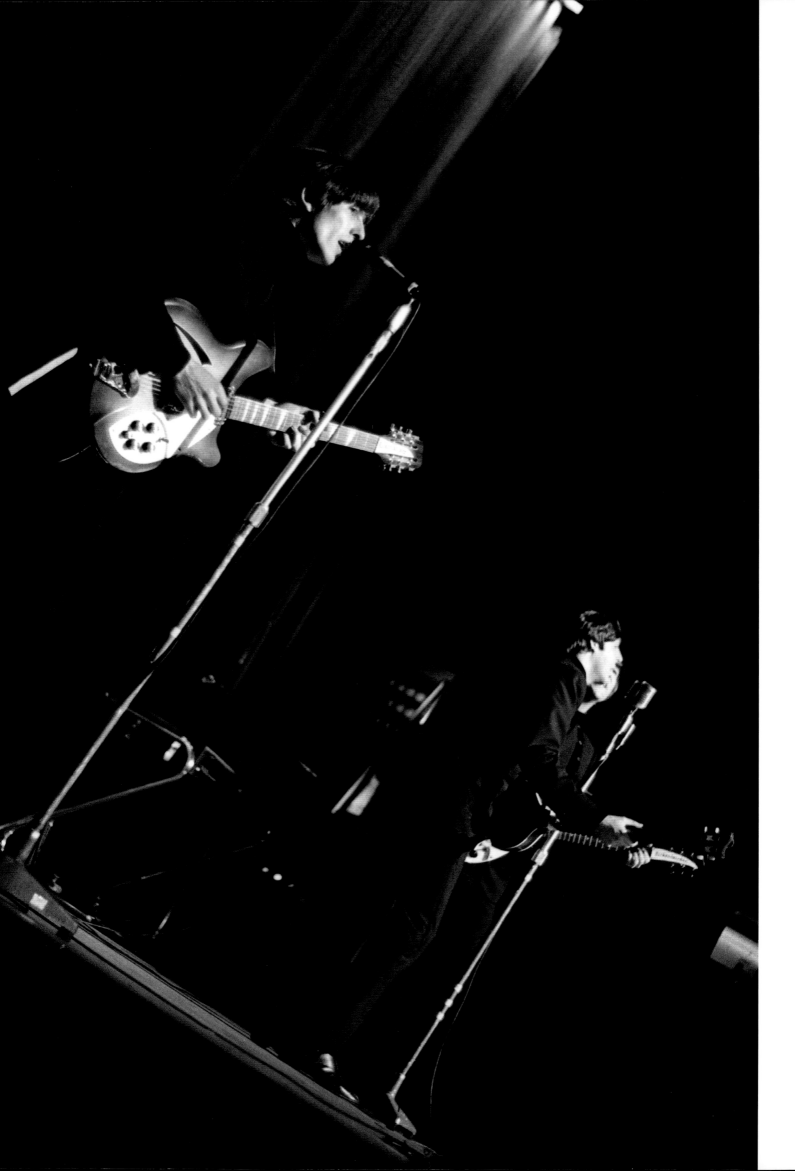

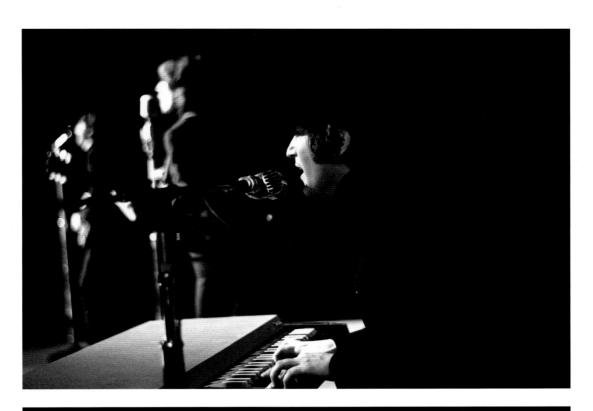

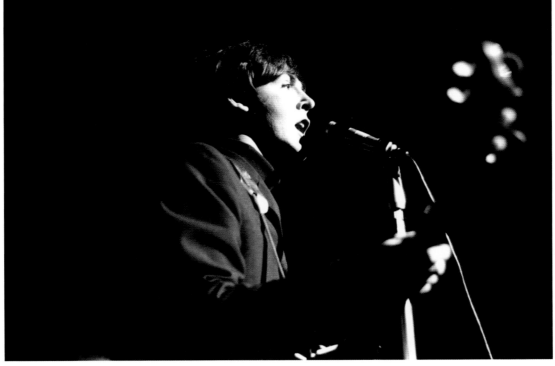

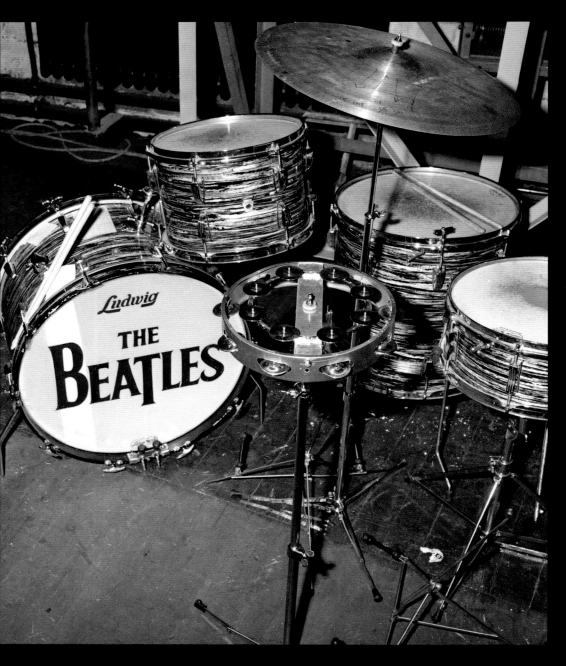

GAUMONT CINEMA, SHEFFIELD
DECEMBER 8, 1965

Fab gear. Notable by its absence is George's Gretsch Country Gentleman which met a calamitous fate during the journey north to the tour's first concerts in Glasgow. For some inexplicable reason, considering The Beatles were the world's biggest entertainment act and could easily afford a spacious equipment van, some of their gear was strapped to the back of the Austin Princess carrying all four Beatles and being driven by Alf Bicknell. Somewhere along the motorway, a lorry flashed them to pull over. "The driver said, 'I don't want to alarm you, but you've just lost a banjo back there,'" Bicknell recalled. "I went back to look and sure enough, one of George's guitars was missing. I was terrified. I said to Neil [Aspinall], 'Go and tell them.' And he said, 'No, *you* tell them.' I opened the passenger door, leaned in and said, 'We've just lost a banjo,' trying to make light of it. John's voice came back. 'Alf, if you can find it, you can have a bonus.' 'What's that?' I asked. He said, 'You can have your job back.'"

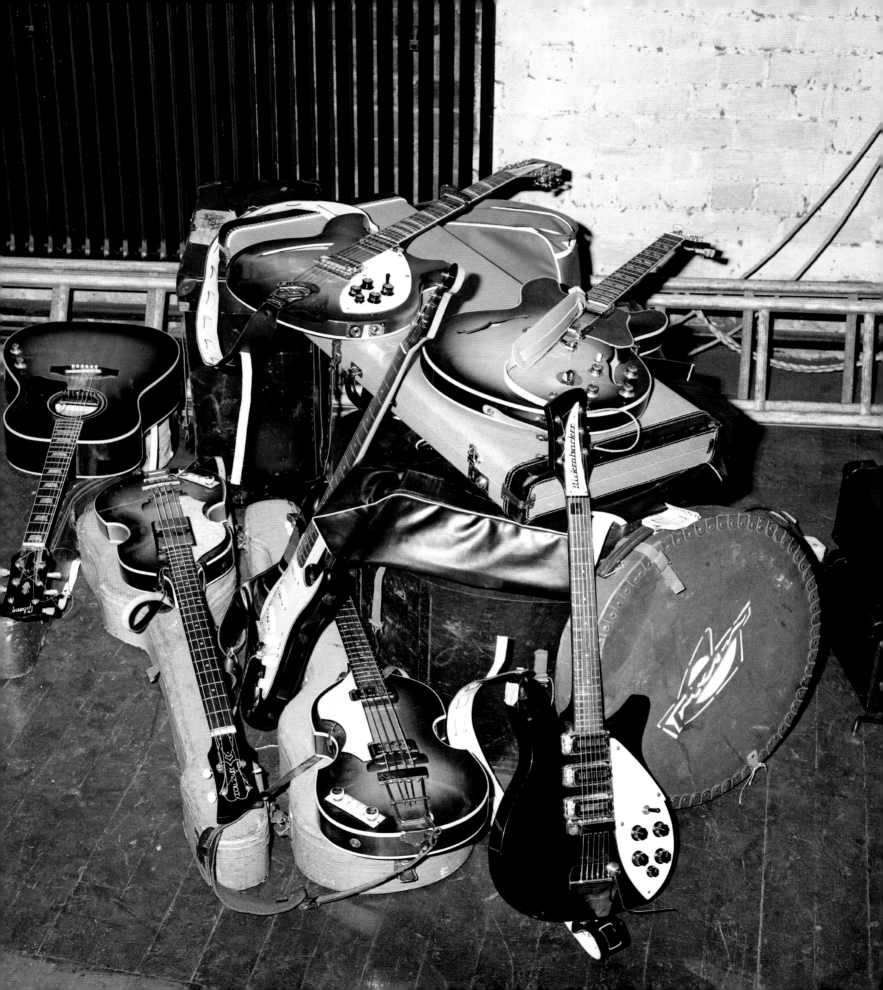

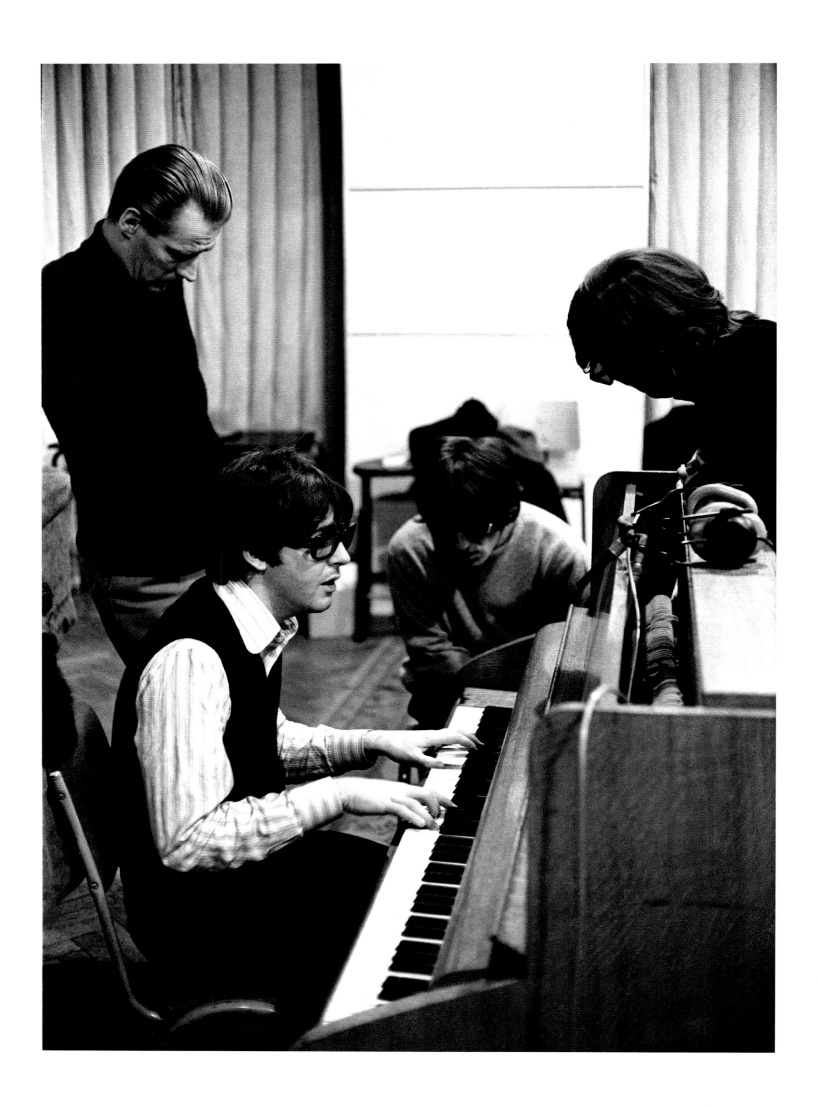

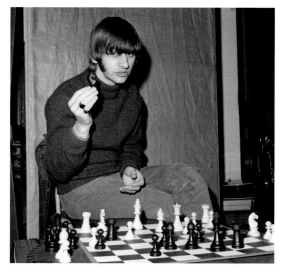

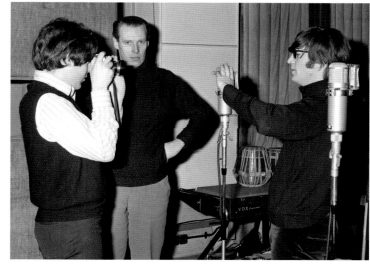

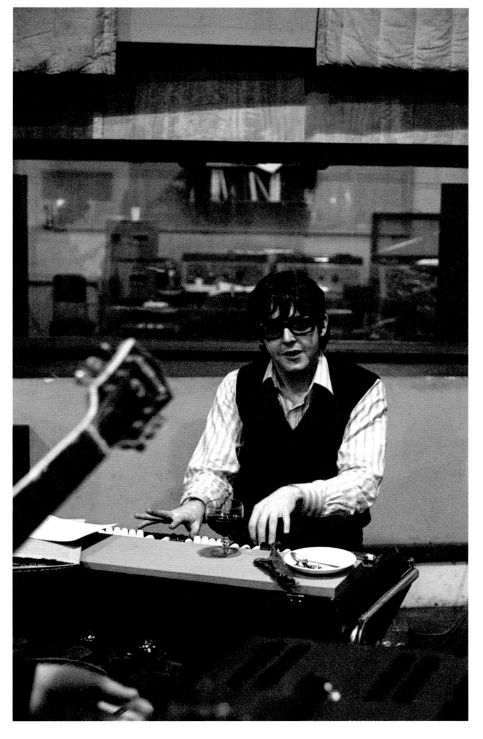

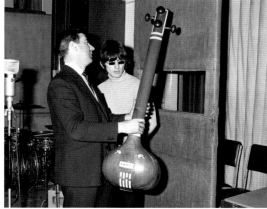

EMI STUDIOS, LONDON APRIL 14, 1966

Following their final British concert tour, The Beatles took four months off – an act of commercial suicide for any lesser group in the heady firmament of mid-1960s pop. The expected output of three singles, two albums and a film was no longer a consideration – The Beatles would work at their own pace until they were satisfied with the result. The sessions for what became *Revolver* commenced on April 6. If critics were taken aback and fans caught unawares by the maturity evident in *Rubber Soul*, they were in for an even greater shock. The die was cast from the first song recorded – John Lennon's 'Tomorrow Never Knows' – which sounded far beyond the realms of ordinary 1966-style pop music with its collage of tape loops, disembodied vocals and lyrics based on *The Tibetan Book Of The Dead*. Paul's 'Got To Get You Into My Life' and George's first full-blown Indian experiment, 'Love You To' (featuring the sitar Sean O'Mahony is holding) followed. A week after the sessions started, Paul's 'Paperback Writer' was crafted to perfection in the smaller No. 3 studio. The lengthy time involved working out ideas for the backing track would mean long chess games for Ringo...

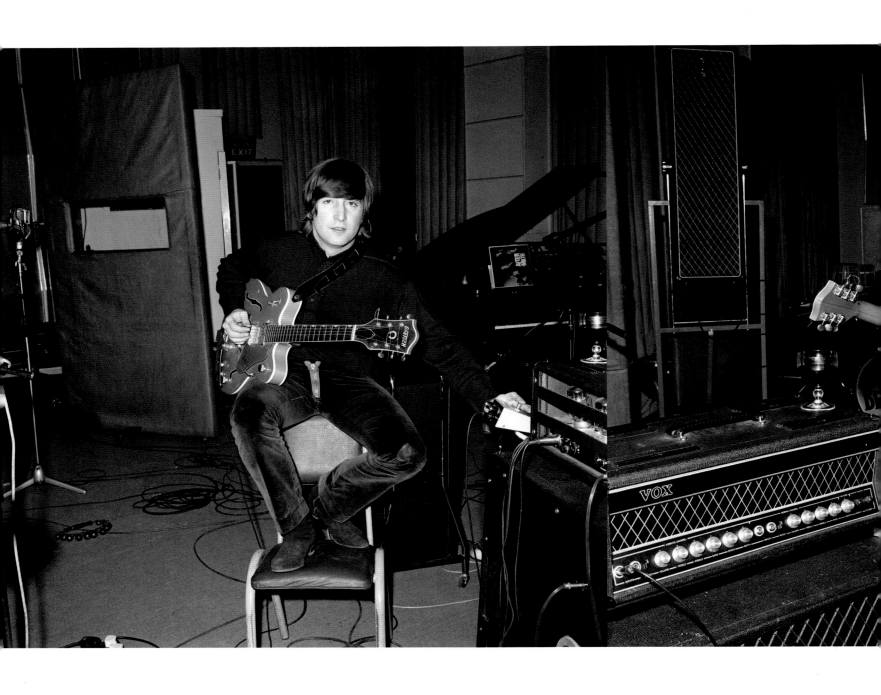

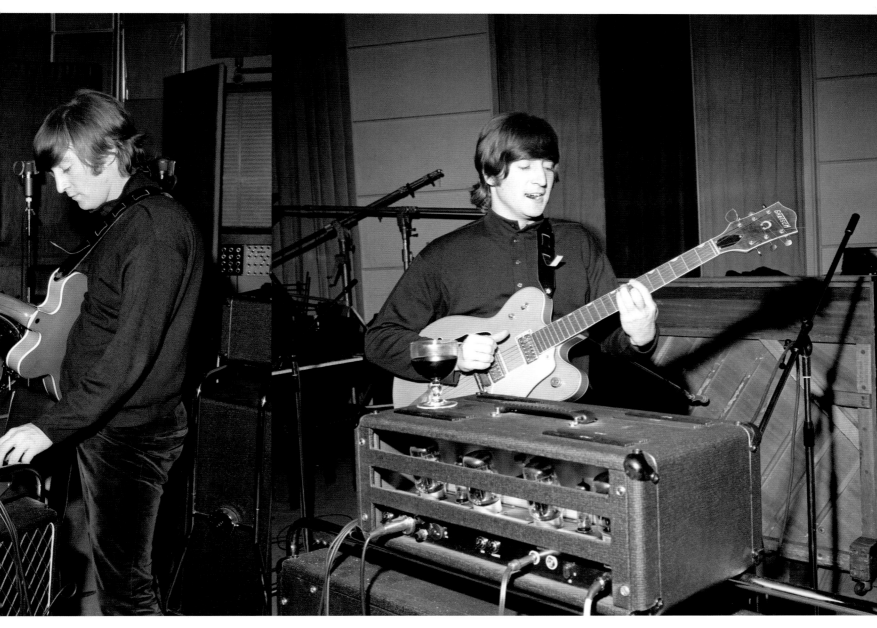

EMI STUDIOS, LONDON
APRIL 14, 1966

Both 'Paperback Writer' and its B-side, 'Rain', were notable for their heavier guitar sound. John's restless imagination was being let loose in the music room at his home, ideas from which he brought in to the sessions, as did Paul and George who also had home studios equipped for experimentation. One of the guitars John used on the 'Paperback Writer' session was an orange Gretsch 6120 Chet Atkins Nashville model which he generously gave to his cousin David Birch the following year. The guitar, which came up for auction in 2014 but failed to reach its reserve price, was subsequently sold privately for $530,000.

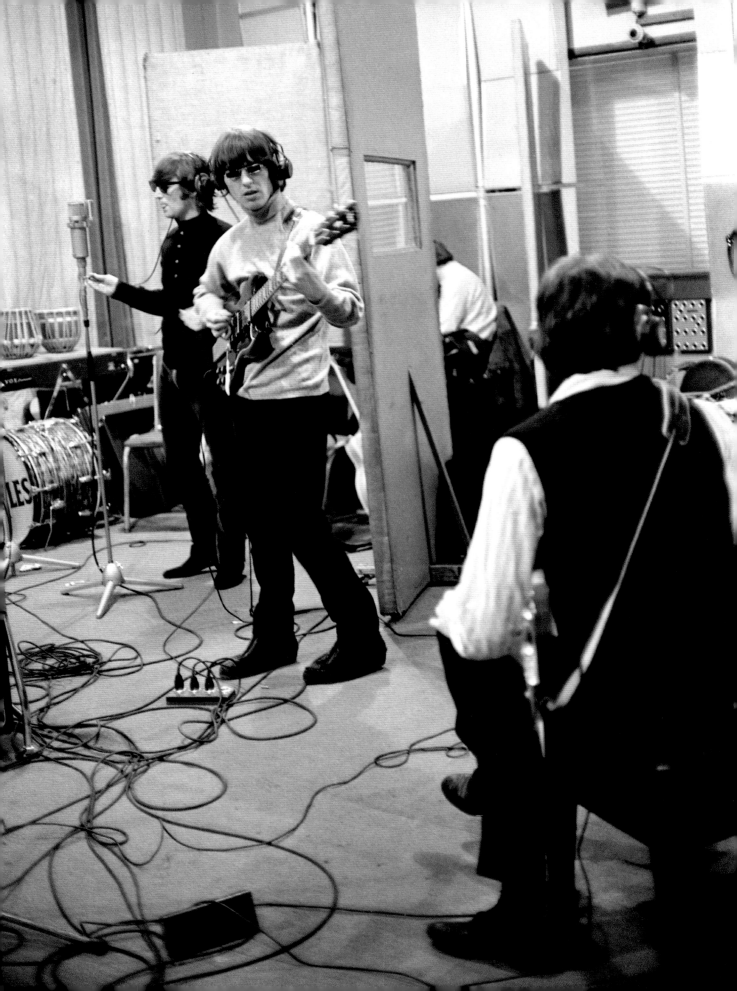

EMI STUDIOS, LONDON
APRIL 14, 1966

The Beatles had originally wanted to record *Revolver* in the United States – at the famous Stax Studio in Memphis, starting on April 11 – where they hoped the sound and groove would rub off but EMI baulked at the idea, mainly due to the cost. Also, the modest set-up in a disused cinema where so many of The Beatles' current favourite records were being created would have proved inadequate, security-wise, to deal with the hordes of Beatle fans descending on McLemore Avenue. Their 'rivals' The Rolling Stones had recorded most of their output in America over the past two years, and *Aftermath*, the Stones' fourth British album, was recorded entirely at RCA Studios in Los Angeles. Released this week, it was their first album to feature exclusively Jagger-Richards compositions and, keen to see what their closest competitors but good friends were up to, the Fabs sent an aide out to purchase copies from the HMV Shop on Oxford Street. He also came back with Peter Cook and Dudley Moore's hilarious soul parody 'Bo Dudley'.

Overleaf: Cool threads, exotic gear, mind-boggling sounds – The Beatles at work in EMI Studio 3.

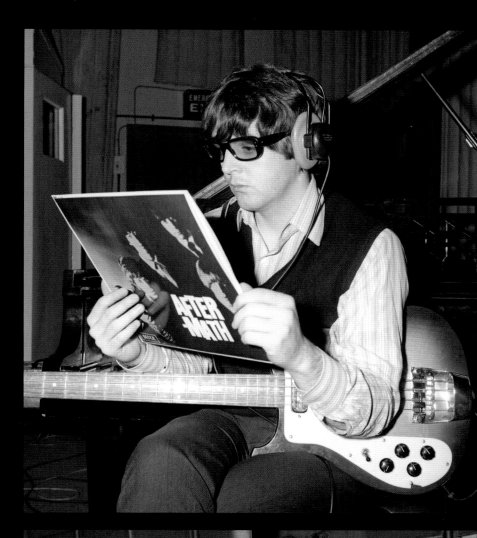

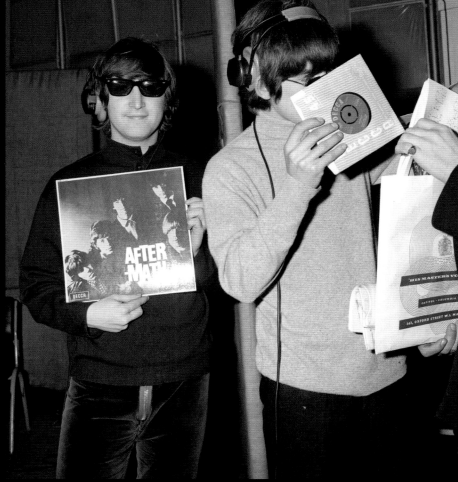

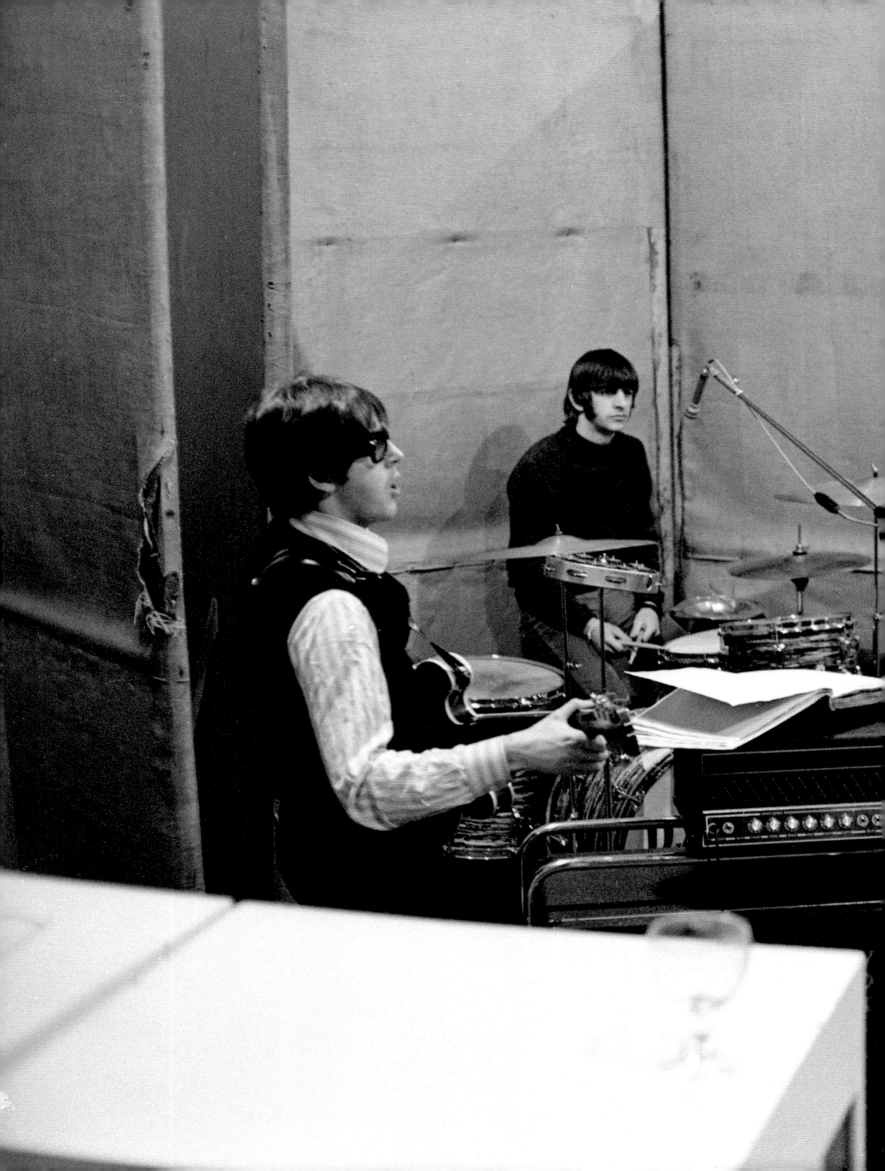

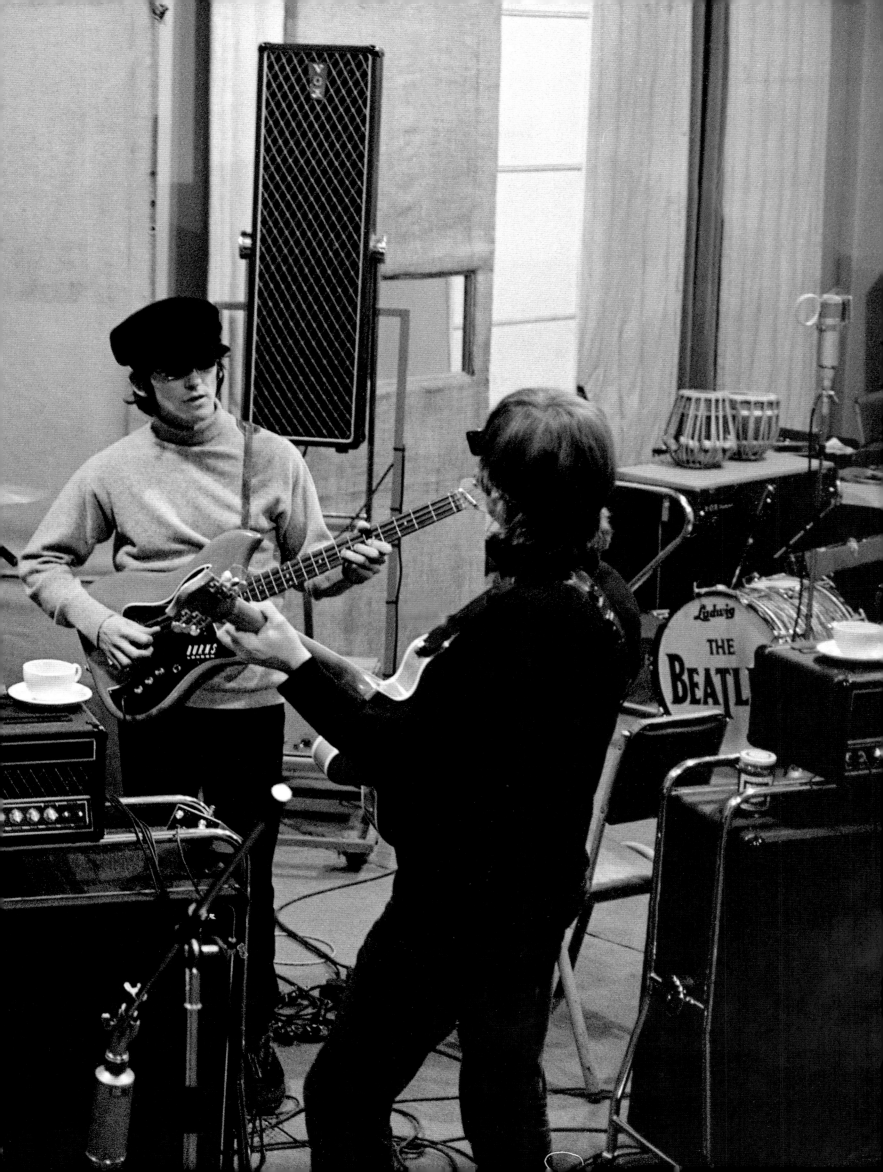

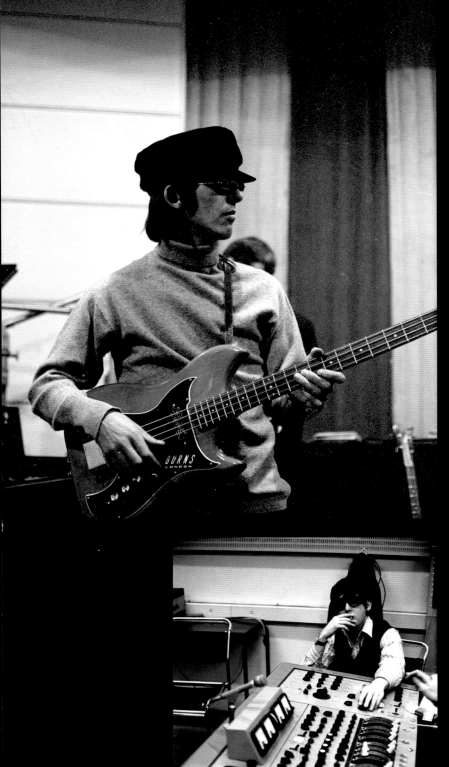

EMI STUDIOS, LONDON
APRIL 14, 1966

As The Beatles worked on 'Paperback Writer', all manner of fashions and instruments were on display including George's black corduroy hat, oblong metal specs and Burns bass (which appears not to have been used on the finished recording). *Beatles Monthly #35* reported: "Paul was perched on a stool thumbing away at a red and white Rickenbacker guitar (moving with the music as he does on stage) whilst the lyrics boomed through the studio speakers – so we were very honoured at being the first to hear their new single besides George Martin, and of course, The Beatles." Released on June 10, 'Paperback Writer' was the first Beatles single since 'She Loves You' not to enter the British *NME* chart at number one. It was kept off by Frank Sinatra's 'Strangers In The Night' – a statistic pounced upon by the "Are The Beatles slipping?" brigade – but true to form it reached the top spot the following week.

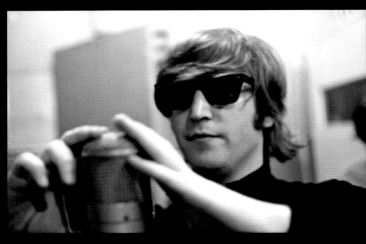

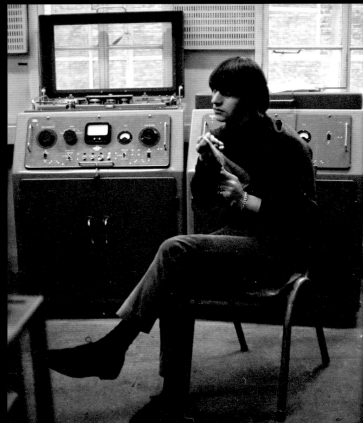

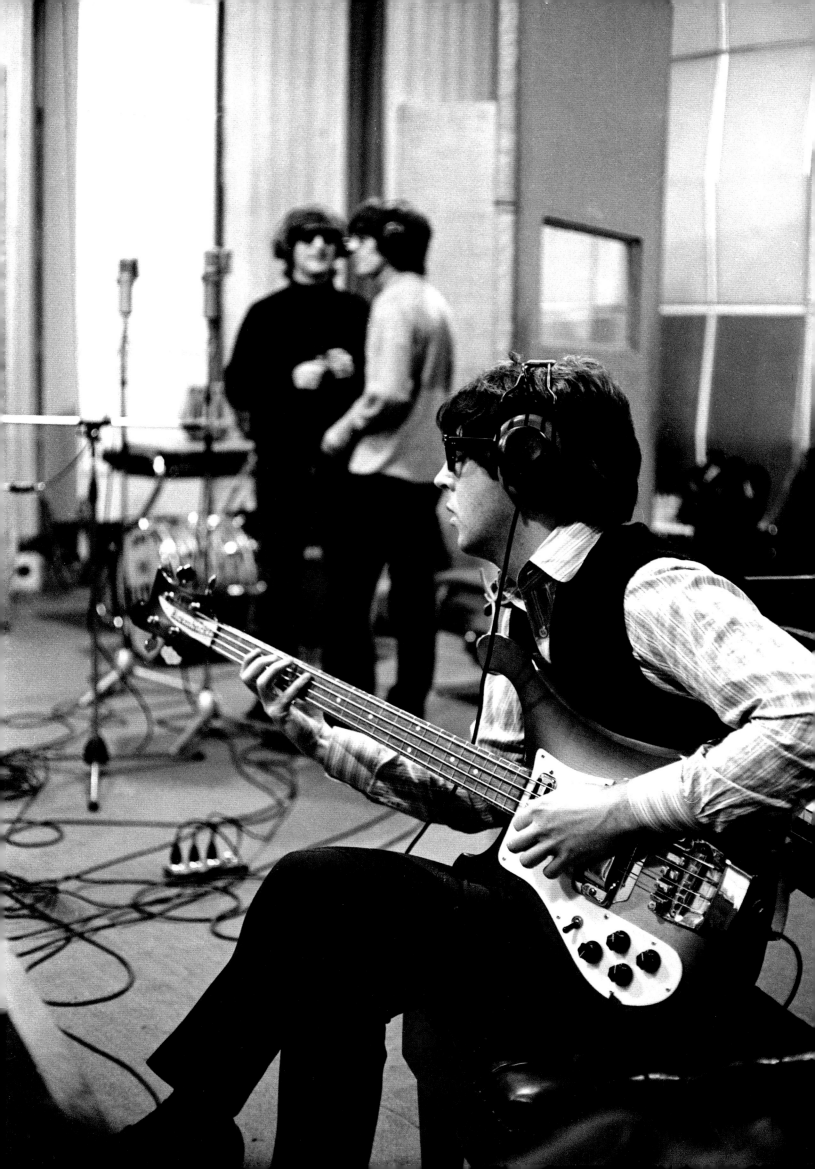

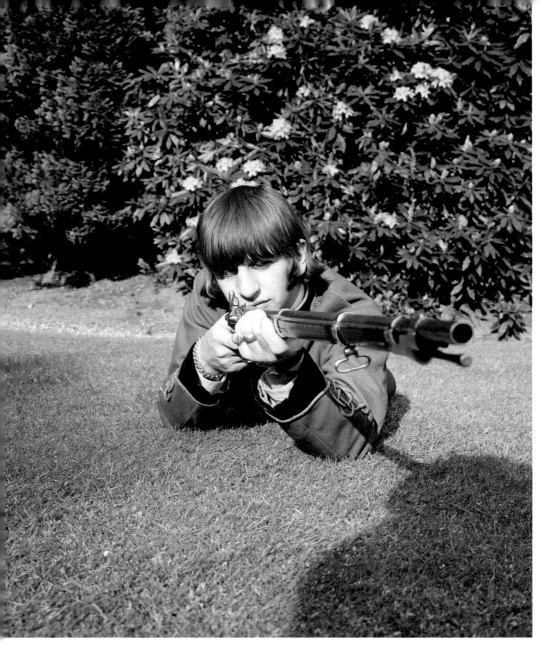
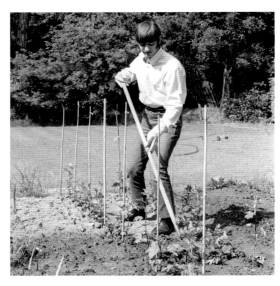
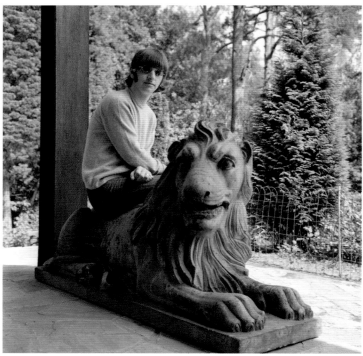
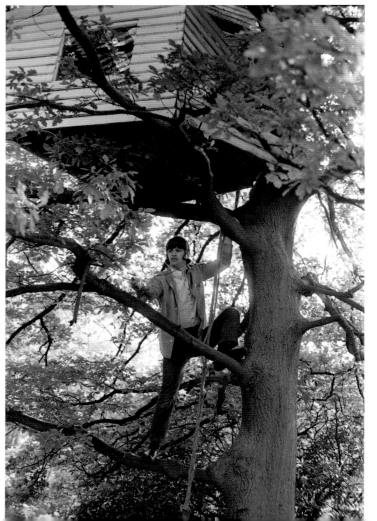

SUNNY HEIGHTS,
WEYBRIDGE, SURREY
MAY 31, 1966

The second 'Beatle at home' subject was Ringo. Bought back in July 1965, his mock-Tudor house Sunny Heights was completely modernised by the firm he co-owned, Brickey Building Company Ltd. Posing in the extensive grounds, Ringo got a chance to dress up in some of the military regalia he collected as well as to pose with one of his antique rifles, climb into a treehouse (with the steadying aid of Sean O'Mahony) and ride a fold-up bike. The session continued inside with Ringo playing mine host behind the bar of his own pub, The Flying Cow. At one point, John dropped by to visit – Ringo, John and George frequently visited one another as their homes were all within easy driving distance of each other. The following day, Ringo was back at Abbey Road with his comrades, adding the hearty backing chorus and zany sound effects to 'Yellow Submarine' courtesy of the contents of Studio 2's storage cupboard.

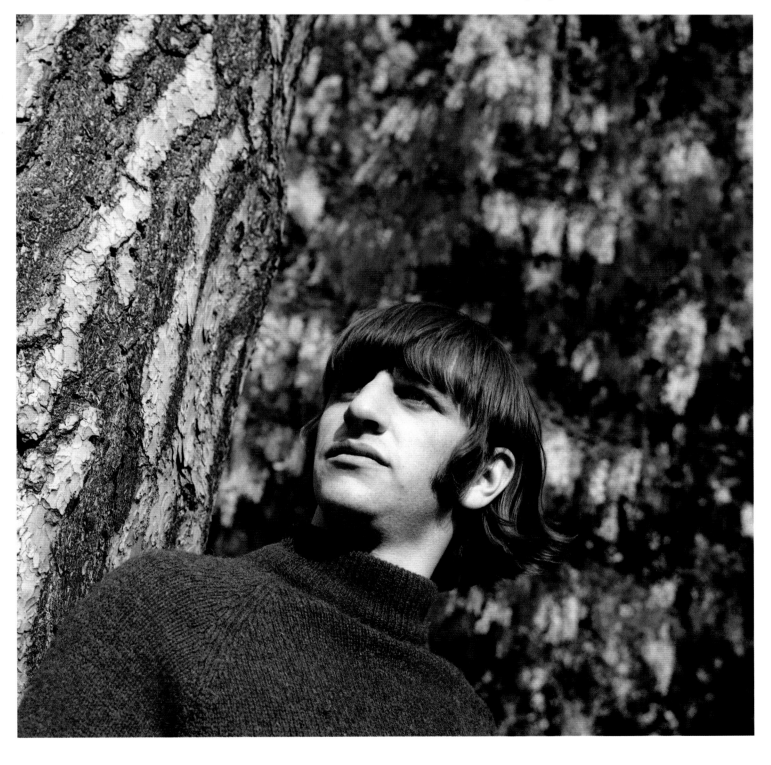

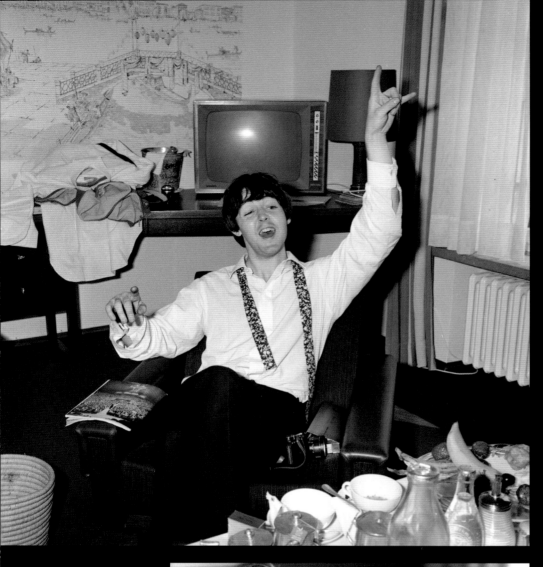

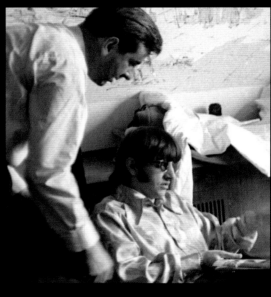

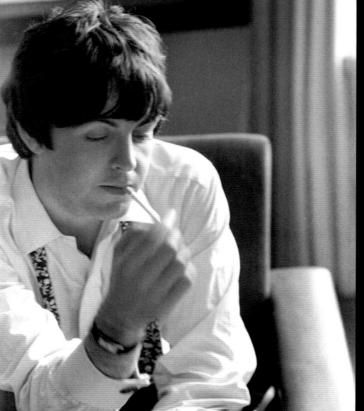

BAYERISCHER HOF HOTEL, MUNICH, GERMANY
JUNE 23, 1966

Six months had passed since The Beatles last toured, and apart from a short set at the *New Musical Express* Poll Winners Concert in London on May 1, they had spent the past 11 weeks ensconced in the studio recording *Revolver*. Brian Epstein had booked a summer tour of Germany and the Far East to start at the end of June so recording had to be completed by then. Arriving in Munich, Sean and Leslie visited The Beatles in their hotel room; here Sean shows Ringo some recent *Beatles Book* pictures. While there, the pair got treated to an advance preview of The Beatles' new album. After listening to the finished running order on George's tape recorder, Paul later remembered expressing concern that some of the tracks sounded out-of-tune. It was McCartney who came up with the name *Revolver* while on tour after other titles such as *Abracadabra* and *Beatles On Safari* were rejected. The title was cabled to EMI in London in time for the album's release on August 5.

CIRCUS-KRONE-BAU, MUNICH, GERMANY
JUNE 24, 1966

As Mal lines up the instruments – including Paul's Rickenbacker bass which he decided not to use onstage – John, Paul and George get ready for their opening concerts. The Beatles' new dark green stage outfits and colourful offstage wear were made by trendy King's Road boutique Hung On You. Support acts on the German tour – sponsored by the country's entertainment magazine *Bravo* hence the prevalent stage signs – were Cliff Bennett & The Rebel Rousers (who, during the tour, arranged to cover 'Got To Get You Into My Life' which Paul later produced), German group The Rattles, and Peter & Gordon, whose recent minor hit 'Woman' was written for them by Paul under the pseudonym Bernard Webb, a ploy to see if people bought Lennon-McCartney songs purely on the strength of the name alone.

Overleaf: Audience bird's-eye view of The Beatles performing in Munich.

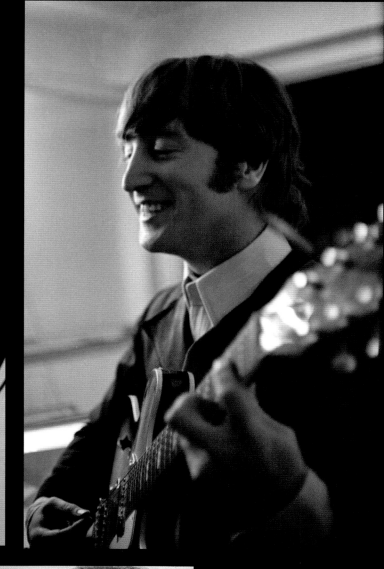

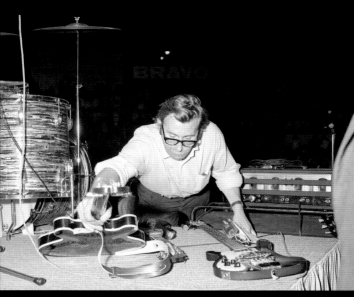

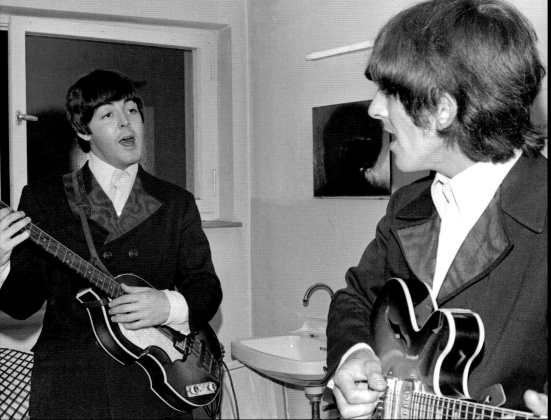

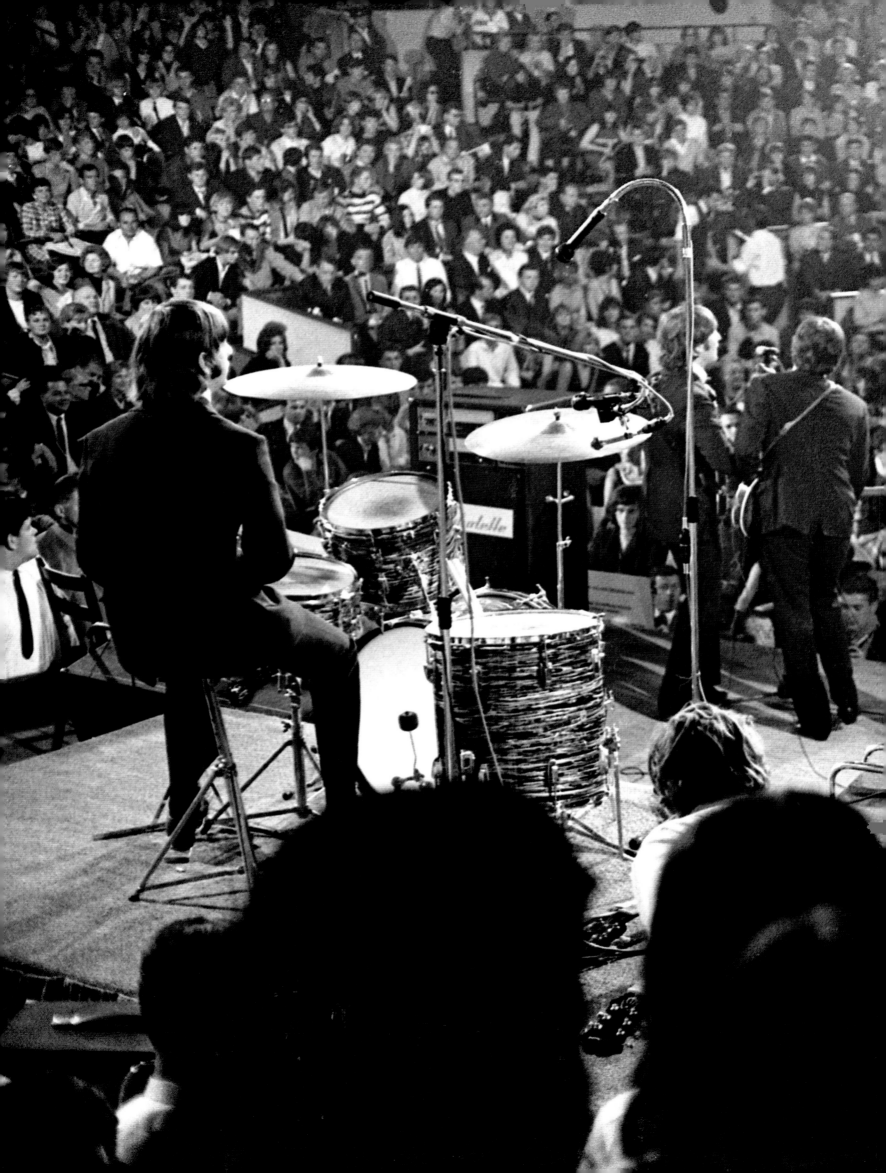

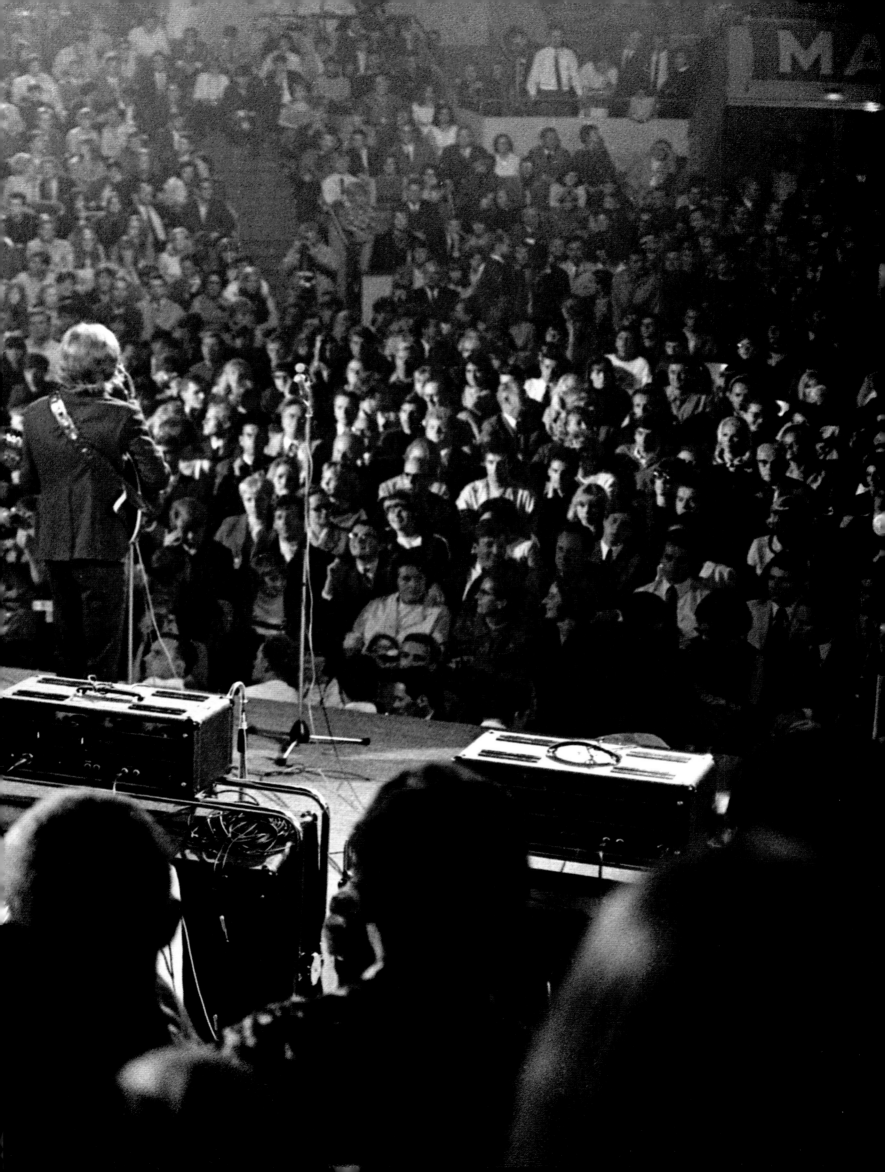

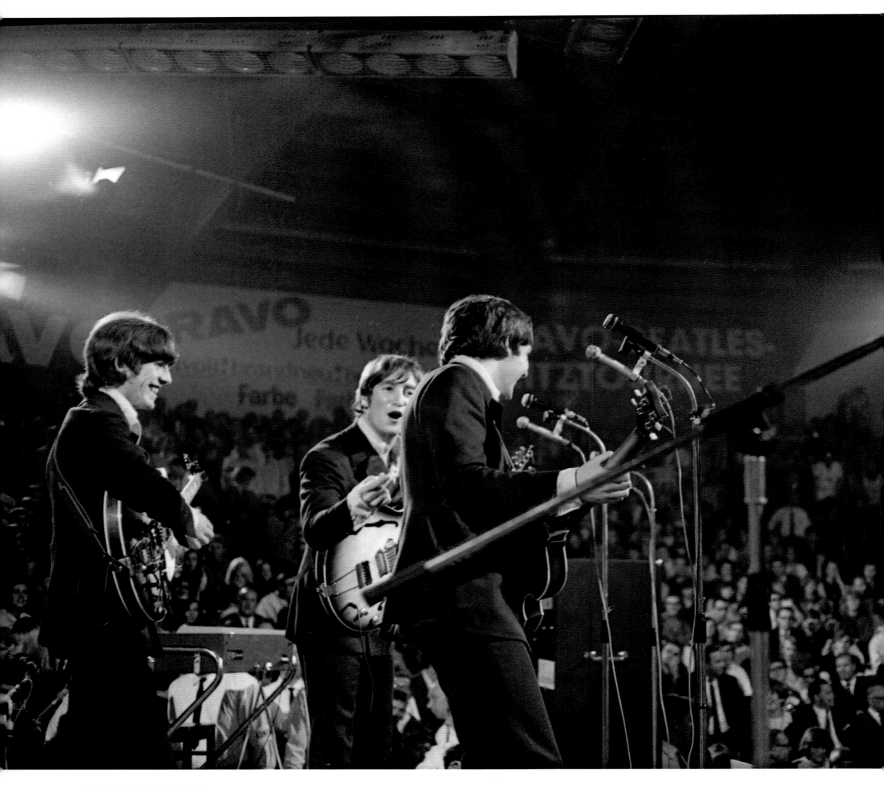

CIRCUS-KRONE-BAU,
MUNICH, GERMANY
JUNE 24, 1966

With only the briefest of rehearsals in their hotel suite,
it was painfully obvious to those who cared to listen that
The Beatles were out-of-shape as a live band, evidenced by
lacklustre playing, forgotten lyrics and often out-of-tune
performances. Ringo struggles manfully through 'I Wanna
Be Your Man' – he later claimed that due to excess crowd
noise and a lack of fold-backs, he often had to guess the
progress of a song – while much to George's amusement,
John reminds a forgetful Paul of the opening lyric to 'I'm
Down' at the finale of the evening Munich show. The fact
that audiences responded in their usual Pavlovian fashion
(page 164) was instrumental in bringing The Beatles'
performing career to its conclusion.

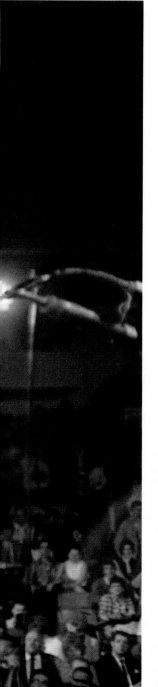

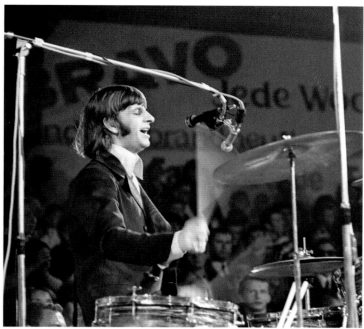

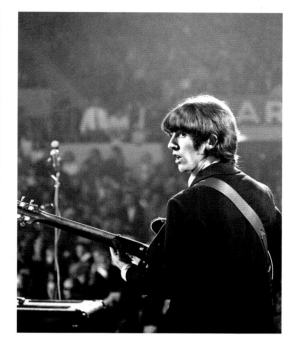

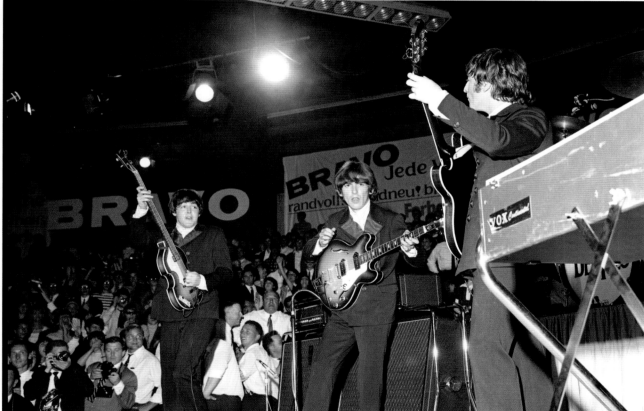

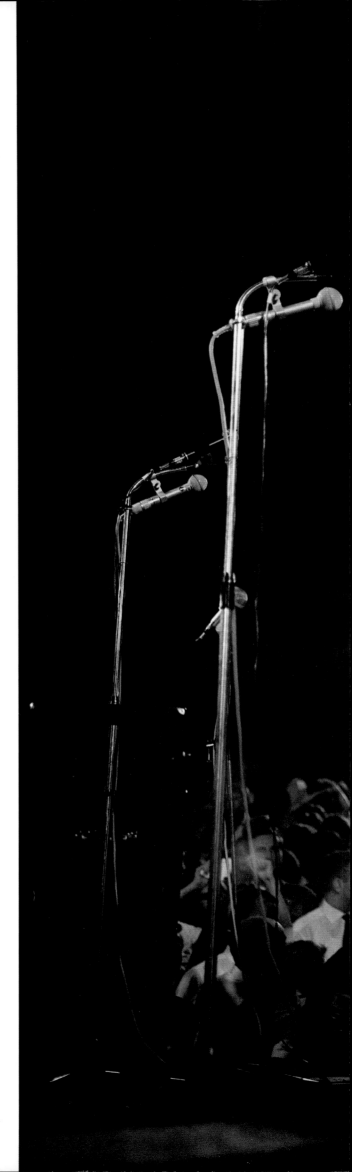

CIRCUS-KRONE-BAU, MUNICH, GERMANY JUNE 24, 1966

The set-list for The Beatles' final world tour was 'Rock 'n' Roll Music', 'She's A Woman', 'If I Needed Someone', 'Day Tripper', 'Baby's In Black', 'I Feel Fine', 'Yesterday', 'I Wanna Be Your Man', 'Nowhere Man', 'Paperback Writer' and 'I'm Down'. Asked (in *Beatles Book #40*) if he considered The Beatles' older hits were a step back in time Paul replied, "Yes. They're a step back in time, and as for performing them on stage, I don't think our audience would like it, but that, of course, depends on where we're playing – Germany, for example, cried out for the old hits because that is what they remembered us for." In *Beatles Book #38*, John was even more candid in his attitude to The Beatles' back catalogue: "I can't play any of *Rubber Soul*, it's been so unrehearsed – the only time I played any of the numbers on it was when we recorded it! I forget about songs, they're only valid for a certain time."

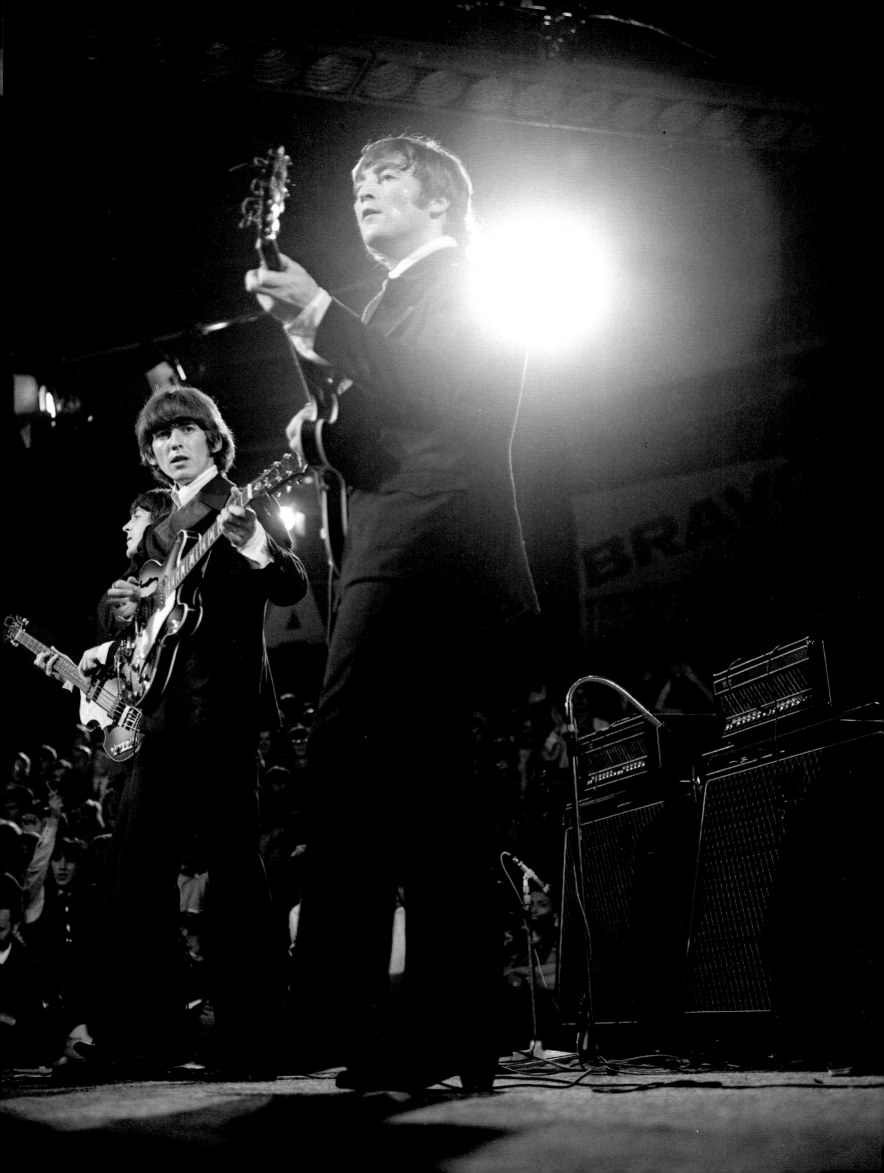

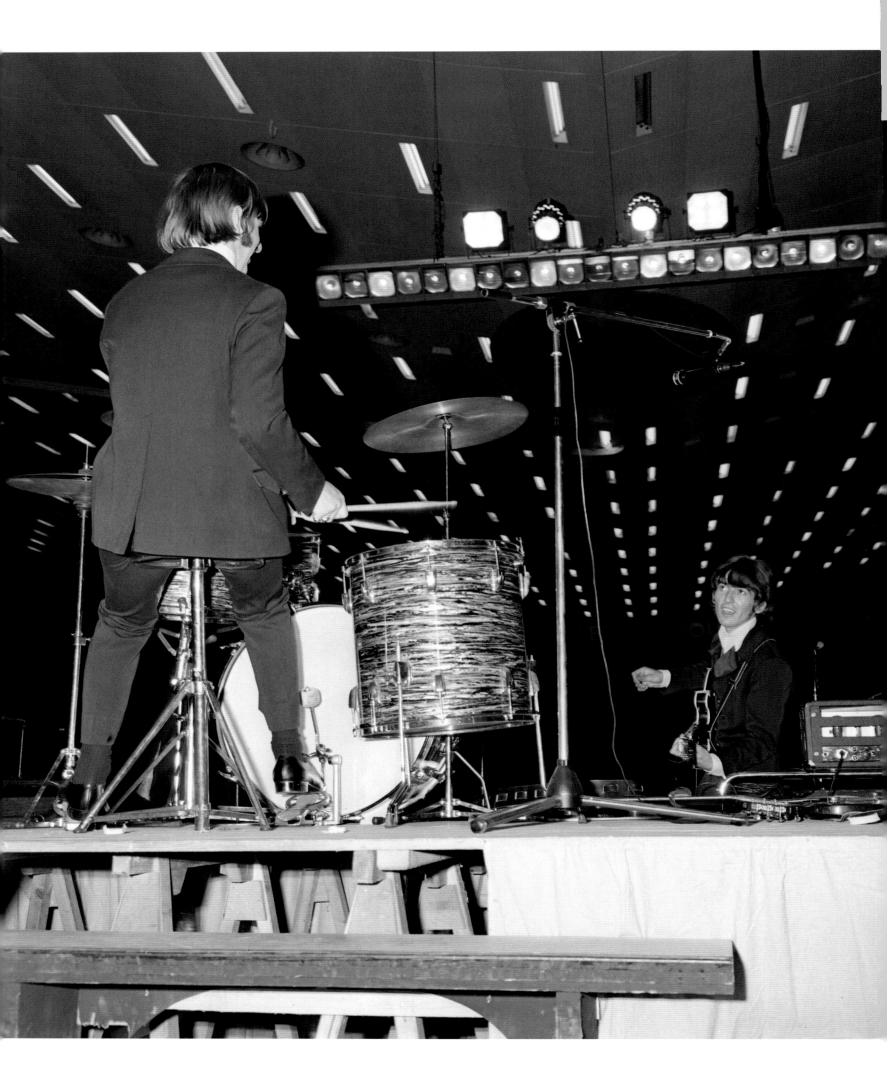

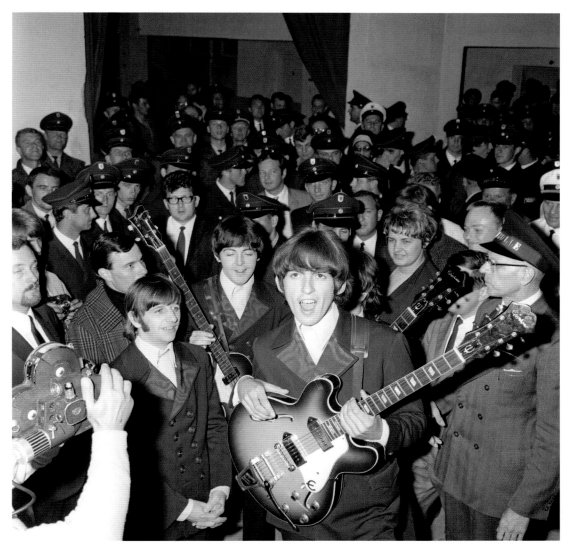

GRUGAHALLE, ESSEN, GERMANY
JUNE 25, 1966

For the journeys between Munich and Essen and from Essen to Hamburg, The Beatles travelled on the luxurious royal train previously used by Queen Elizabeth II and Prince Philip during their 1965 royal visit; the private carriage boasting a large dining room, a lounge, four bedrooms and bathrooms. While run with typical German efficiency, The Beatles were dismayed at the heavy police presence employed to keep fans at bay and the brutal treatment that was often meted out. This was minor compared to the security in Japan, the tour's next port of call, where 3,000 police guarded audiences totalling 9,000 at each show.

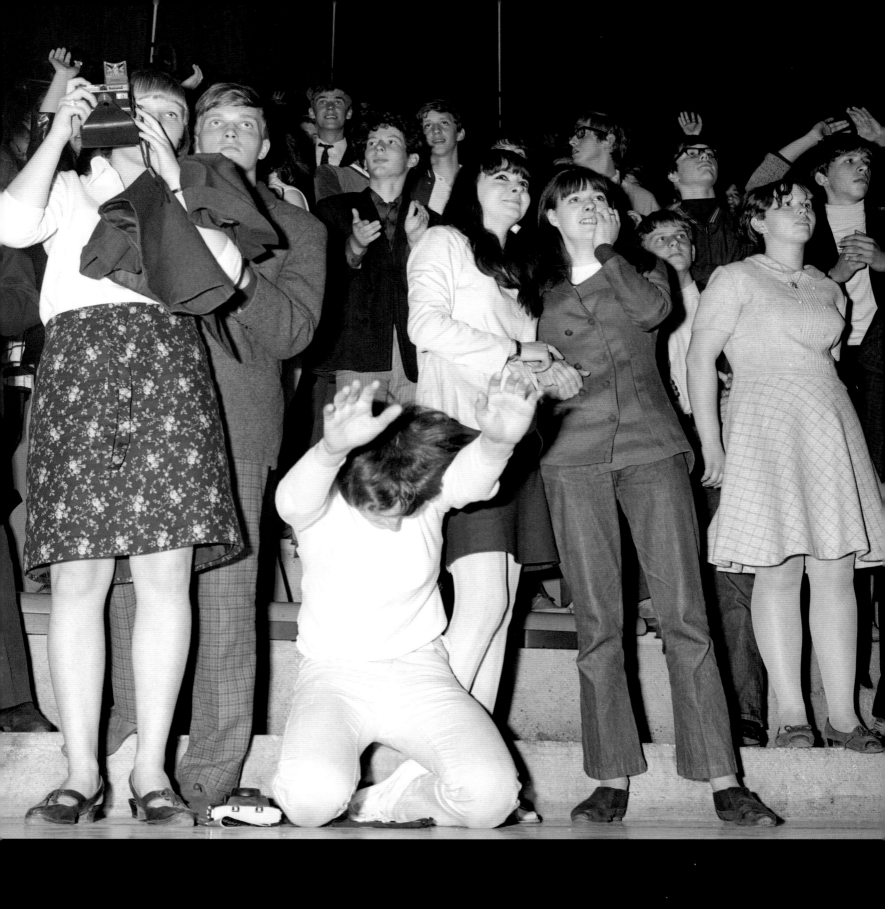

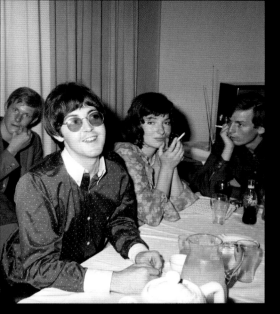

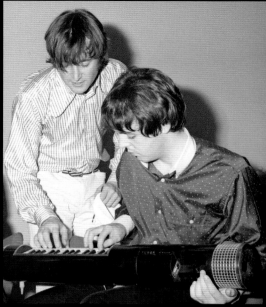

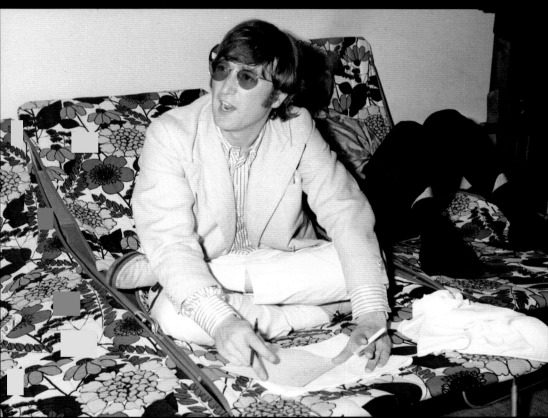

ERNST-MERCK-HALLE, HAMBURG, GERMANY
JUNE 26, 1966

Backstage between shows in Hamburg, The Beatles caught up with old friends including Astrid Kirchherr and bandleader Bert Kaempfert, the producer of their early recordings backing Tony Sheridan. Kaempfert coincidentally composed Frank Sinatra's 'Strangers In The Night' that had recently impeded their UK chart progress. John and Paul broke into a rousing rendition when he entered the dressing room. Behind Paul is journalist Jochen von Bredow, and seated next to him is Kathia Berger, a friend/fan from the Hamburg days, and tour photographer Robert Whitaker. Frank Dostal, singer with German band The Faces, brought with him a gift of a Tubon keyboard – a cylindrical instrument with a small keyboard that produced different tones not unlike an electric organ.

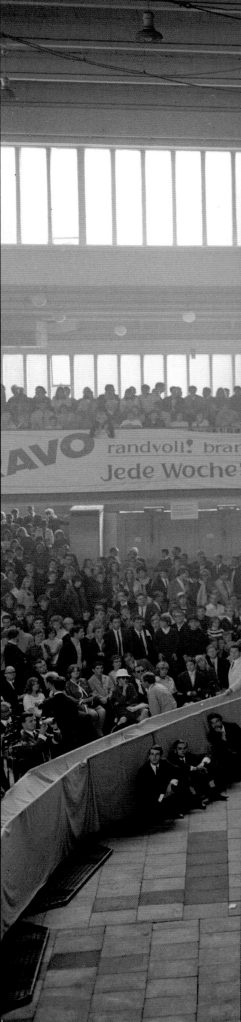

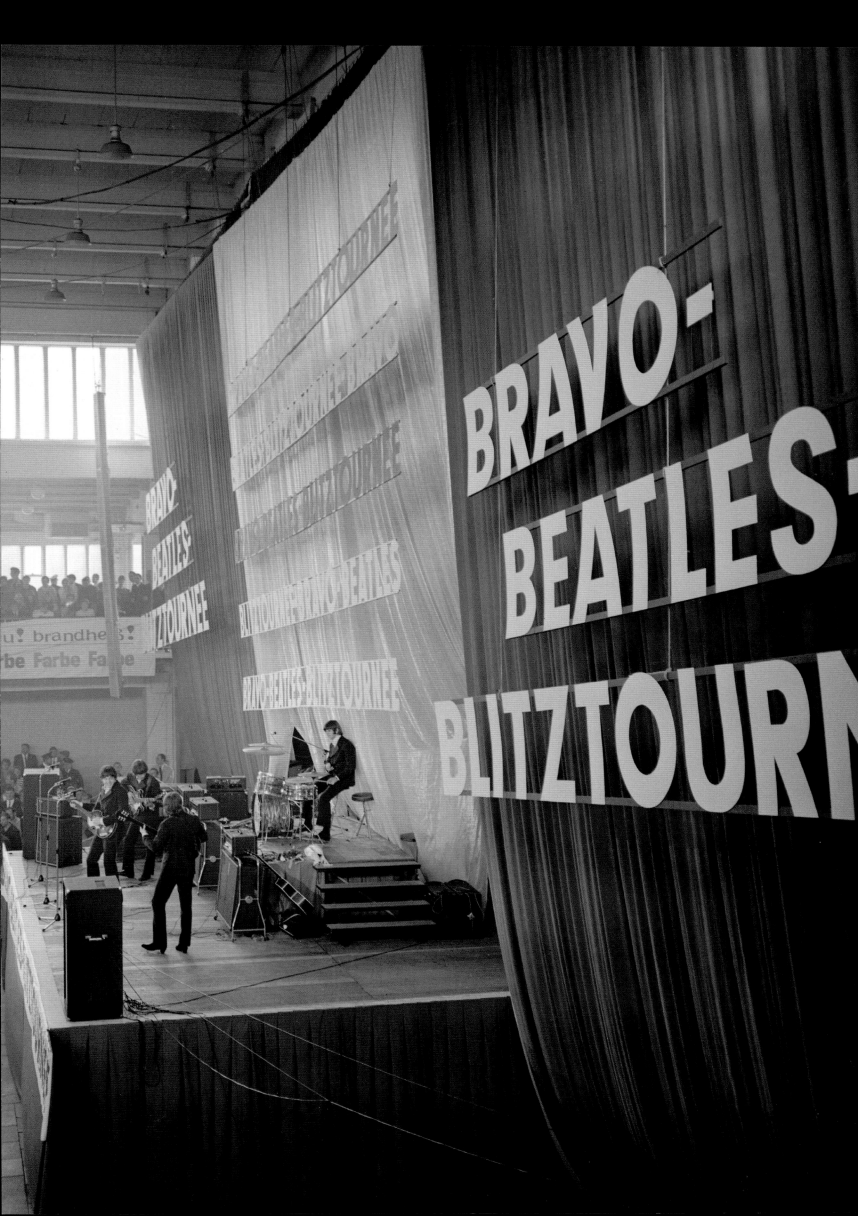

EMI STUDIOS, LONDON
FEBRUARY 22, 1967

With the final Beatles concert to a paying audience taking place at San Francisco's Candlestick Park on August 29, 1966, the decision was made privately to end touring for good. Having projected a fixed group personality to the public for the past three years, they were now eager to step outside the circle and explore new avenues as individuals while still remaining Beatles.

In September John went off to Germany and Spain to film his role as Private Gripweed in Richard Lester's *How I Won The War*; Ringo visited him on the set in Almeria but otherwise pottered around; George went to Bombay studying sitar under Ravi Shankar as well as absorbing Indian philosophy and culture; and Paul was busiest of all, decorating the Georgian town house he'd bought in St John's Wood, writing the score for the Boulting Brothers film, *The Family Way*, and embarking on a Kenyan safari accompanied by Mal Evans. Asked in India if he would be a Beatle forever, George responded, "I do not even think about next week."

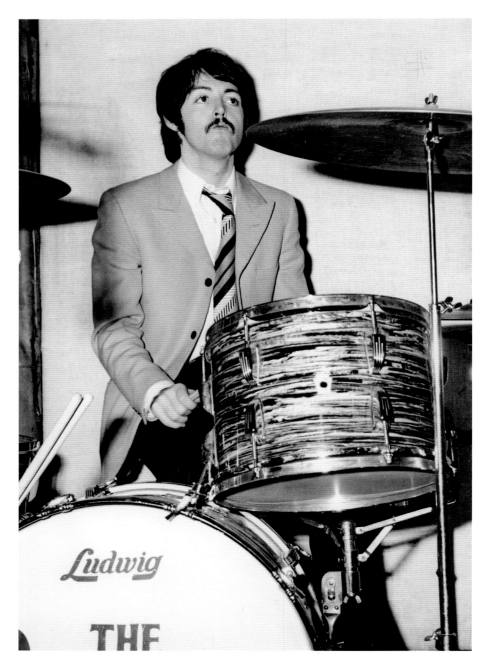

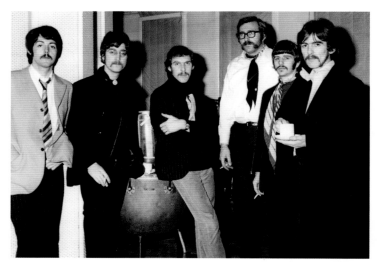

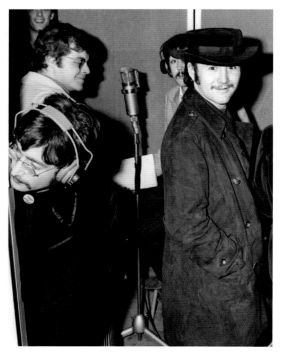

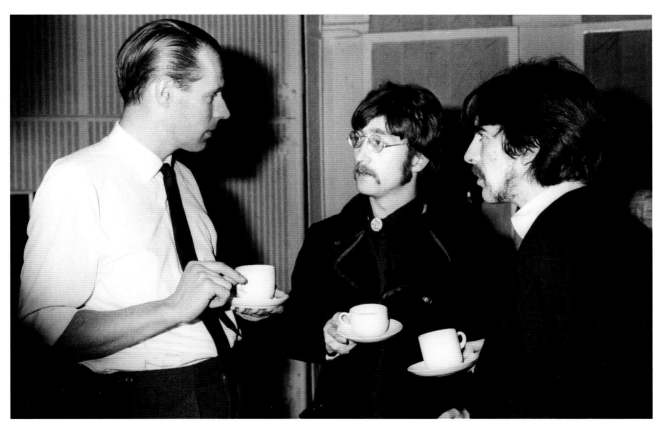

EMI STUDIOS, LONDON
FEBRUARY 22, 1967

With rumour and conjecture in the British press surrounding their future, The Beatles went back into Abbey Road on November 24, 1966, their imaginations full to brimming with the experiences of recent months, not least the influence of mind-expanding substances. George Martin was now even more integral to the process of translating the sounds in their heads for what became the landmark album *Sgt. Pepper's Lonely Hearts Club Band*. Neil and Mal too, seen here emulating their bosses' new moustachioed look, provided invaluable suggestions. These pictures show them working on John and Paul's combined epic, 'A Day In The Life'. During a brief promotional European tour with The Byrds, the Fabs' friend David Crosby popped by to check out his peers' progress. Crosby recalled, "I walked in, and they were acting silly and strange and having fun, because I think they were thrilled with what they had done. They knew what they had created. They sat me down in the middle of a room on a stool, and they rolled over two of those huge, coffin-sized speakers up on either side of me, and then they played me 'A Day In The Life'. And when they got to the end of the piano chord – man, I was a dish-rag. I was floored. It took me several minutes to be able to talk after that."

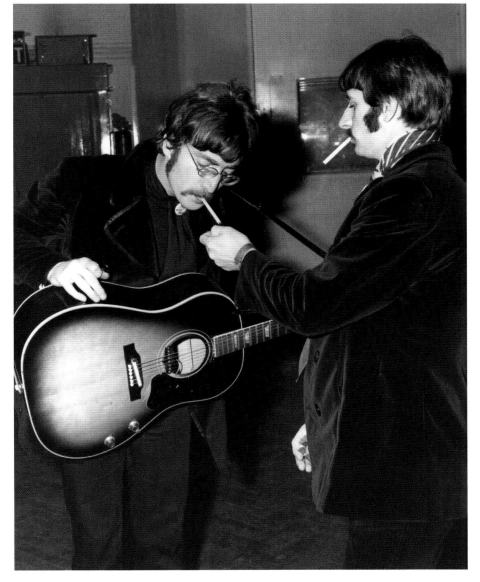

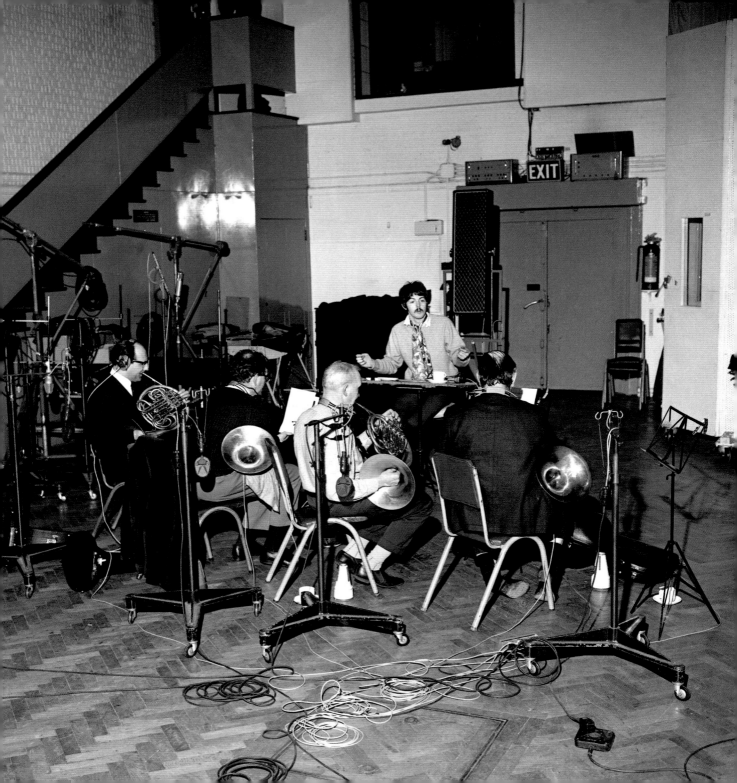

to London's underground and avant-garde scenes. In the control room George Martin lends a sympathetic ear to another of Paul's ideas while seated at the console, a sign of how The Beatles now took a far more active role in the sound mixing process. Tape operator Richard Lush (sitting behind) awaits instructions.

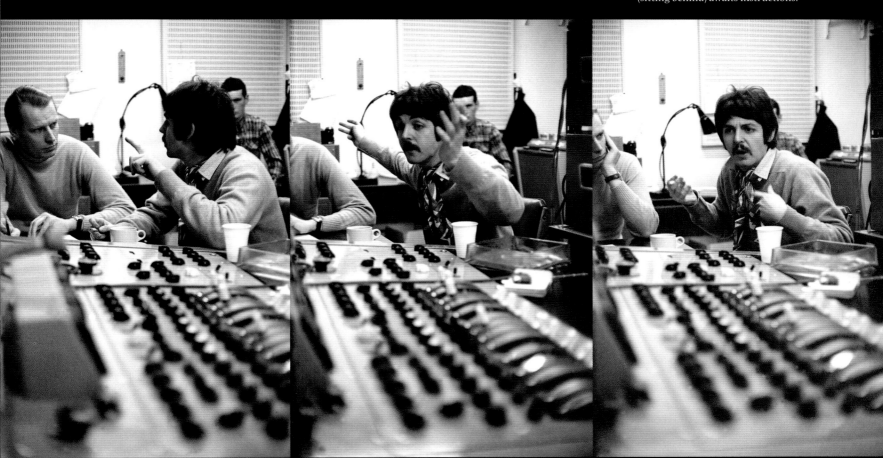

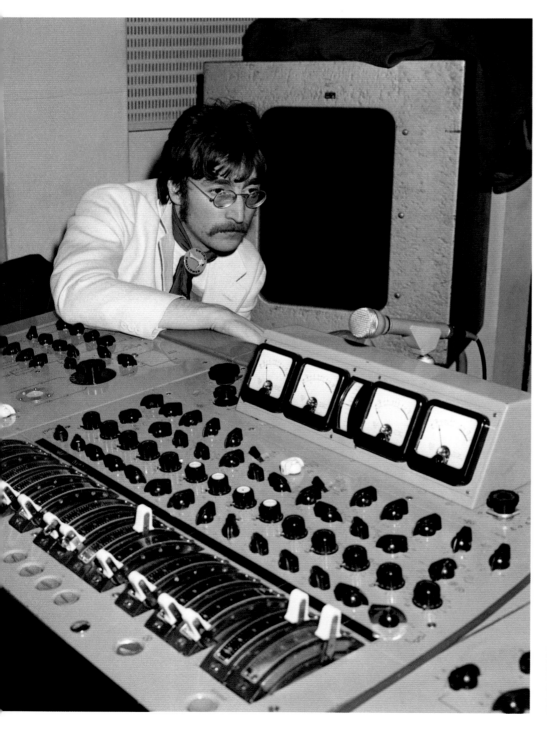

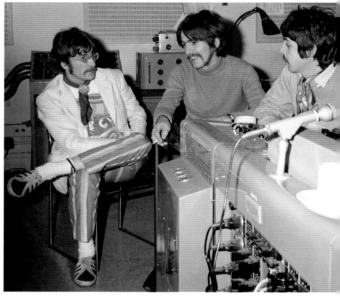

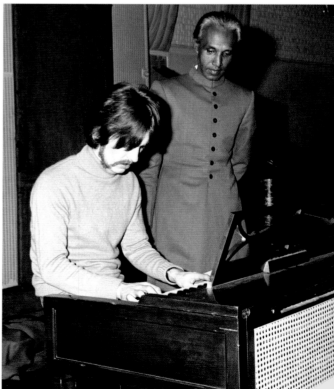

EMI STUDIOS, LONDON
MARCH 3, 1967

In 1963, the first Beatles album was completed in a day. Four years on, sessions now ran through the night into the early hours. A song might start with only a basic melody so copious studio time was spent on building up the arrangements and rehearsing and recording a basic track, slowing or speeding up the tape or playing it backwards, adding parts as they went along. Session musicians were brought in to augment the track where necessary. John listens intently to a playback and watches with Paul while George makes a point. In retrospect, *Sgt. Pepper* could be seen as the last unified Beatles project where all four were working towards and co-operating on a common purpose. George's main contribution was the philosophical 'Within You, Without You' and he is seen going through the arrangement on a harmonium watched by visiting Indian musician, Amiya Dasgupta, erroneously identified in *The Beatles Book* as Ravi Shankar's brother. Other visitors to the session included Sean O'Mahony (talking to Mal) and Dick James (seen behind George Martin).

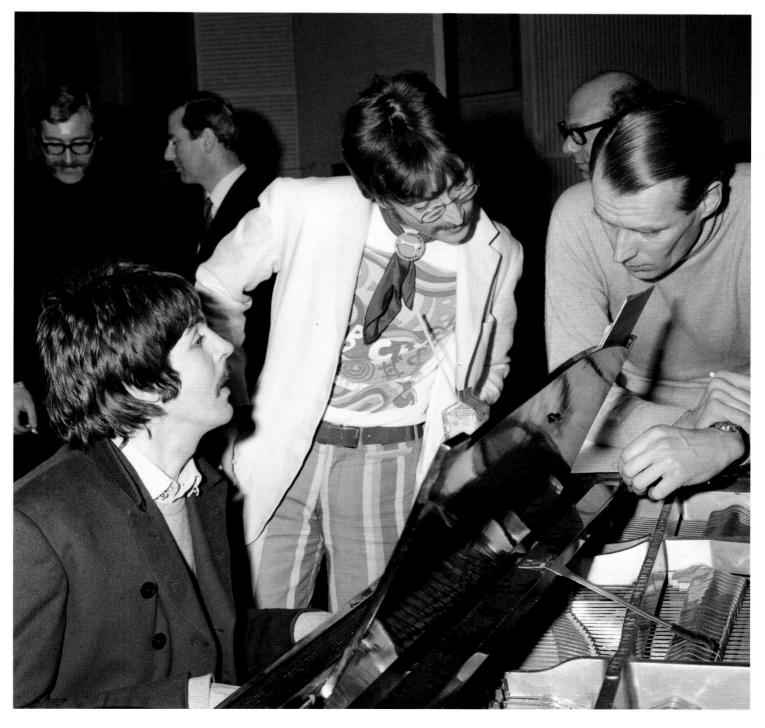

The recording of 'Being For The Benefit Of Mr Kite' was a veritable kitchen sink of a production – all in a successful attempt to convey the sound of a circus ring as John wished. Tapes were cut up, randomly reassembled and played backwards within the mix to recreate an old steam organ, and to virtually complete the recording on this day, John and George blew bass harmonicas. Next on the agenda was knocking Ringo's song for the album into shape. John and Paul had started writing 'With A Little Help From My Friends', under the working title 'Bad Finger Boogie', in Paul's music room on the top floor of his house just a short distance away in St John's Wood, where they would often meet before continuing on to the evening's session. A mirthful John and Ringo listen as Paul works out an idea on his Epiphone while a dinner tray balances precariously on an amp. Moving over to the piano, Paul goes over the lyrics for Ringo.

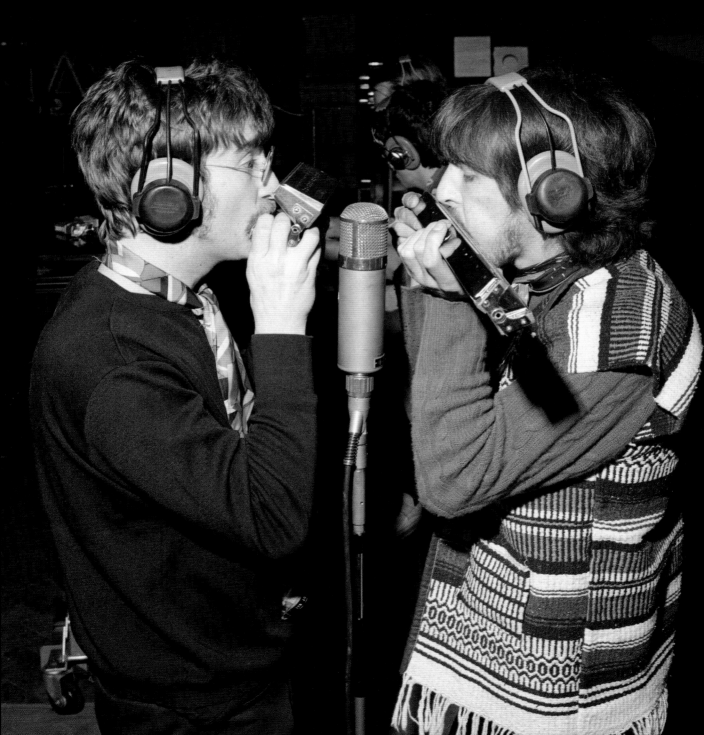

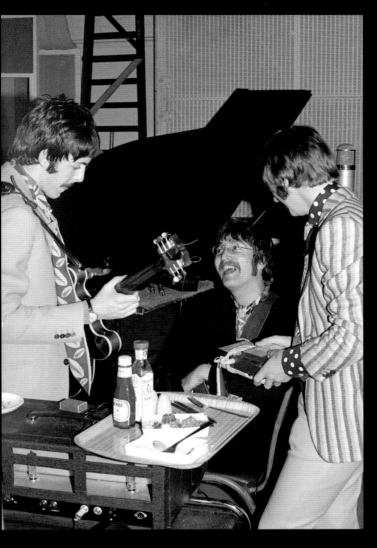
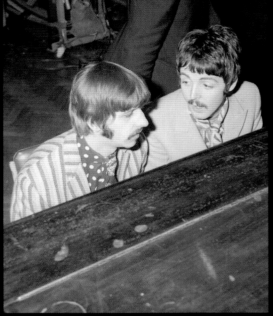
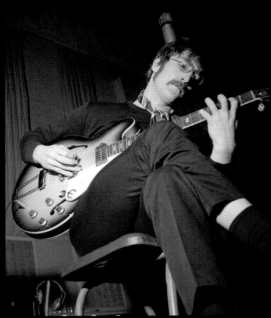
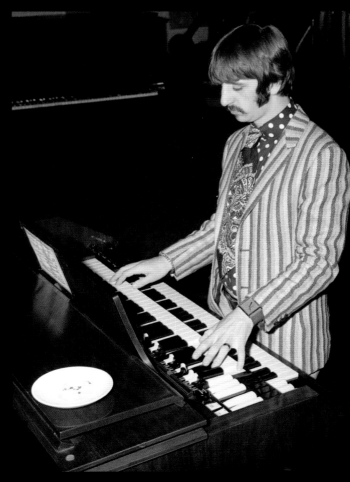

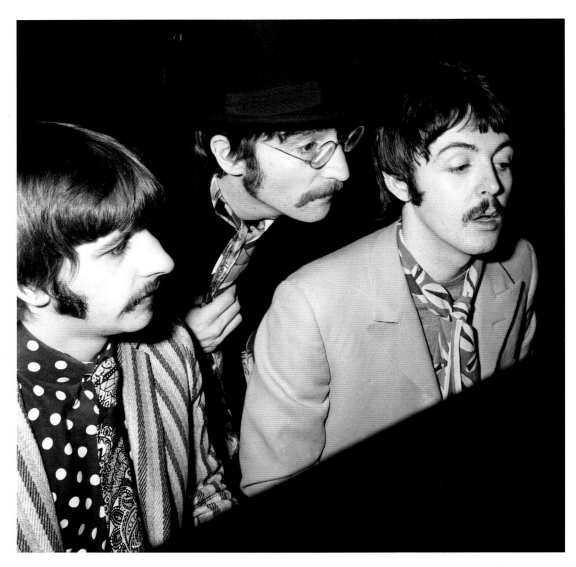

EMI STUDIOS, LONDON
MARCH 29, 1967

A homburg-hatted John joins in on working out the
arrangement of 'With A Little Help From My Friends'
for Ringo's benefit. Lennon was presumably in a
more coherent state than the previous week when
he accidentally ingested some LSD during a session.
George Martin, blissfully unaware of the drug's powerful
hallucinatory effects, had lead John up to the roof to get
some air after he'd complained of feeling ill. On learning
of this Paul and George both dashed upstairs to rescue
him. Paul clutches an acetate of one of the *Pepper* tracks
while George pulls up a chair to work with John on the
guitar parts.

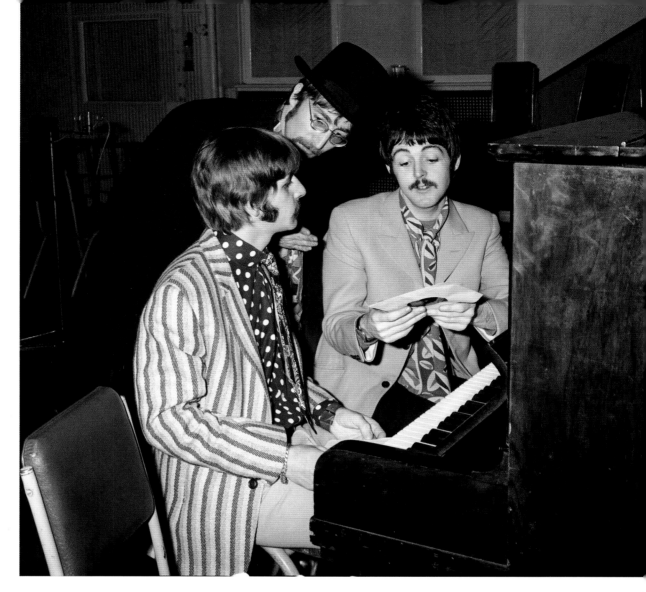

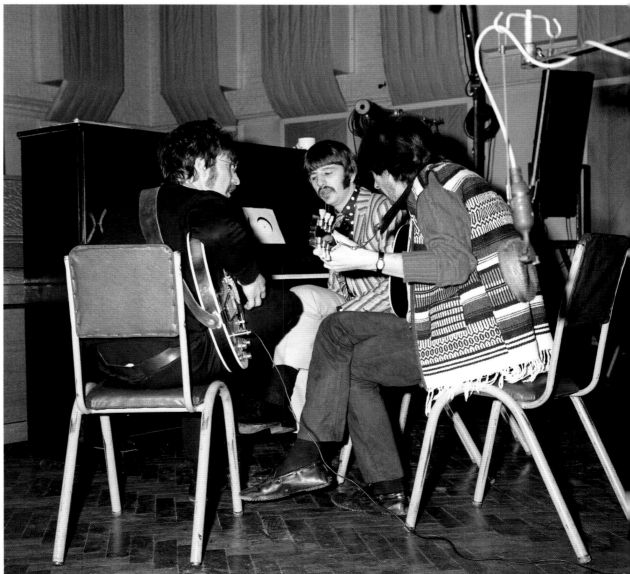

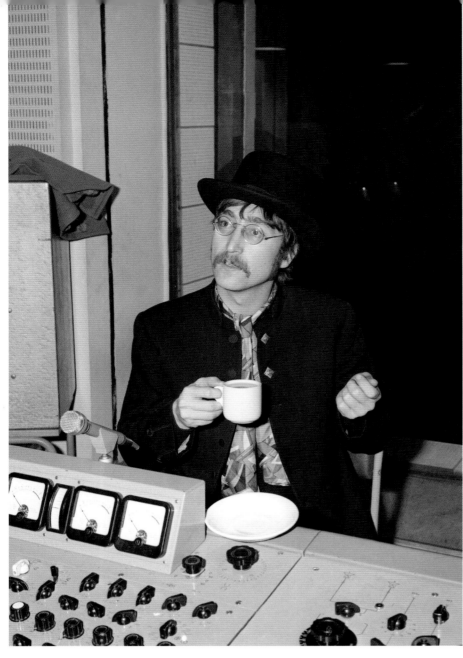

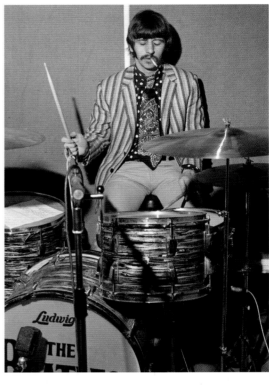

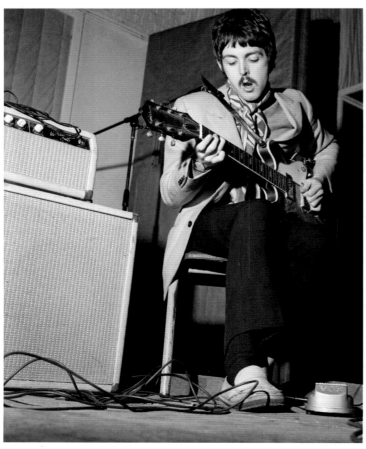

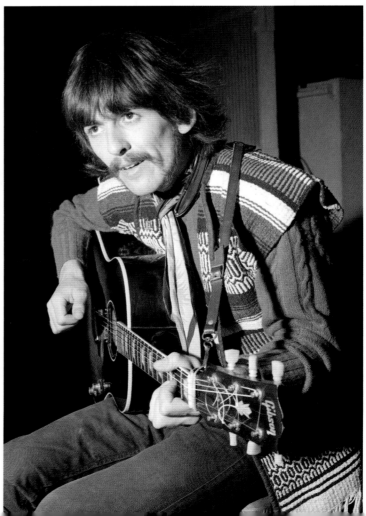

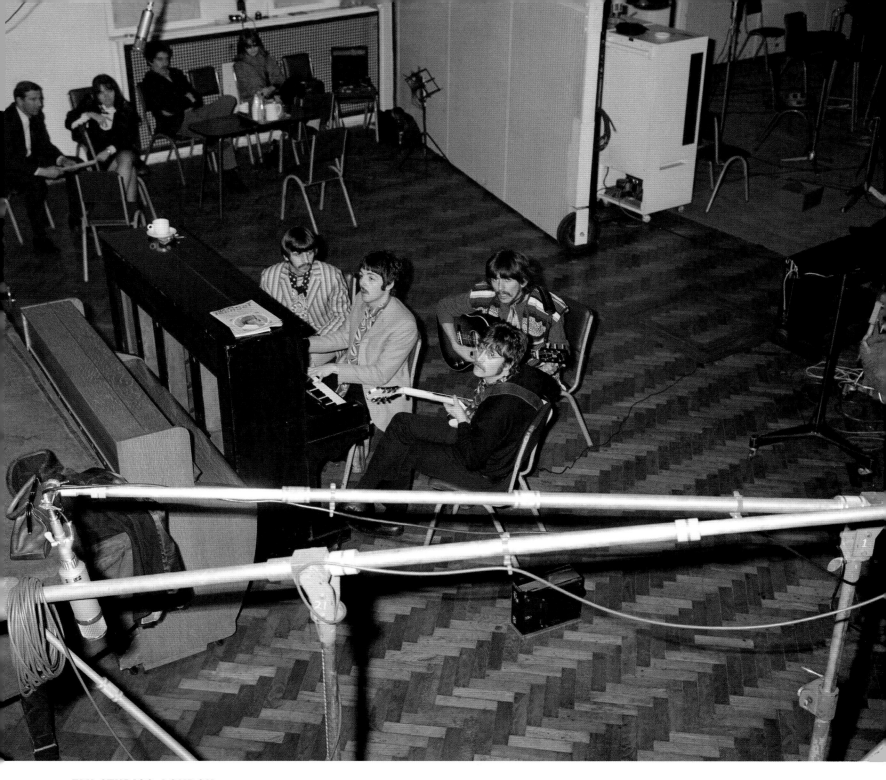

EMI STUDIOS, LONDON
MARCH 29, 1967

John and George meet the gaze of Leslie Bryce's camera, taken from the vantage point of the stairs leading to the control room. Studio visitors sitting in the background are (l-r) Sean O'Mahony, Judy Sims (the editor of US magazine *Teen Set*), Beatles assistant and car dealer Terry Doran (the line "meeting a man from the motor trade" in 'She's Leaving Home' being a nod in his direction), and Cynthia Lennon. During a break in the session, Sean grabbed a chat with Paul who attempted to clear the Beatles break-up rumours that continued to persist. On April 3 Paul flew off to America (accompanied by Mal Evans) for a holiday and to visit Jane Asher, on a repertory tour with the Bristol Old Vic, who was celebrating her 21st birthday there. In his absence, George, John and Ringo added finishing touches to certain tracks while George Martin and engineer Geoff Emerick prepared mixes and worked out the running order. With the final brush strokes – gobbledegook designed for the record's run-out groove and a high-frequency note heard only by dogs – being applied on April 21, *Sgt Pepper's Lonely Hearts Club Band* was complete, taking some 700 hours of solid studio time to produce.

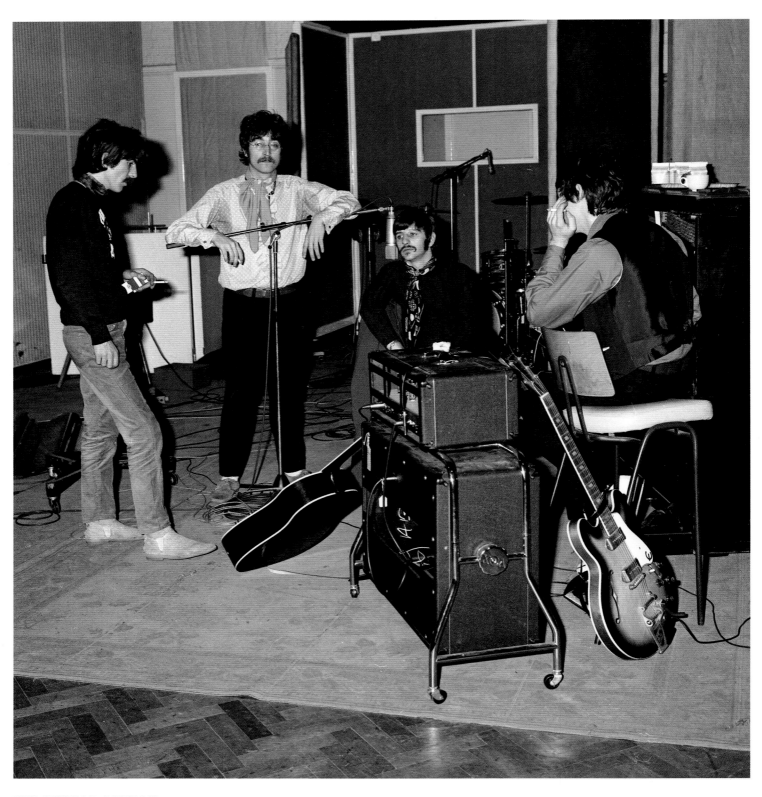

EMI STUDIOS, LONDON
MAY 17, 1967

Despite having spent endless hours in the studio
creating both a single ('Penny Lane'/'Strawberry Fields
Forever') and album (*Sgt Pepper*) of stunning originality,
The Beatles' creativity seemingly knew no bounds. They
continued to record sporadically from April into June –
not just at Abbey Road but at two independent London
studios, Olympic and De Lane Lea. Many of these sessions
resulted only in aimless, formless jams while others had
a more structured, if undefined (at that point) purpose
such as this session for 'You Know My Name (Look Up
The Number)', one of The Beatles' most bizarre songs.
Essentially a novelty, inspired when John noticed an
advertisement in the phone book with these words,
The Beatles started recording the backing track this day.

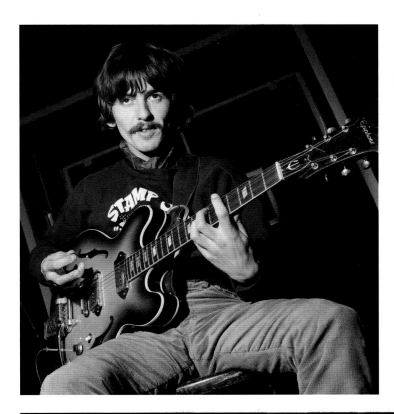

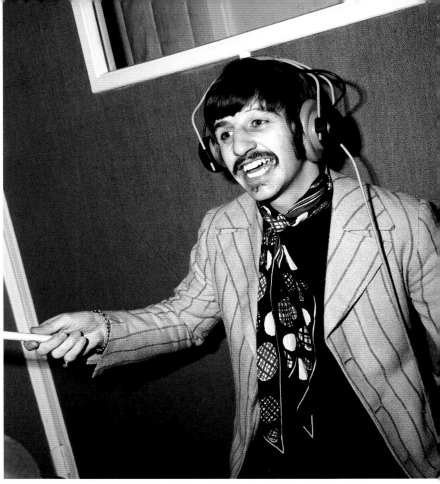

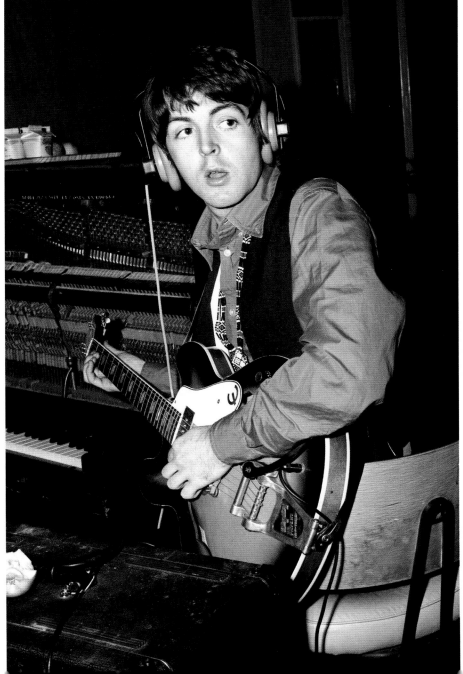

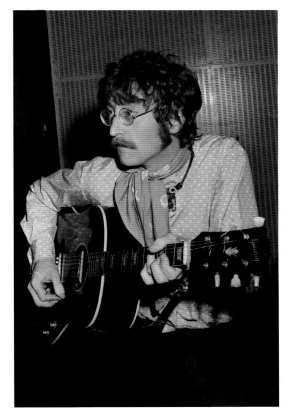

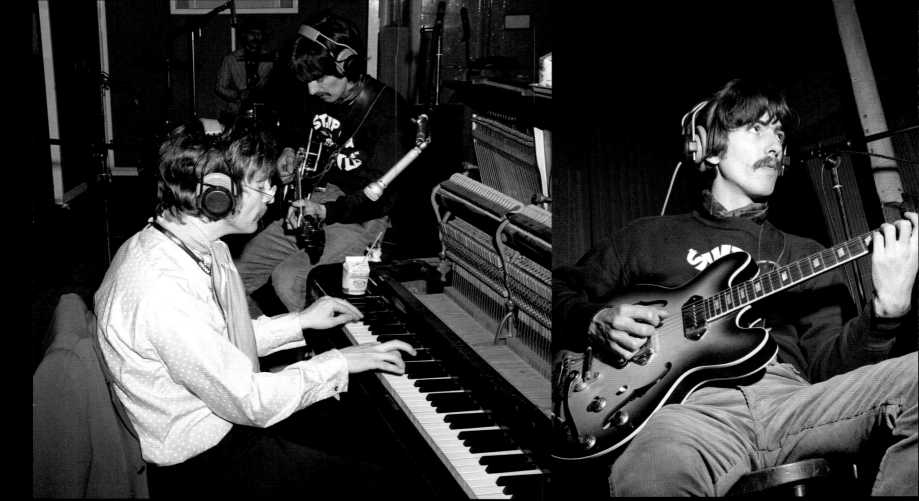

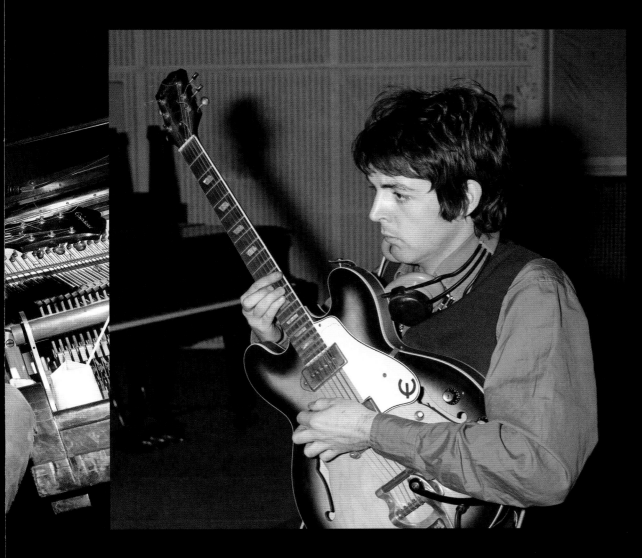

EMI STUDIOS, LONDON
MAY 17, 1967

Interestingly the heading given on
The Beatles Book archive listing for
this date states: 'EMI No 2 Studio
recording 'All You Need Is Love', 'You
Know My Name'. In his editorial for
Beatles Book # 49 Sean recalled how
he first heard 'All You Need Is Love'
in embryonic form; the basic track
lasting "about 10 minutes long".
Mark Lewisohn's *Recording Sessions*
and *Chronicle* tomes, taken from EMI
documentation prepared at the time,
list only 'You Know My Name'. The
track had quite a convoluted history –
it was revisited in June when Rolling
Stone Brian Jones contributed alto
sax, but sat on the shelf until April
1969 when John and Paul added their
vocals. Lennon originally wanted it
released – along with another Beatles
leftover (from the 'White Album'
sessions), 'What's The New Maryjane'
as a Plastic Ono Band single in
December 1969. The release got as
far as test pressing stage but was
cancelled. 'You Know My
Name' eventually appeared – in
edited form – as the B-side of The
Beatles' final single, 'Let It Be', in
March 1970.

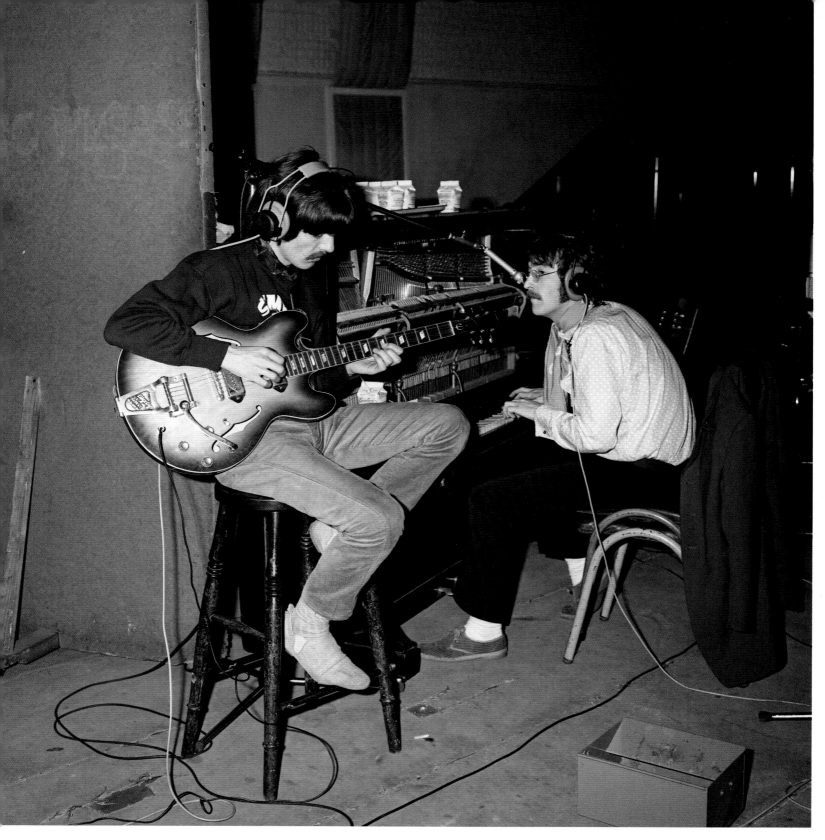

EMI STUDIOS, LONDON
MAY 17, 1967

George and John work at the Steinway, on which lies a tray of Sunfresh lemon drinks that were constantly sipped. Paul works the control desk with engineer Geoff Emerick who produced the session in George Martin's absence. Emerick's procedure of close-miking The Beatles' instruments made a considerable difference to the sound of their recordings at this time. Throughout the *Sgt Pepper* sessions and beyond, The Beatles sported a flamboyant collection of clothes in keeping with the psychedelic era. Colourful scarves, hats and badges with nonsense slogans such as Sword Swallower and Down With Pants were all par for the course. Back in 1964, when the group first arrived in America, a group of Detroit students had started a Stamp Out The Beatles campaign. Brian Epstein had worn a purple sweatshirt made up with the slogan and now so did George Harrison (whether it was the same garment remains unknown). The sentiment contrasted nicely with the 'Yellow Submarine For Peace' badge George is wearing, distributed by the anti-war organisation WIN (Workshop In Non-Violence) from New York. On the subject of *Yellow Submarine*, it had now been agreed that the full-length cartoon film in production would feature a soundtrack of Beatle songs – several being leftovers from various sessions.

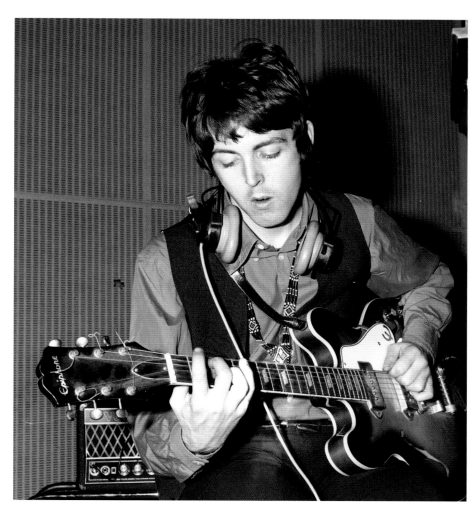

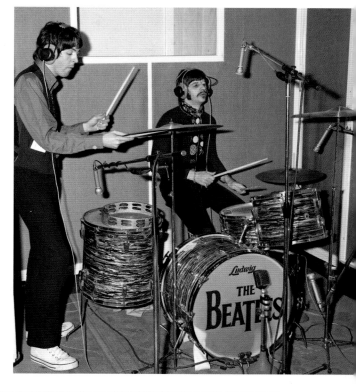

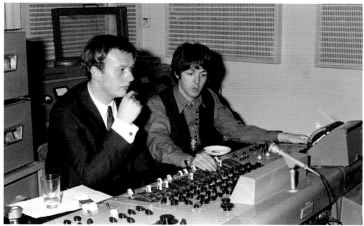

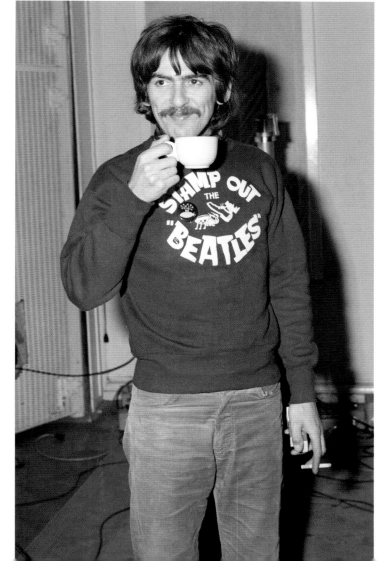

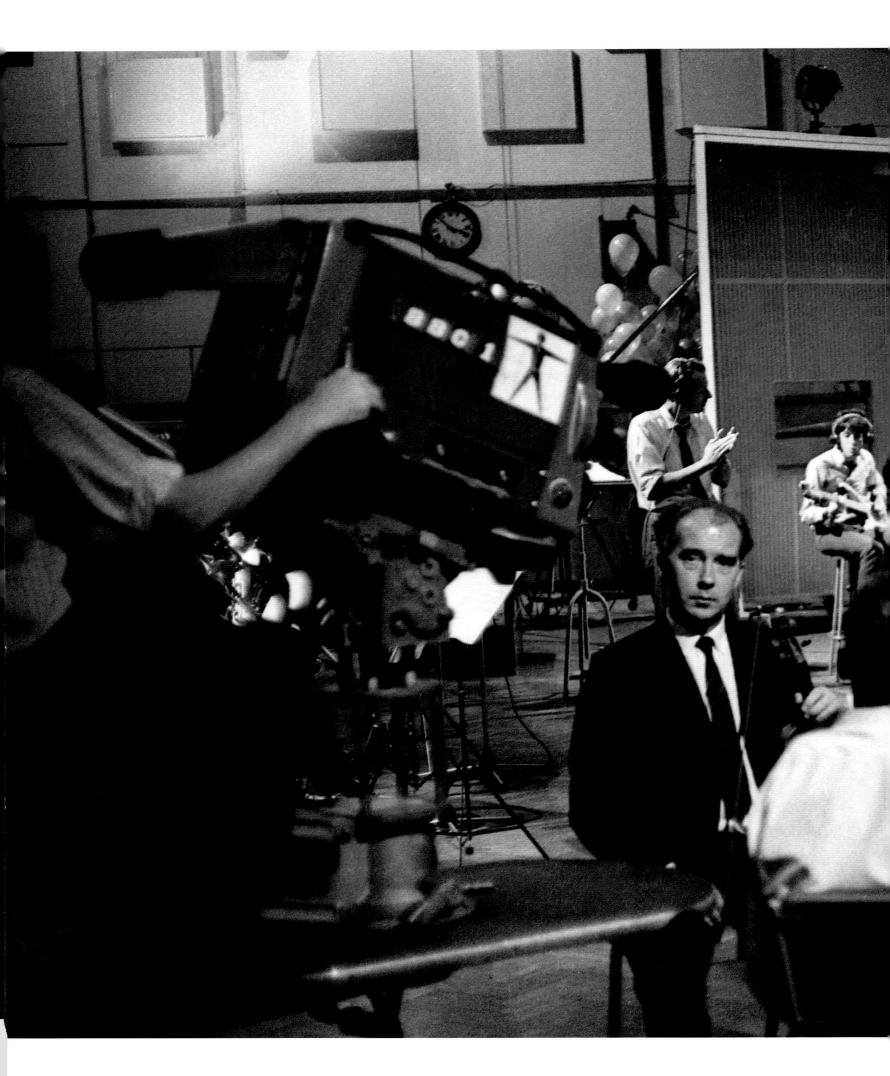

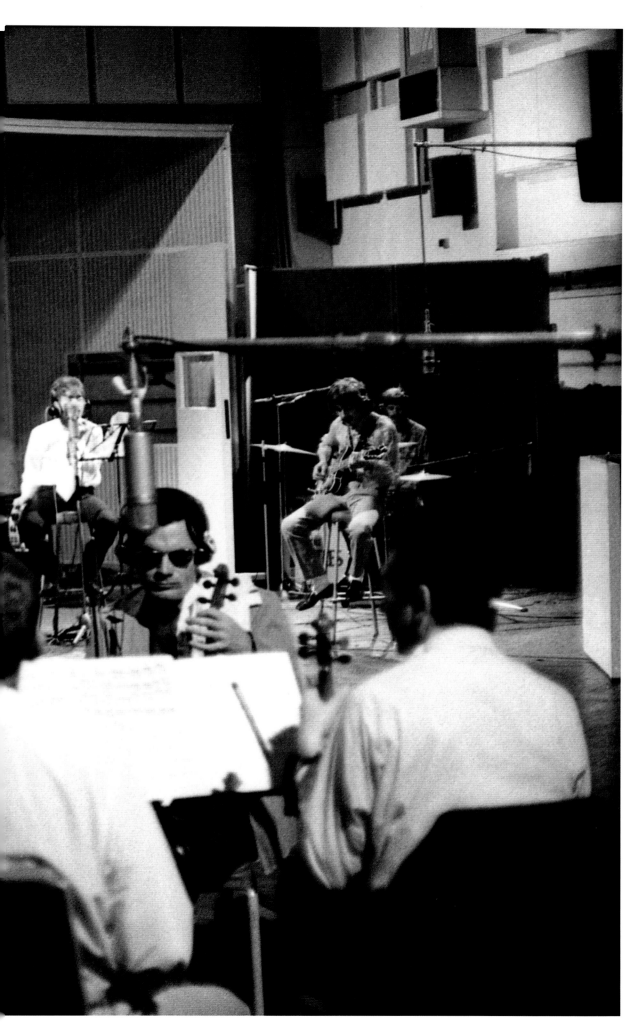

EMI STUDIOS, LONDON
JUNE 24, 1967

On May 18 it was announced
The Beatles had been chosen to
represent Great Britain in the first
televised worldwide satellite link-up
programme *Our World*, broadcast
during the evening (UK time) of
June 25. The cameras would show
the group working in the studio
on a new song which turned out to
be John's panacea anthem, 'All You
Need Is Love', written specially for
the event and an acute celebration
of the Summer of Love which was
nearing its height. Naturally, for
such an august occasion, the press
were invited to a photo call in the
cavernous Studio 1 the day before
the broadcast. The Beatles were
surrounded by balloons, flowers
and banners with the word 'love'
translated into several languages.
Once the photographers had
dispersed the BBC film crew sorted
out their camera positions as The
Beatles, George Martin and the
orchestra rehearsed.

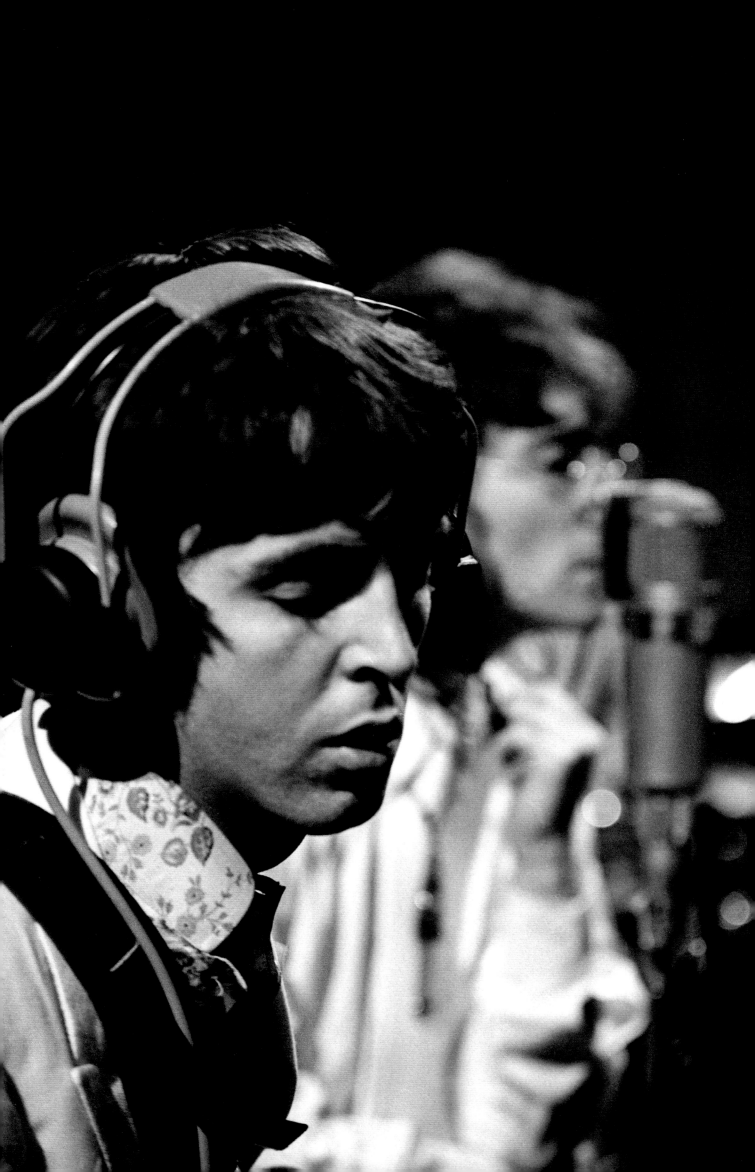

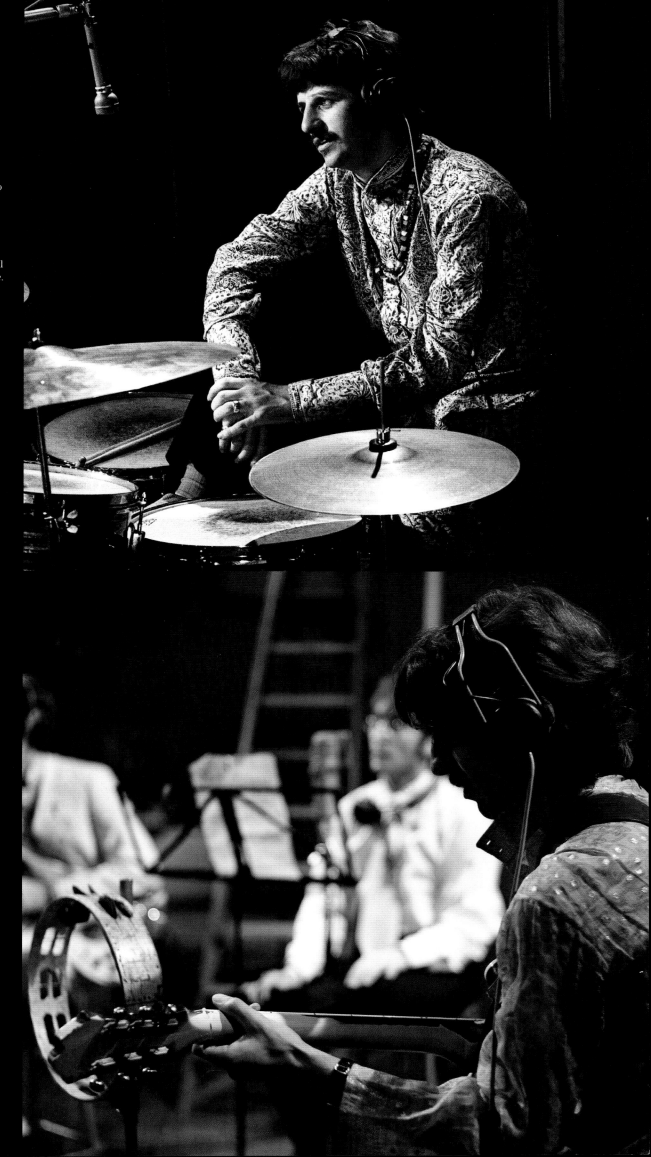

e two-hour camera rehearsal
mplete, The Beatles taped
overdubs for the take to
hey would mime for the
g day's important telecast. To
increase the chances of the
st passing smoothly without
ir musical hiccups, The
simply played along to the
recorded backing track with
ass, George's solo, John's vocal
orchestra being recorded live.
Martin and Geoff Emerick
ed 'on the fly' and fed the
he BBC van parked outside
tudio car park which was
oadcast to an estimated 400
around the world.

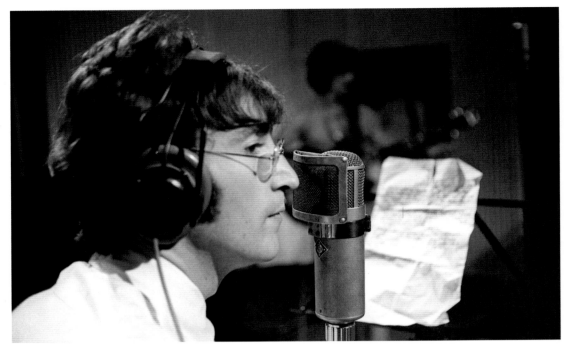
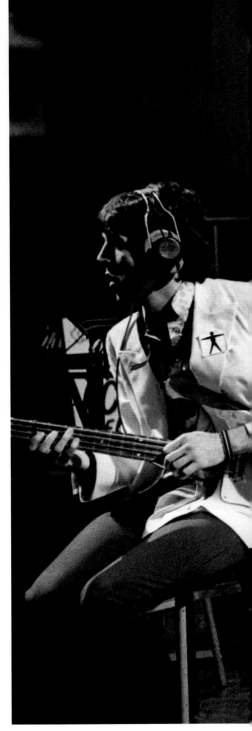
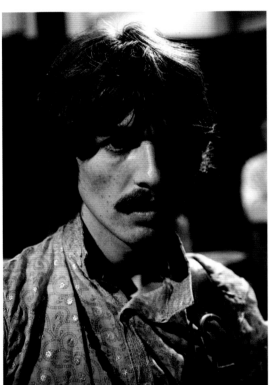
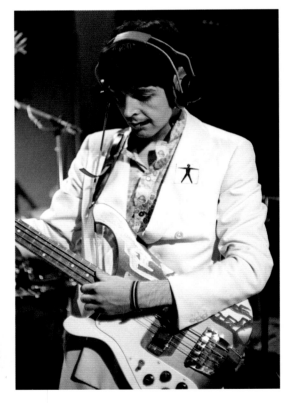

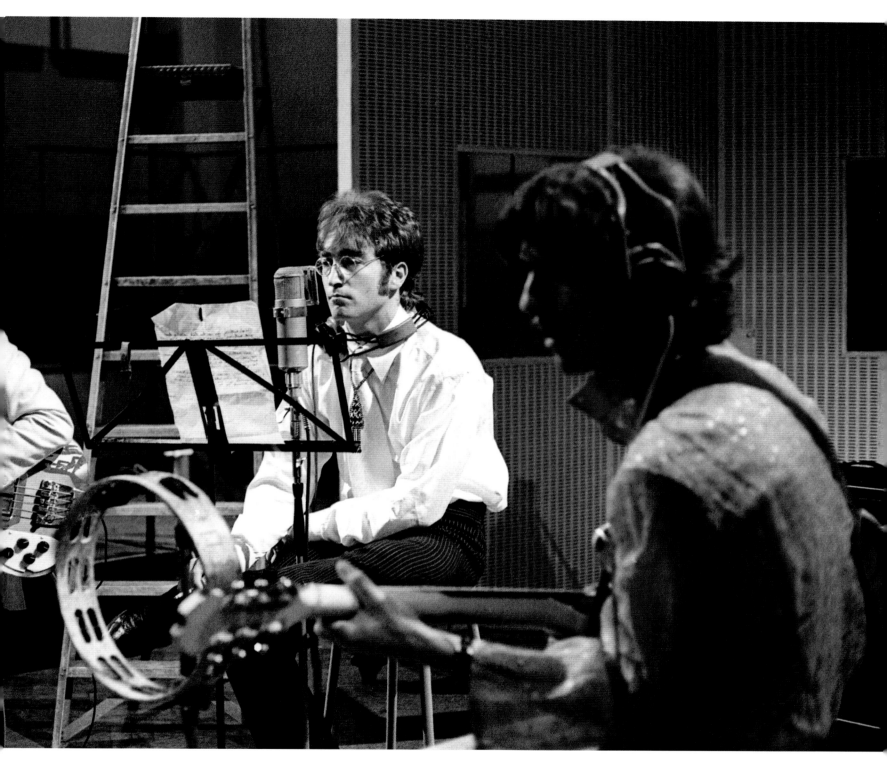

EMI STUDIOS, LONDON
JUNE 24, 1967

Paul's lapel badge features the *Our World* project logo. These rehearsal pics reveal his Rickenbacker bass had been hand painted in white, silver and red. The finish of some of George and John's guitars were also altered to reflect the psychedelic age – George covered his Stratocaster with dayglo paint in various rainbows and symbols while the back of John's Epiphone was aerosol sprayed – the surface got sanded down the following year. Even Ringo's drum head wasn't spared the brush and now featured an orange backdrop with the words 'LOVE' and 'The Beatles' painted in yellow.

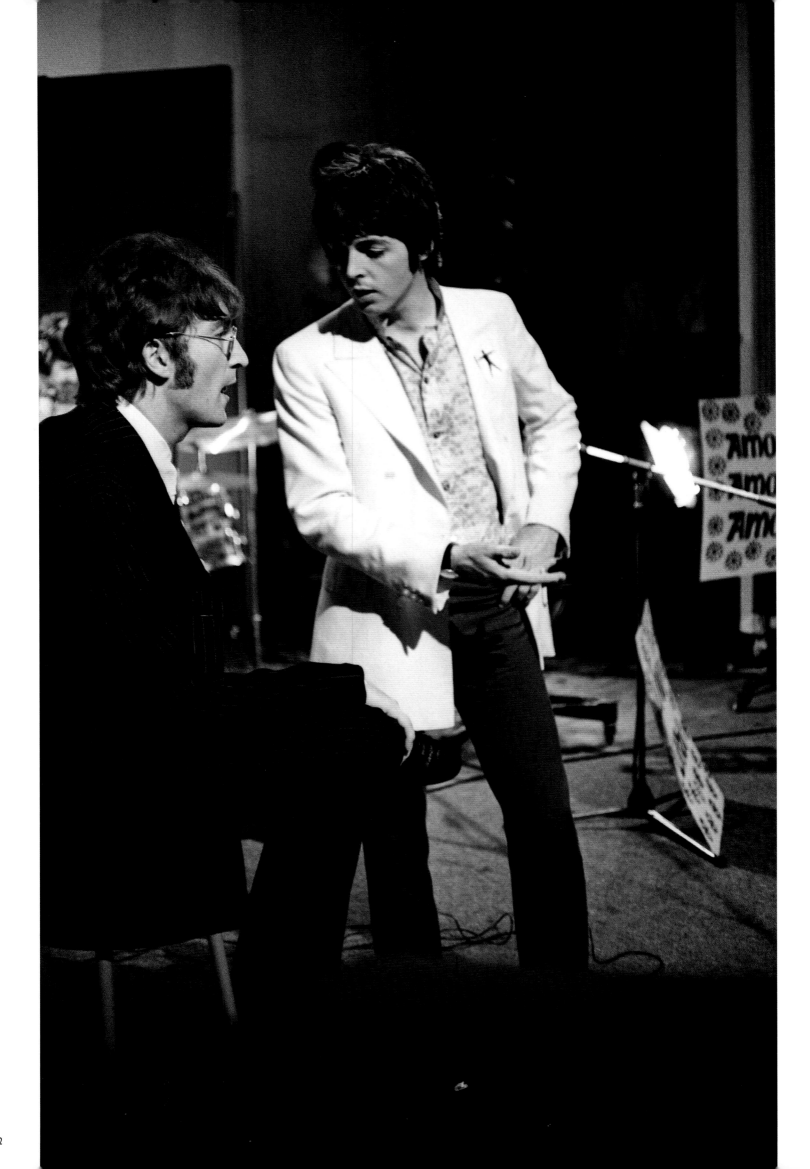

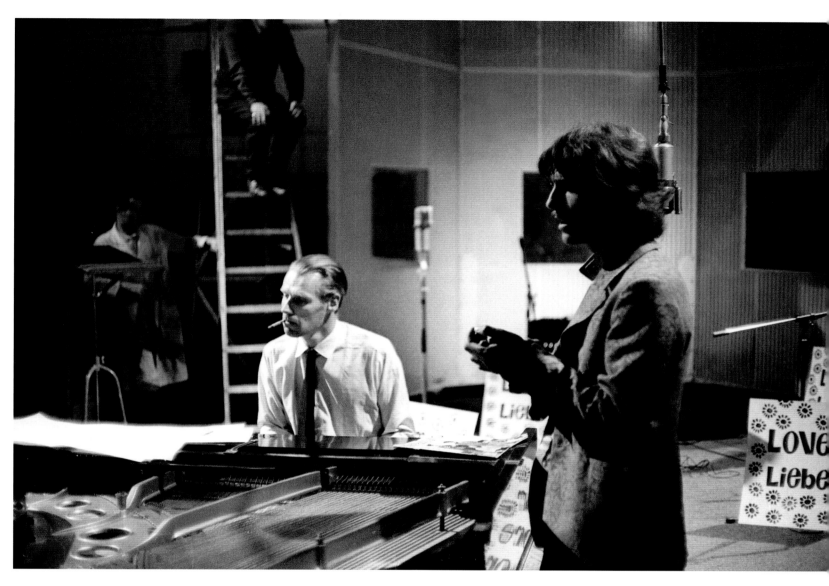

EMI STUDIOS, LONDON
JUNE 24, 1967

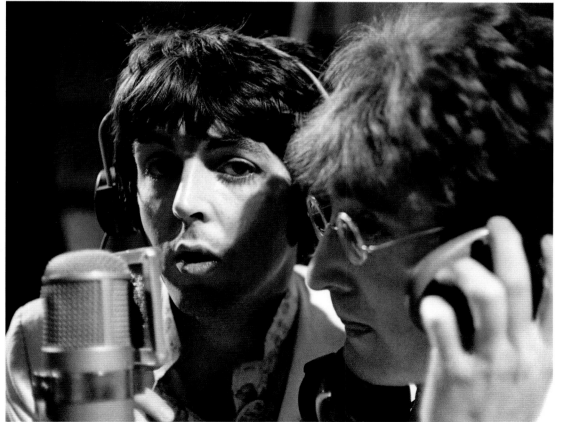

Paul makes a serious point to John; knowing that they were going to be watched by millions in 24 hours' time did little to soothe the nerves. The basic directive given to The Beatles by the *Our World* producers was that their contribution should be simple and direct with easy-to-understand phrases due to the number of foreign nations that would be watching. In keeping with the international flavour, from the outset 'All You Need Is Love' began with the distinctive opening bars of the French national anthem 'La Marseillaise'. Paul's contender for the programme, 'Hello, Goodbye', was equally basic enough to understand by most but was held over, being recorded and released as The Beatles' third 1967 single in November.

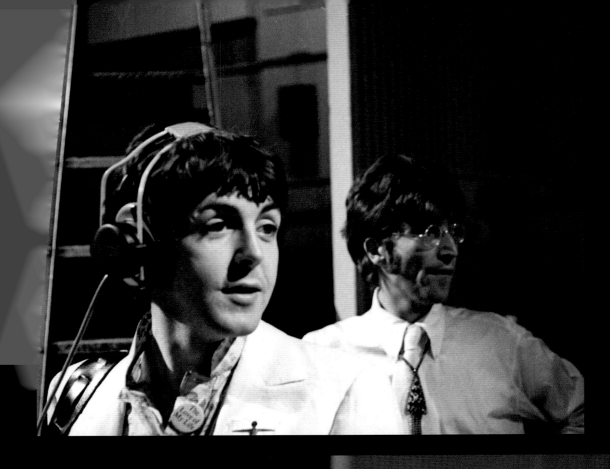
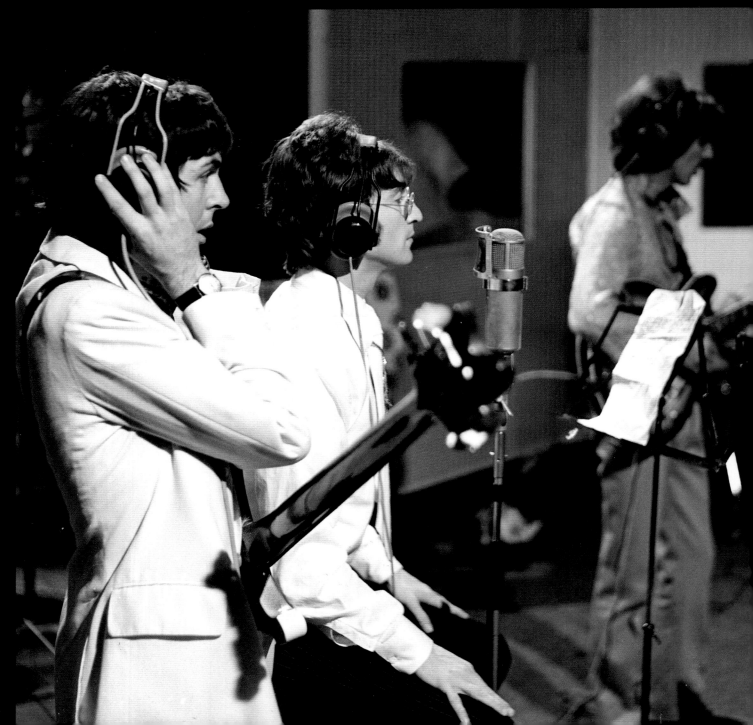

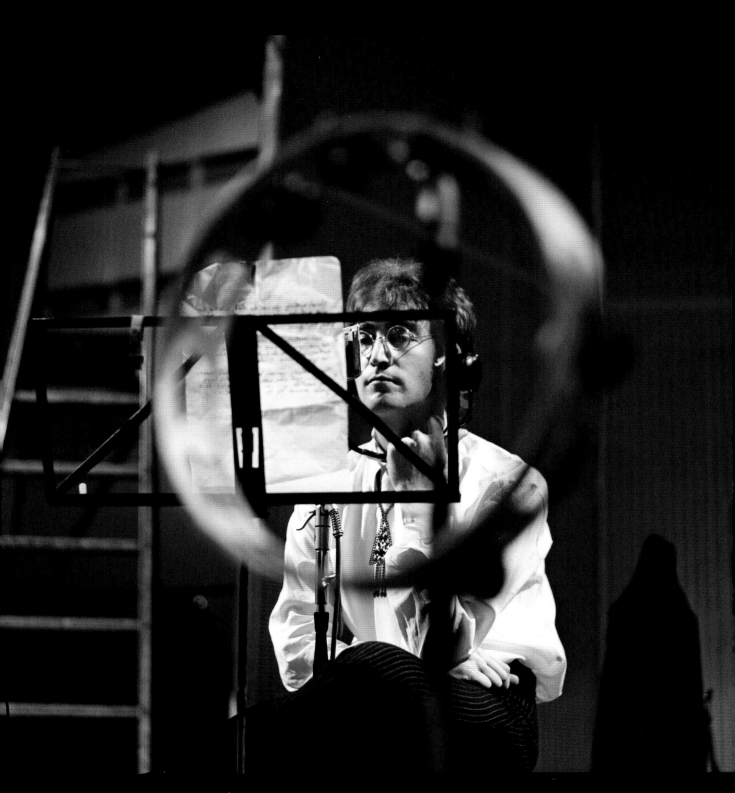

EMI STUDIOS, LONDON
JUNE 24, 1967

The backing track for 'All You Need Is Love' was unusual in that John, Paul and George each played unfamiliar instruments – John a harpsichord, Paul a double bass and George a violin. Recording began at Olympic Studios on June 14 and continued to completion at Abbey Road. To help sing along on the infectious chorus for the actual broadcast, The Beatles invited various friends and acquaintances including Mick Jagger, Keith Richards, Marianne Faithfull, Eric Clapton, Keith Moon, Graham Nash, Gary Leeds, Mike McCartney, and writers Barry Miles and Hunter Davies into the studio. As a postscript, the handwritten lyric sheet from which John is reading in these pictures was picked up by a BBC employee from where it had been discarded. When sold at auction in 2005, it realised a staggering one million dollars.

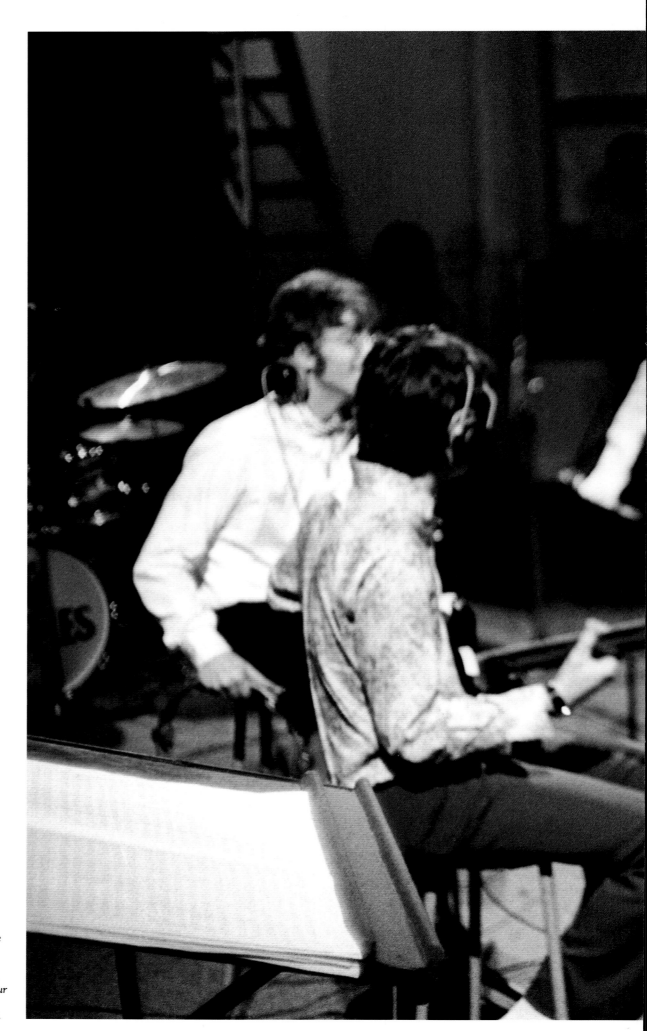

EMI STUDIOS, LONDON
JUNE 24, 1967

For the extended orchestral finale to 'All You Need Is Love', George Martin wove in popular tunes like 'Greensleeves' and 'In The Mood', the latter not out of copyright so Glenn Miller's estate received a settlement. Compared to the methods The Beatles had used on *Sgt Pepper*, sometimes taking weeks to complete a song, 'All You Need Is Love' came together quickly because of the television deadline and EMI's decision to rush-release it as a single to capitalise on the exposure. Released within a fortnight of the *Our World* broadcast, it gave The Beatles yet another worldwide number one.

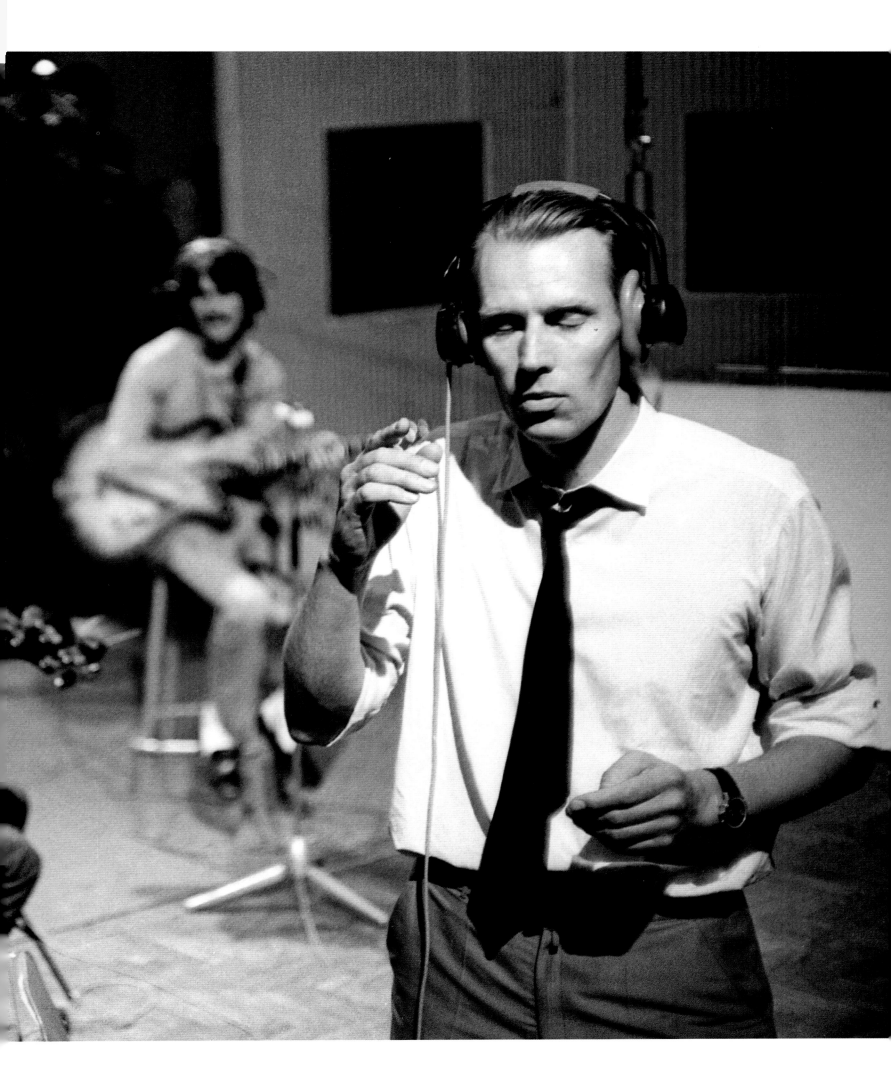

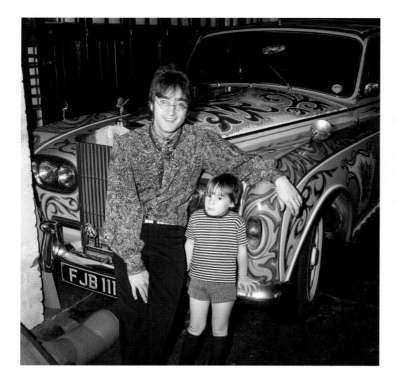

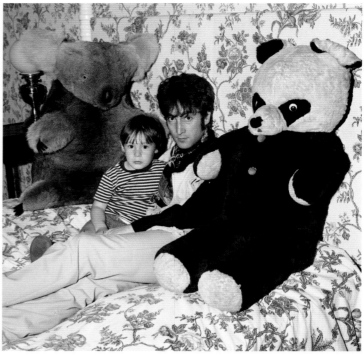

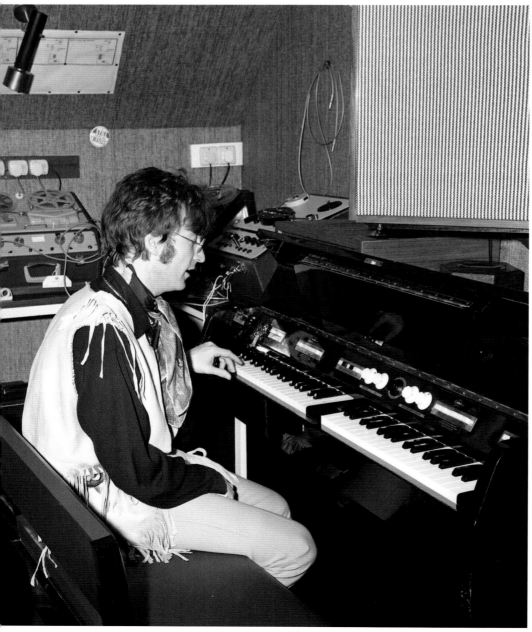

KENWOOD,
WEYBRIDGE, SURREY
JUNE 29, 1967

The final 'Beatle at home' subject was John. Paul had allowed *The Beatles Book* access to his St John's Wood house earlier in the year for an article but insisted on no photographs. John seemed not to have cared either way and while Cynthia kept out of the frame, four-year-old Julian got to pose with his dad. As Simon and Marijke of Dutch design collective The Fool painted John's Bechstein piano, photos were taken around the estate of the large mock Tudor mansion. In the double garage was Lennon's Rolls-Royce Phantom V which local fairground painter J P Fallon had recently made over in vivid yellow paint and Romany patterns to match its owner's colourful imagination. Moving indoors – and with John changing clothes, sporting a badge from a US fan proclaiming 'I STILL Love The Beatles' – shots were taken in the music room at the top of the house where John is seen tinkering at the Mellotron, and in Julian's room with a large koala and panda. On to the master's den, where he is seen reading British countercultural broadsheet *International Times*, two *Safe As Milk* stickers from Captain Beefheart's album on the cupboard doors behind him. The visit ended by the swimming pool where, as Beatles biographer Hunter Davies confirmed, John would spend idle hours in contemplative silence.

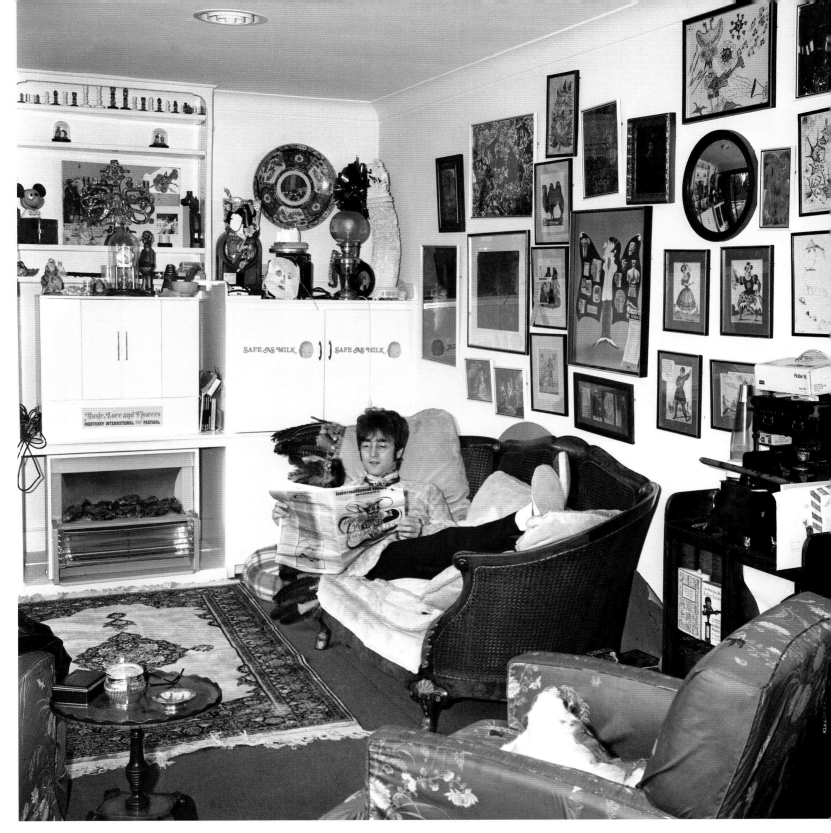

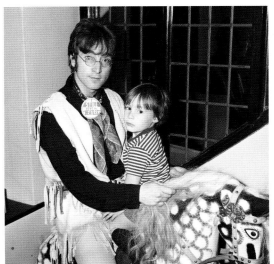

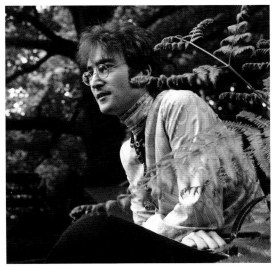

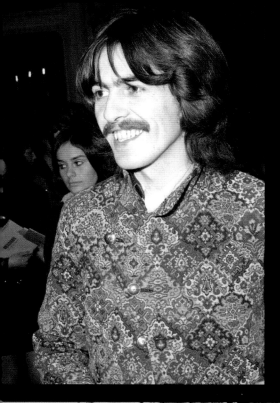

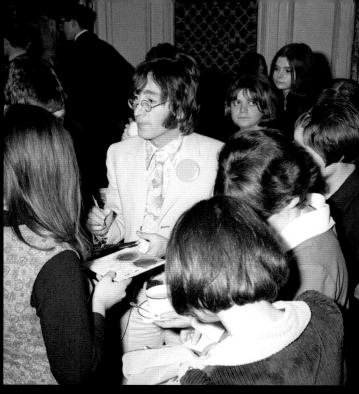

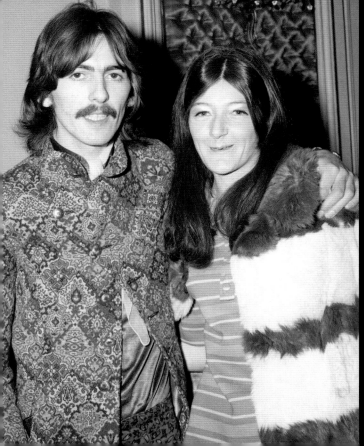

HANOVER GRAND HOTEL, LONDON
DECEMBER 17, 1967

The Beatles' third film was still conspicuous by its non-appearance. Tentative plans had been made for a television special using songs from *Sgt. Pepper*, but while some preparation and filming occurred, the venture went unrealised. In April Paul had returned from his US holiday with the idea of a mystery coach trip, from which the next Beatles' project germinated. The self-directed *Magical Mystery Tour*, made for television in the wake of Brian Epstein's tragic death, was shot during September and October in the West Country and at an aerodrome in West Malling, Kent, followed by 11 weeks spent editing the footage in a Soho cutting room. The hour-long film was bought by the BBC and scheduled for peak Christmas viewing. For the 40 British Fan Club area secretaries – three of whom were on the bright yellow coach and appeared in the film – the opportunity of an all-expenses paid trip to attend a special preview with two Beatles in attendance was too good to turn down. (Paul was away on his farm in Scotland and Ringo was in Rome filming his first solo movie role *Candy*). John and George happily mingled, signed autographs and posed for photos (George puts his arm around Freda Kelly, Joint National Secretary of the Official Beatles Fan Club). The wider British public got their chance to see *Magical Mystery Tour* on Boxing Day on BBC 1. While most fans predictably lapped up anything new from The Beatles, the TV critics were less kind. The morning papers were full of scathing reviews, *The Daily Express* calling it "blatant rubbish". A second screening on the colour BBC 2 channel did little to alter first impressions. Paul, the prime instigator behind the projec was stung. It was The Beatles' first serious failure.

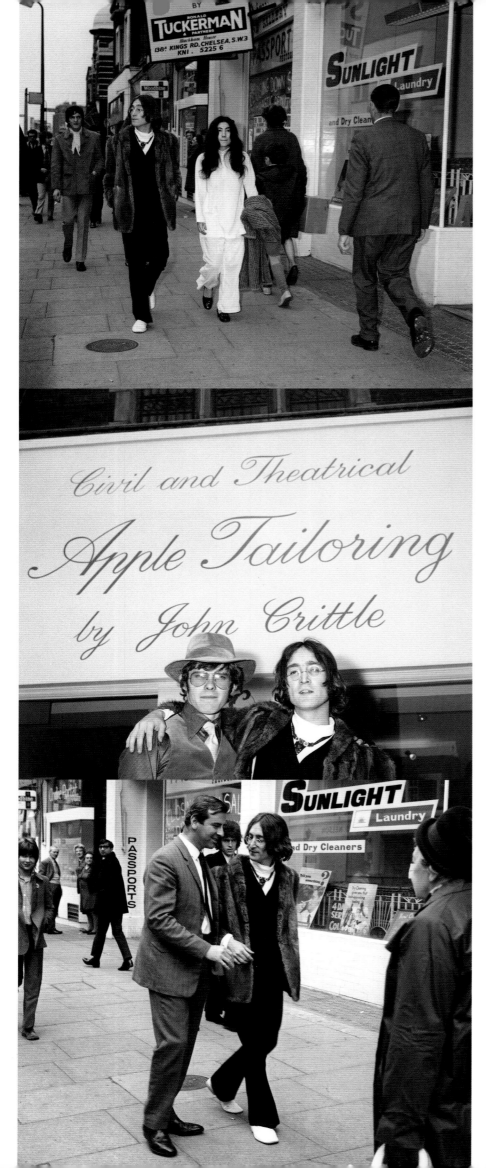

KING'S ROAD, CHELSEA
MAY 22, 1968

The Beatles spent most of the first half of 1968 in Rishikesh with the Maharishi Mahesh Yogi, whose teachings of transcendental meditation they had begun to follow the previous August. However as each grew disenchanted with the guru for various reasons they returned from their time in India to, as John Lennon described it, "play businessman". This was a reference to their newly-formed company Apple Corps Ltd, a multi-media operation involving music, books, films, electronics and clothes. In December 1967, the Apple shop at 94 Baker Street opened selling all manner of trendy psychedelic clothing, posters and knick-knacks. John and George with partners Cynthia and Pattie attended its opening, and six months later both Beatles were present again for the launch of a similar ill-fated venture, Apple Tailoring (Civil and Theatrical) at 161 King's Road. However there was a difference; John was now accompanied by his new artistic muse and partner Yoko Ono (so new in fact they had only properly got together over the previous weekend when recording the avant-garde *Two Virgins* at Lennon's home). This was the couple's first public outing although the press were seemingly unaware of their union as was Sean O'Mahony who greeted John on the walk along Chelsea's famous fashion thoroughfare.

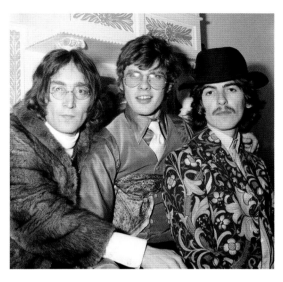

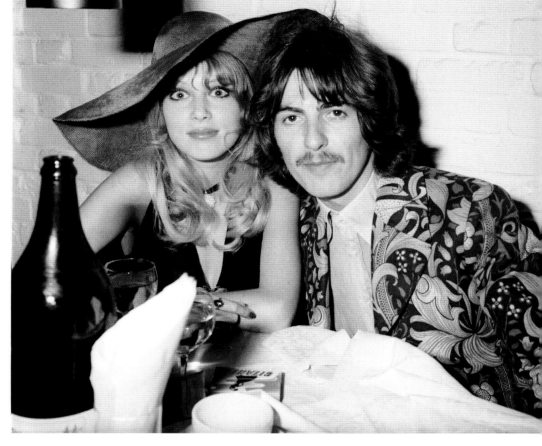

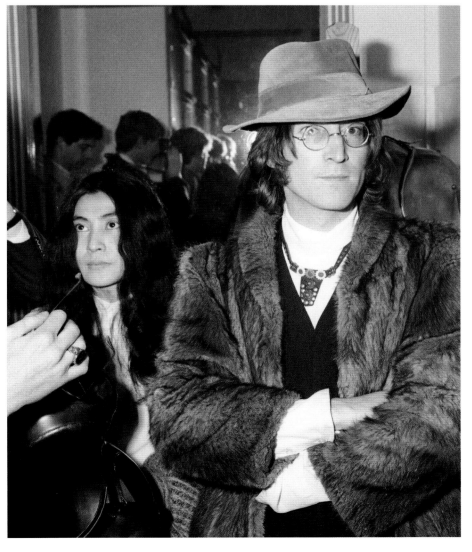

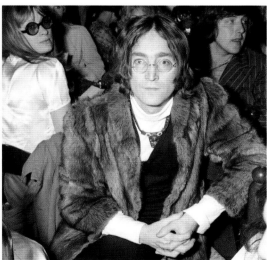

KING'S ROAD, CHELSEA
MAY 22, 1968

A lunchtime launch party was held up the road at the trendy Club Dell'Aretusa attended by Derek Taylor (who had just returned from America to begin his second term as Beatles press officer), Peter Brown, Julie Felix, TV personality Simon Dee and the group Grapefruit, who were signed to Apple Publishing. Running the new tailoring venture was designer John Crittle, seen here with John and George. One of the wave of young Australians making a name for themselves in the arts, Crittle was behind Dandie Fashions, previously run on the same King's Road premises, in partnership with socialite Tara Browne, a friend of The Beatles who had died in an auto accident (and to whom the line "he blew his mind out in a car" in 'A Day In The Life' refers). Crittle is now better known in some circles as the estranged father of ballet dancer Darcey Bussell. Like many things connected to The Beatles' chaotic creation, Apple's fashion venture was short-lived.

203

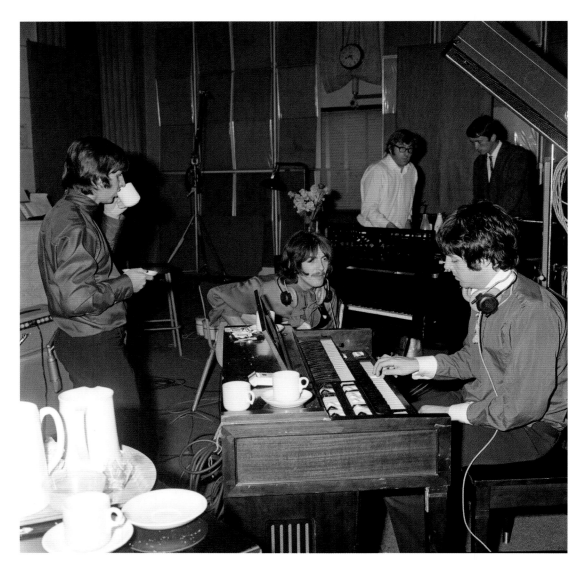

EMI STUDIOS, LONDON
JUNE 4, 1968

The three songwriting Beatles had come away from their time in India with a collection of around 30 new songs. On May 28, John, Paul and George demoed their new compositions at George's house Kinfauns using his four-track tape machine. Two days later they entered Abbey Road to begin what would be the protracted sessions for the double 'White Album'. Having relied on others for up-to-date photographs, Sean O'Mahony, accompanied by Leslie Bryce, was admitted to this session for John's 'Revolution' in Studio 3. Others present were the ever-loyal Mal Evans, assistant Tony Bramwell (who was also taking photos) and two new Beatle partners, Francie Schwartz, a New York writer currently seeing Paul, and the omnipresent Yoko Ono. While The Beatles' wives and girlfriends paid visits to recording sessions but stayed in the background, it was soon apparent that Yoko had no such intention and was to become a permanent fixture at John's side. Unsurprisingly, this new regime conspired to create an uptight atmosphere, which these photos can't help but convey.

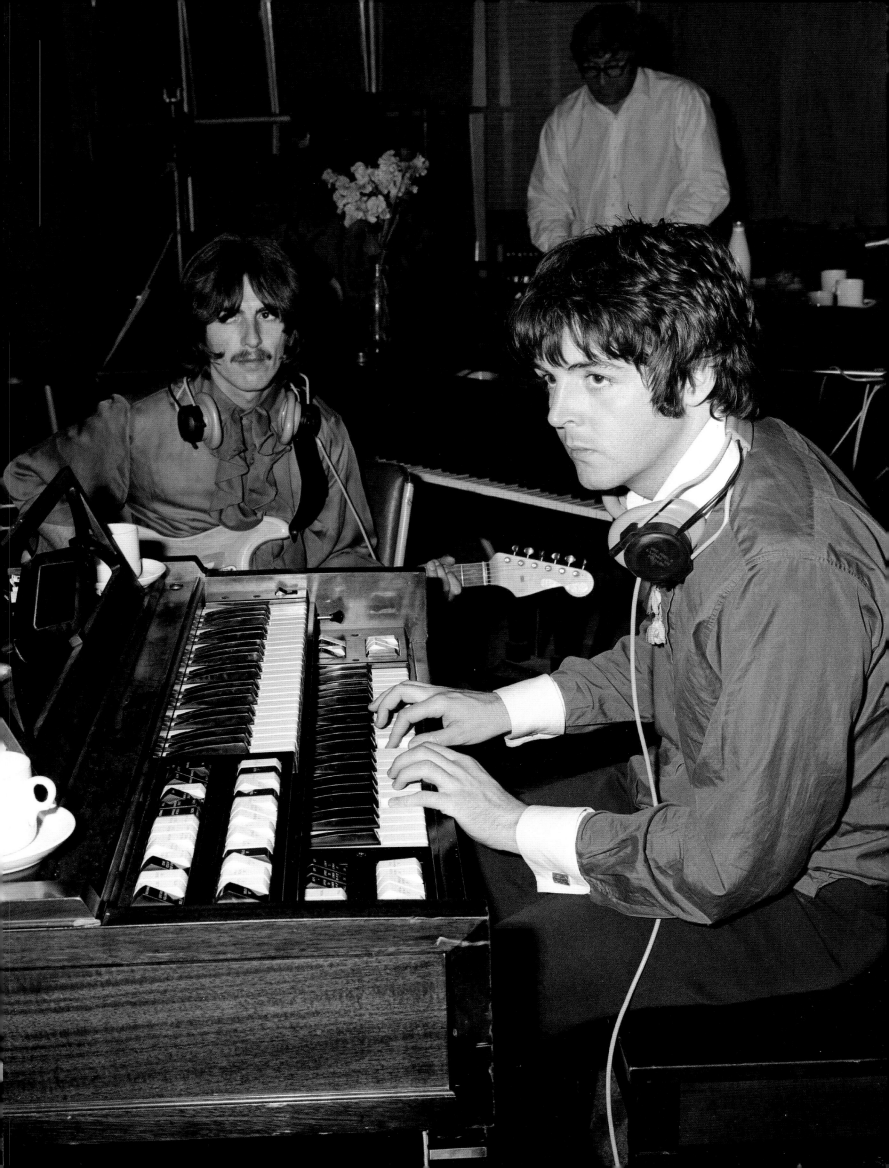

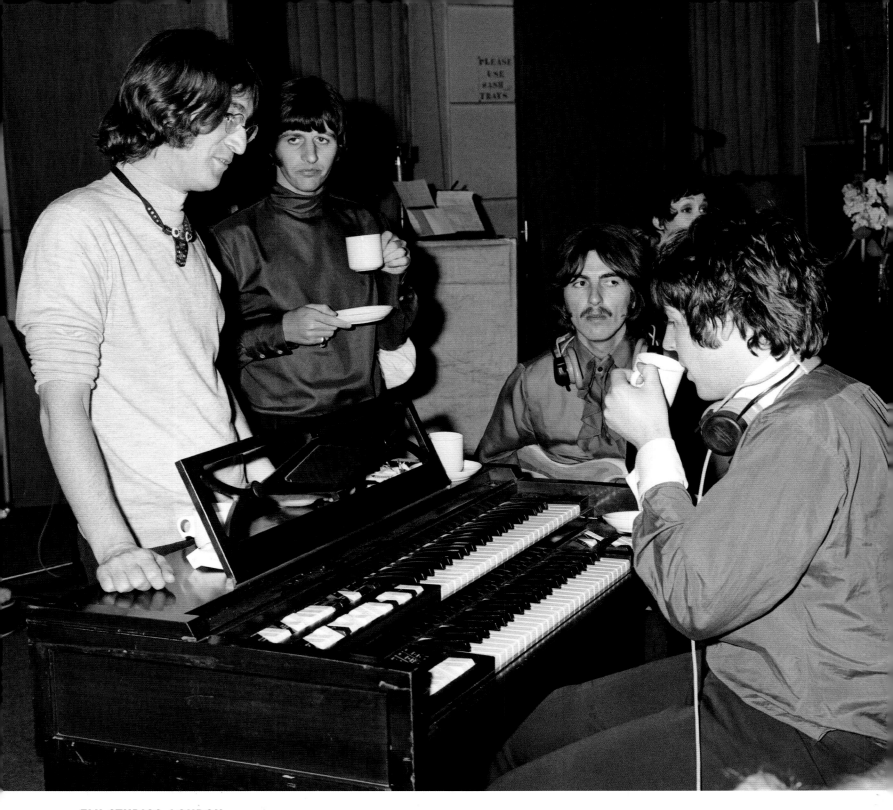

EMI STUDIOS, LONDON
JUNE 4, 1968

By some form of psychic coincidence, the 'Revolution' session fell between the shooting of Andy Warhol in New York and the assassination of Robert Kennedy in Los Angeles. It was symptomatic of the changing times and of the turbulence that would surround the remainder of The Beatles' astonishing career. As the four gather around the organ for a discussion, George's expression says it all. "There were terrible vibes in the studio," Sean recalls. "Everything was wrong. I told Leslie to shoot a few pictures quickly and then Mal Evans came over and suggested we leave. I think we shot one roll, 12 shots. And that was the last time. It was very sad."

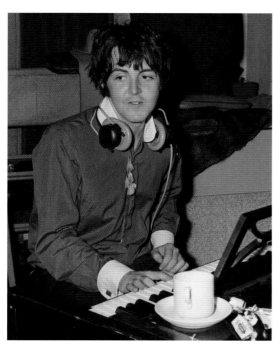

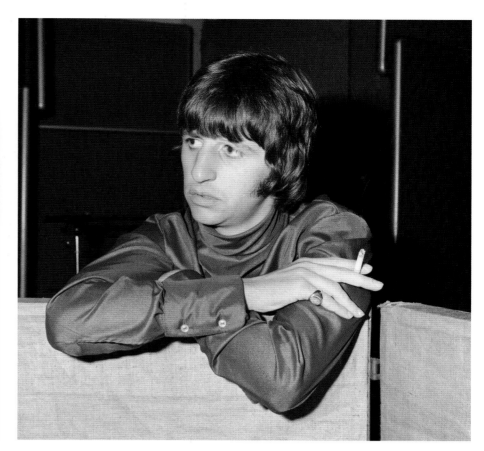

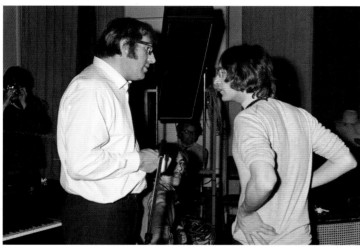

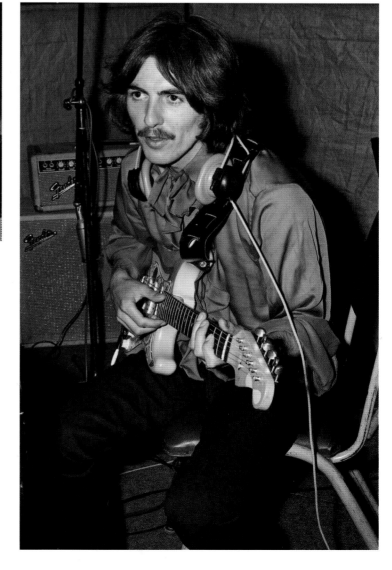

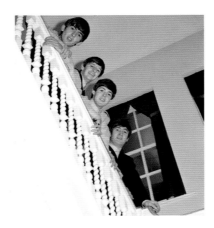

This book would not have been possible without the help of a number of people,
first and foremost of whom is Sean O'Mahony without whose foresight in 1963 this
extraordinary collection could not have been put together. Sean himself would be
first to thank his wife Jackie for her love and support over the years.

We would also like to thank Leslie Bryce for having the eye to capture such magnificent
photographs of The Beatles, Lora Findlay for her understated but sophisticated design and Andy
Neill for the introductory essay and his impeccable research in dating and captioning the pictures.

Others to thank include Beatles historian extraordinaire Mark Lewisohn, for general input
and for kindly allowing Andy access to his unpublished interviews with Sean and Leslie, Thorsten
Knublauch for his help in identifying the locations and people in the German tour pictures,
Frits Broekema for corrections to this updated edition, Pete Nash at the Beatles UK Fan Club,
Phil Smee, our editor Chris Charlesworth at
Omnibus Press and agent Andrew Lownie.

Finally, thanks must go to Brian Epstein for agreeing to Sean's proposal to publish
The Beatles Book all those years ago and, of course, to John, Paul, George and Ringo
for creating some of the most enduring music of the 20th century.

Jo & Tom Adams, March 2015.

This edition published by Omnibus Press and distributed in the United States and Canada by
The Overlook Press, Peter Mayer Publishers Inc, 141 Wooster Street, New York, NY 10012. For
bulk and special sales requests, please contact sales@overlookny.com
or write to us at the above address.

Copyright © 2016 Omnibus Press
(A Division of Music Sales Limited)
14/15 Berners Street,
London, W1T 3LJ UK.

Cover and interiors designed by Lora Findlay

ISBN: 978-1-4683-1275-1

Every effort has been made to trace the copyright holders of the
photographs in this book but one or two were unreachable.
We would be grateful if the photographers concerned would contact us.

Printed in China.

A catalogue record for this book is available from the British Library.

Cataloguing-in-Publication data is available from the Library of Congress.

Visit Omnibus Press on the web at www.omnibuspress.com

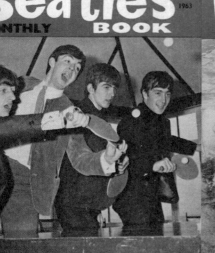
Beatles
MONTHLY BOOK
SEPT. 1963

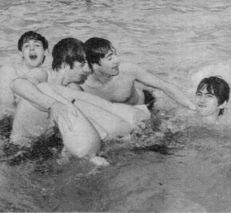
Beatles
MONTHLY BOOK
OCT. 1963

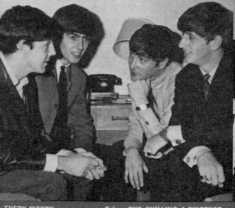
Beatles
MONTHLY BOOK
NOV. 1963

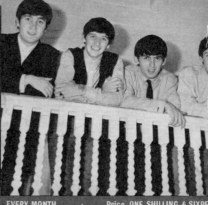
Beatles
MONTHLY BOOK

EVERY MONTH · Price ONE SHILLING & SIXPENCE
EVERY MONTH · Price ONE SHILLING & SIXPENCE
EVERY MONTH · Price ONE SHILLING & SIXPENCE
EVERY MONTH · Price ONE SHILLING & SIXPEN

No. 10
The **Beatles**
MONTHLY BOOK
MAY 1964

No. 11
The **Beatles**
MONTHLY BOOK
JUNE 1964

No. 12
The **Beatles**
MONTHLY BOOK
JULY 1964

SPECIAL FEATURE BY PAUL
No.
The **Beatles**
MONTHLY

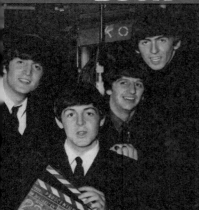
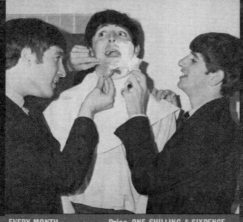
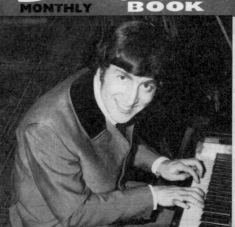
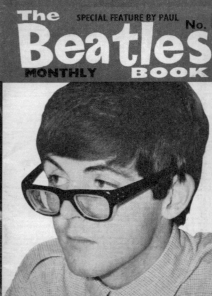

MONTH · Price ONE SHILLING & SIXPENCE
EVERY MONTH · Price ONE SHILLING & SIXPENCE
EVERY MONTH · Price ONE SHILLING & SIXPENCE
EVERY MONTH · Price ONE SHILLING & SIXPEN

No. 18
The **Beatles**
MONTHLY BOOK
JAN. 1965
2nd YEAR

No. 19
The **Beatles**
MONTHLY BOOK
FEB. 1965
2nd YEAR

No. 20
The **Beatles**
MONTHLY BOOK
MAR. 1965
2nd YEAR

No.
The **Beatles**
MONTHLY BOOK

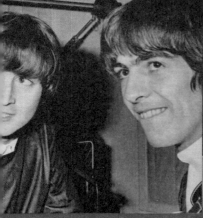
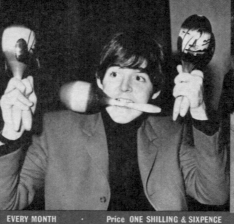
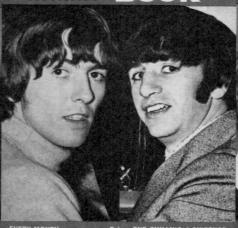
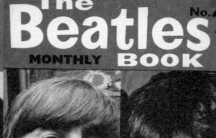
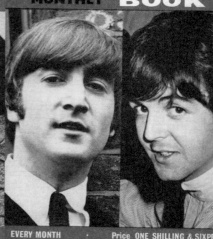
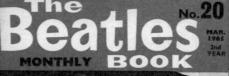

MONTH · Price ONE SHILLING & SIXPENCE
EVERY MONTH · Price ONE SHILLING & SIXPENCE
EVERY MONTH · Price ONE SHILLING & SIXPENCE
EVERY MONTH · Price ONE SHILLING & SIXPEN

No. 26
The **Beatles**
MONTHLY BOOK
SEPT. 1965
3rd YEAR

No. 27
The **Beatles**
MONTHLY BOOK
OCT. 1965
3rd YEAR

No. 28
The **Beatles**
MONTHLY BOOK
NOV. 1965
3rd YEAR

XMAS ISSUE
No. 2
The **Beatles**
MONTHLY BOOK

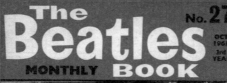
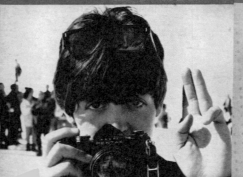
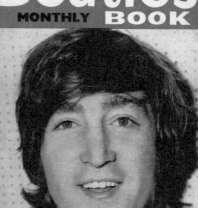